C000263755

Imaginal Macl

Autonomy & Self-Organization in the Revolutions of Everyday Life

<:..MinOr..:>
.cOmp0siti0ns.
Autonomedia

To my favorite little Deleuzian. Hope you like it. cheers,

Imaginal Machines: Autonomy & Self-Organization in the Revolutions of Everyday Life
Stevphen Shukaitis

ISBN 978-1-57027-208-0

Cover & design by Haduhi Szukis
Cover images by Mike Strunk & Renée DeMund

Credit to the images used (page number indicated in parenthesis) goes to the following: Tim Nebel (30), Arley-Rose Torsone (112), Haduhi Szukis (1, 7, 8, 53, 225-226).

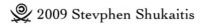
Released by Minor Compositions, London/NYC/Port Watson
Minor Compositions is a series of interventions & provocations drawing from autonomous politics, avant-garde aesthetics, and the revolutions of everyday life.
WWW.MINORCOMPOSITIONS.INFO
Email: |info@minorcompositions.info

Distributed by Autonomedia
PO Box 568 Williamsburgh Station Brooklyn, NY 11211
Phone/fax: 718-963-0568
Email: info@autonomedia.org
WWW.AUTONOMEDIA.ORG

Table of Contents

Acknowledgments

This text owes an immense debt, far beyond that which I could ever hope to repay, to years of conversation and dialogue with friends, comrades, and colleagues. At the end of the day, if its creation and circulation (as well as further development in circulation) can bring back to and replenish the commons and collective creativity from which it has drawn so much, then it will have achieved its goal. Having said that, there are individuals whose effort and time has been absolutely indispensable in the process leading to the formation of this solidified, and temporally stopped-in-motion text. Among those who have been so kind and wonderful, and from whom I have learned a great deal, are Franco 'Bifo' Berardi, Erika Biddle, Jack Z. Bratich, Lindsay Caplan, George Caffentzis, Massimo De Angelis, Dave Eden, Jim Fleming, David Graeber, Jamie Heckert, Nate Holdren, Brian Holmes, Silvia Federici, Malav Kanuga, Darren 'Deicide' Kramer and everyone from Ever Reviled Records, Sophea Lerner, Bernard Marszalek, Alan Moore, Rodrigo Nunes, Spencer Sunshine, Saulius Uzpelkis, Kevin Van Meter and Team Colors, and Will Weikart. Thanks to the wonderful folks from 16Beaver for the chance to present and discuss this project as a whole. Many thanks to Peter Case and Saul Newman for their timely interrogation. Drifting greetings and appreciations to the London Micropolitics Research Group. Cheers and solidarity to Cindy Milstein and everyone from the Institute for Anarchist Studies (who provided funding for the research that was the initial basis of this project). Appreciation to the Asian bourgeois for sending their children to UK universities and thus inadvertently providing funding for autonomist social research. Special thanks to all my comrades and colleagues from the University of Leicester Centre for Philosophy and Political Economy (especially Stephen Dunne and Eleni Karamali) and the Autonomist Front Group at Queen Mary (particularly Arianna Bove, Emma Dowling, Peter Fleming, Matteo Mandarini, and Angela Mitropoulos). Stefano

Harney and Martin Parker have been of immeasurable value for their constant discussion, encouragement, and constructive prodding when necessary. Much love to my family for being supportive of me, even though they probably think most of this book is gobbledygook. I give my thanks in all possible senses to Emma Chung, who has brought more joy and wonder to my life than can possibly be contained within the space of an acknowledgment. This book is dedicated to my sister Becky Shukaitis (who did not stick around long enough to see it published) and my grandmother Nancy Shukaitis, who taught me all I needed about maintaining a balanced and joyous relationship with the struggles of life and politics, under whatever name they may appear.

IMAGINAL

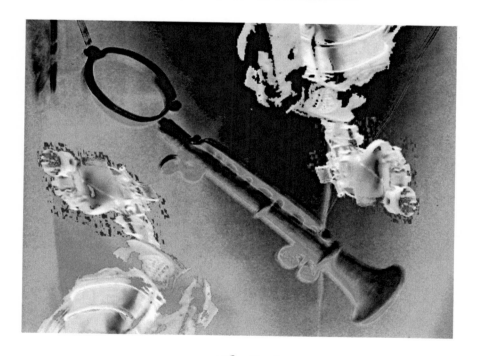

Machines

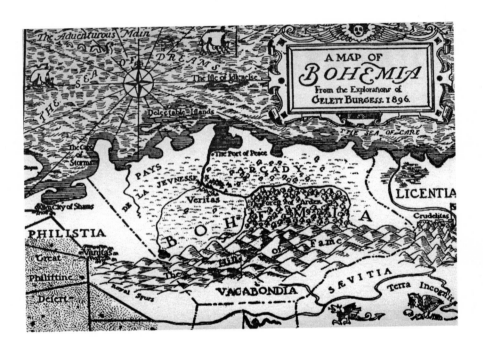

:: 0 :: Introduction ::

The geography of the imagination should have a little bit more wilderness to it; I hate it when it becomes subdivided. – Tom Waits (2005: 72)

Social technical machines are only conglomerations of desiring-machines under conditions that are historically determined; desiring-machines are social and technical machines restored to their determinant molecular conditions. – Gilles Deleuze and Félix Guattari (1977: 129)

This intervention has no beginning or end.[1] To begin an exposition on the mutation and transformation of the radical imagination with something alleged to be a 'beginning' would be almost as absurd as declaring the 'end of history' or the end of time itself. History has a funny way of not ending, despite numerous and exaggerated rumors of its impending demise. The banal requirements of form necessitate what appears to be a beginning, but this is purely incidental, or perhaps born of habit, repetition or trauma. We actually begin in a middle, in a muddle, perhaps a puddle, running across the street. We are in the gullet of a chicken without a road to cross. Likewise, the beginning and end may very well represent the same location, a non-place of (im)possibility, containing seeds for a radically alternative present, continually folding over itself and refracted through patterns, modulations and intensities: spasms and shifts divided by recurrences and undercurrents. This may be an intervention with no end, potentially present, existing before its visible self-institution and creation. It is not a roadmap or blueprint set out beforehand where sentences and pages unfold logically from one location to the next, moving through well-charted territory. It is a series of gestures, a means without ends, an arrangement and collision of bodies, texts, concepts and formations that generates the space it inhabits as it collapses its multidimensional self-fractured form. It implodes and bends dimensions back over itself, producing tesseracts.

< one / second / space >

To invoke the *imagination* as underlying and supporting radical politics, over the past forty years, has become a cliché. A rhetorical utilization of ideas that are already in circulation that invokes the mythic unfolding of a self-institutionalizing process of circulation. At a certain point, the recourse to the imagination as a source of potentiality in radical politics was no longer enacting new forms of creativity, but continually circulating forms that already existed and perceiving them as newly imagined. What exactly is *radical imagination*? And what are the compositional capacities created by the emergence, transformation, mutation, and decomposition of collective imagination within social movements? Imagination is not ahistorical, derived from nothing, but an ongoing relationship and material capacity constituted by social interactions between bodies. While liberatory impulses might point to a utopian (no)where that is separate from the present, it is necessary to point *from* somewhere, from a particular situated imagining. The task is to explore the construction of imaginal machines, comprising the socially and historically embedded manifestations of the radical imagination. Imagination as a composite of our capacities to affect and be affected by the world, to develop movements toward new forms of autonomous sociality and collective self-determination.

What does it mean to invoke the power of the imagination when it has already seized power (through media flows and the power of the spectacle)? Does any subversive potentiality remain, or are we left with simply more avenues for the rejuvenation of questionable fields of power and rearticulating regimes of accumulation? Perhaps it is only honest to think in terms of a temporally bound subversive power, which like the mayfly has already had its day in the sun. Maybe imaginal machines, like all desiring machines, only work by breaking down. That is, their functioning is only possible, paradoxically, by their malfunctioning. By reopening the question of recuperation, the inevitable drive to integrate the power of social insurgency back into the workings of capital and the state, we create possibilities for exploring a politics continually reconstituted against and through the dynamics of recuperation, to keep open an antagonism without closure that is continually composed and recomposed, to develop the necessary tools to resist the pervasive subdivision and suburbanization of the radical imagination.

People without imagination are beginning to tire of the importance attached to comfort, to culture, to leisure, to all that destroys imagination. This means that people are not really tired of comfort, culture and leisure but of the use to which they are put, which is precisely what stops us enjoying them.
– Raoul Vaneigem (1994: 17)

Notes

1. In an essay on research militancy, *Colectivo Situaciones* (2005), comment that footnotes do not constitute a complementary set of references, but operate as a fundamental articulation of the text operating on a different level. This is similar to the role of allusions and unmarked references in many forms of political writing and aesthetic composition. An awareness of the reference, while not absolutely essential to the main point of the piece, enhances the ideas contained within it (one perhaps could think of footnotes and references as somewhat akin to shout-outs in hip hop). In this text, the notes continue and extend the main line of argument of the text, and feedback on and through the body text. Despite the reality that this text could really have no beginning or end, that it always starts within the middle, this does not mean that one can find an almost infinite amount of space for elaboration; an 'imaginal limit function.' In the same way, there is an infinite number of theoretical points on any line leading up to but never actually reaching a given point. Here, the notes create a conduit for microcircuits of feedback and interaction within a text that moves towards, but never reaches, an end. The open space of the radical imagination exists both through extensive and intensive elaboration, continually growing in fractal patterns.

:: I :: Of Imaginal Machines & Compositional Inquiries ::

A sociological tradition has diagnosed the collective imagination as a system of correlative *representations* of... even reducible to a series of *situations*; in this diagnosis the collective imagination is constituted more or less in the last analysis by the constraints of reality. Could there not be another sociological tradition – linked however to the preceding one – in whose terms the phenomena of collective imagination would assert themselves as phenomena of a *constituent* imagination, in the name of, if not a last analysis, at a leading role played by it in the constraints which give social *facts* their *meaning*, conferring on reality a surreality which this reality would not be itself?

How does a collective imagination – hanging, it seems, on ideas 'up in the air,' judged by reasoning reason as factitious, fantastic, erroneous, empty ideas, indeed even as mumbo-jumbo or as pernicious ideas – how does this imagination exert a force of attraction, mobilizaton, dynamization, activation or reactivization, a force such that populations hang on to it themselves, and which holds them, maintains them and supports them? Briefly, how does imagination take power? – Henri Desroche (1979: 146-147)

The concept of an imaginal machine is coined, but never fully developed, by Peter Lamborn Wilson, in his work on the traditions of initiatic dreaming and automatic writing within Sufism and Taoism, *Shower of Stars* (1996). He deploys these techniques as a means of exploring what he describes as the deep structures that underlie various kinds of religious experiences and traditions (although these are not deep structures in the structuralist sense). The task set out for analysis is not to find structural similarities from an external perspective (as might typically be the case in most works of comparative religion), but to locate "resonant patterns that emerge directly from the material under consideration" (1996a: 10). Rather than seeking to impose patterns and bases for comparison from an external perspective, to overlay and impose them upon the social phenomena, the aim instead is to develop categories of comparison within these quite different, but also quite resonant, traditions of religious and mystical practice. It is in the reverberations of these 'imaginal powers' (*quwwat al-khayal*), that the workings of an imaginal machine are constituted.[1]

An imaginal machine enacts the production and interpretation of images, or the production of images by the body through its experiences and interactions. The *imago* is also the last stage in the development of an insect, after emergence from the pupae when metamorphosis is complete. This is ironic since the manifestations of collective imagination considered in this text can never really be said to be fully mature. They mutate, multiply, ossify, die and renew themselves again and again in successive cycles of social movement. For the purposes of this exposition, the term imaginal machine will indicate a particular arrangement or composition of desires and creativity as territorialized through and by relations between bodies in motion. The machine, as Deleuze and Guattari explain, is not a perceptive state of memory, but rather an "affective state" (1977: 122). Imaginal machines are composed by the affective states they animate, reflecting the capacities to affect and be affected by the worlds that are contained within them. They activate a cartography of thought: space is where the relation between subject and object blurs: "Each new act of connective seeing develops in oneself a new organ of perception" (Sacks 2007: 37).

Just as Wilson's analysis strives to avoid imposing categories by working with and elaborating forms of resonance, any formal exploration of imaginal machines requires searching for patterns of resonance rather than imposing them. To restore the social-technical machines of a particular organization or movement, we need to attempt to identify forms of resonance between desiring machines, between imaginal machines constructed and animated by constituent power. To pursue a form of conceptual development that resonates with the materials and questions under consideration requires techniques that closely resemble those described by Charles O. Frake as "cognitive ethnography" (1968), which involves working within categories and concepts used by people involved in a social situation to understand how that social situation functions.

Themes of imagination, creativity and desire run throughout the radical left movements, and the so-called "other workers' movement," to borrow Karl Heinz-Roth's phrasing. An emphasis on these themes did not appear on a mass scale until the late 1960s, but they exist within a secret drift of history that runs from medieval heresies to bohemian dreams of the Big Rock Candy Mountain in the 1930s. It is a drift that connects Surrealism with migrant workers, the IWW with Dadaism, and back again. Although these undercurrents are often renounced by the left's institutions, they find channels of influence in collective dreams and a pervasive yearning for freedom. The radical imagination can be found in Marx's assertion of the architect's superiority to the bee because of the act of imagination which precedes execution, or Spinoza's placing of the imagination as the primary mode of knowledge, an eminently material capacity that is a necessary prerequisite for any other kind of knowledge to exist. Even prophecy (and its political role), for Spinoza, is based far more on the particular imaginative capacities of the prophets than anything that is miraculous or exceptional to the unified order. Imaginal machines are constituted of god and/or nature (2004).

The importance of the imagination finds its fullest expression in the work of Cornelius Castoriadis (1975) and his conception of the social imaginary as a radical, self-instituting form: the very capacity to create new forms of social relations and organizations that determine the course of social and historical development. The social imaginary is not a network of symbols, or a series of reflections, but the capacity for symbols and reflections to be created in the first place. It is these shared capacities, and their ability to give rise to new forms of what is thinkable, of new social possibilities or organizations and new modes of understanding. Social imaginaries are not emergent in and of themselves, they are composed through the workings of many imaginal machines, devices created through social relationships and struggles that do not necessarily encompass the entire social field (even if they aspire to).

With imaginal machines it is important not to assume the homogeneity of a particular machinic composition over an entire movement or social sphere. Moments of minor mutation, while often occupying a seemingly insignificant role within the larger social fabric, act as a fulcrum on which larger transformations in collective imagination are initiated. This is how the ideas of the Situationists and *Socialisme ou Barbarie* found traction and expression in massive forms of social contestation. They can also be seen in the Italian movement of '77. New ways to socialize and expand the ideas and tactics of the avant-garde into mass methods for social conflict and insurgent creativity are only revealed by not assuming a unified character over the situation. James

Scott (1979) refers to this as the "revolution in the revolution," or the constant movement and transformation contained within. Here one uncovers a minor tradition of rebellion whose ideas and structures often diverge from stated goals, ideas, and methods: the everyday life of revolution is renewed everywhere a new imaginal machine is constructed.

Beneath the Bored Walk, the Beach

The everyday has this essential trait: it allows no hold. It escapes. It belongs to insignificance, and the insignificant without truth, without reality, but perhaps also the site of all signification... hence the weight and enigmatic force of everyday truth. – Maurice Blanchot (1987: 14/20)

While the classic 1968 slogan "beneath the pavement, the beach" was used to indicate that beyond industrial technology and mundanity one could still find a passionate drive for a vibrant life, something more profound seemed to be hinted at. One would not want to abandon the inquisitiveness and joy of 'uncovering' something precious, despite this being the very same emotion that has been mined constantly since the 1960s to fuel new shopping campaigns, designer holidays, and produce countless other forms of commodification. The point is not to ignore the commodity and its fetish, its shimmering appearance of general equivalence that is constantly denied, but rather to turn the gaze in the direction of the bored walk, and pay attention to the one who walks slowly because there is no reason to walk any faster. That is, to consider more carefully the constant silent war taking place on the factory floor (or any number of workplaces), as work and domination are stealthily avoided, not through open resistance, but through foot dragging, feigned respect, or feigned stupidity. As Anton Pannekoek argues, "Every shop, every enterprise, even outside of times of sharp conflict, of strikes and wage reductions, is the scene of a constant silent war, of a perpetual struggle, of pressure and counter-pressure" (2005: 8). Rather than focusing too much on the spectacle and spectacular forms of resistance (which risk falling into a consumerist critique), this focus keeps the emphasis on the production involved in the labor of the social itself.

Digging deeper, but beginning at the end, one curiously encounters a revolution of everyday life. Why revolution, and why everyday life? Following the ideas of the Situationists and many related currents of thought (particularly the ideas of Raoul Vaneigem), the idea is to refuse to fetishize particular dramatic, visible moments of transformation. This is not to say that those moments do not have any importance, particularly in the generation of new dramatic and mythical imagery, but rather to avoid the tendency to reduce the entire and much larger process of social transformation to these particular moments. This is to understand radical politics and social transformation taking place in a much broader and diffuse social milieu marked by points of materialization and the condensation of cycles of struggles, where the outward appearance and consciousness of the struggle is not the process in itself. These compressions in history might make for good film sequences, but not for substantive political transformation. As Huey P. Newton argues (2002), mistaking a moment in the revolutionary process for the entire process itself is to risk falling into mystifications of bourgeois thought. After all, if that is both the model and the expectation, if that magic moment never comes, then the long process and turmoil that that gives birth to another world can simply be written off as not being revolutionary because it lacked that fetishized moment.

Revolutions in their everydayness, as movement through and of the entire social field, are nearly impossible to describe without imposing closure on them as open and constantly fluctuating processes. It is this everydayness that Blanchot describes as insignificance that escapes signification, yet at the same time, is the source of all signification. It is this paradox that much of the creativity of radical thought over the past forty years has worked with or tried to work around. This can be seen clearly in the work of Michel De Certeau, who understands the everyday not as a background or container but rather the space of multiform, tricky, and stubborn tactics of resistance that lack a proper locus of their own. The tactics of everyday life that shift between and around fields of power and define the spaces of their existence, can be drawn from the consideration of "a certain kind of *rationality* and an imagination" that marks successive stages in the elaboration of radical politics (1984: xxii).

Rather than assert the scope of investigation as a totality let us then break things down into the simplest bodies of meaning and build up from there. What could be simpler? The problem is that even starting from the simplest aspects possibly might not be that simple.[2] For instance, what do autonomy and self-organization, the substance of the compositions forming and animated through imaginal machines, mean? The problem is that both concepts are notoriously hard to pin down. There are also long and complex histories of how these concepts have developed. As George Caffentzis notes, notions of autonomy used within the radical left include:

(0) The ability of workers to transcend the "laws of capital"

and the confines of their roles as dependent variables in the
surplus-value producing machine
(1) The attempt by the Italian extra-parliamentary left in the
early 1970s to "go beyond the contract" into the "territory"
(self-reduction of rents, electricity bills, transport, etc.)
(2) Feminists who argue that women should make their political decisions independently of male organizations
(3) The politics of the squatters' movement in Europe (especially Berlin) that reject any negotiations with city authorities
and other traditional "left" unions and parties
(4) The politics of Hakim Bey's "Temporary Autonomous
Zones" and related actions by groups like Reclaim the Streets
(5) Negri's notion of autonomy – in *Marx Beyond Marx* – as
the power of the working class to self-valorize through its use
of the wage not for the reproduction of its work function
(6) Harry Cleaver's notion of "autonomous Marxism" (2006a)

In this text, autonomy broadly refers to forms of struggle and politics that are not determined by the institutions of the official left
(unions, political parties, etc.). In other words, extraparliamentary
politics; a rejection of the mediation of struggles by institutional forms,
especially since representation and mediation are all too often the first
step in the recuperation of these struggles. To borrow Wolfi Landstreicher's description (n.d.), autonomous self-organization is characterized by non-hierarchical organization, horizontal communication
and relationships, and the necessity of individual autonomy in relation
to collectivity. The last point is important for Landstreicher (otherwise
there is no reason why states or corporations could not argue that
they were also forms of autonomous organization). It is also a key debate within radical politics as to the relation between the realization
of individual and collectivity autonomy, and how best to go about creating spaces for realizing these relationships. For Landstreicher, "autonomous self-organization is the development of shared struggle
based on mutuality for the full benefit of each individual involved"
(n.d.: 3).

It is important to think critically about the notion of autonomy
and calls for its realization. As David Knights and Hugh Willmott
wisely remind us, the call to become autonomous can have a potentially dark side, especially when the nature of that autonomy and its
emergence is not considered. For example, autonomy may function
as a mechanism for the self-discipline of the subjects in question. As
they emphasize, autonomy does not in itself describe or even point toward a condition or state of mind that exists within the world; rather,
it is a "way of imbuing the world with a particular meaning (or

meanings) that provide a way of orienting ourselves to the social world" (2002: 60). And that is why the question of the *composition*, and the compositional process, is important, precisely because the point is not to fall back on the unstated assumption of the existence of forms of autonomy possessed by the enlightened subject inherited from liberal political discourse. Autonomy is not something that is possessed by an individual subject so much as a relation created between subjects; that is, it is a form of sociality and openness to the other created through cooperative relations. Relations composed of individual subject positions in the process of emergence, rather than something that is possessed by isolated individuals before an encounter. The assumption of the existence of autonomy, whether by individuals or collectively, might well be an important precondition in creating conditions for its emergence. Autonomy is more a notion that is useful in mutual shaping and crafting of the social field, rather than something that precedes it. Similarly, it is important to heed Randy Martin's insightful exploration of how taking a notion of autonomy as a privileged 'first cause' or explanatory dynamic from which other processes are emergent can serve to limit the ability to appreciate forms of agency and social antagonism that emerge (2002: 73-89; 1994; 2006: 206-211). Martin suggests a politics founded on the formation and emergence of ensembles, a concept that has a good deal of resonance with the more open forms of (class) compositional analysis to be explored here.

And this self that is contained within the phrase, what is it and where does it come from? Are we talking about a self-contained and autonomous individual subject or some form of collectivity? Or perhaps we are talking about a particular kind of subjectivized individual self that emerges in the process of and in relation to the formation and maintenance of a larger form of social collectivity. What are the processes involved here? Are these forms of interactions involved in the formation of our various 'selves' a form of labor in themselves? It is these questions and queries that are to be explored, even if from the beginning we acknowledge that the territories of the question are almost inexhaustible, and that social movements by their very nature will niftily side-step our questions by constituting new arrangements on which the same questions are revisited within a different context. But perhaps the most important element here, further complicating the mix, is the hyphen in self-organization. The hyphen conjoins and brings together words but also transforms the joined elements that are at the time kept separate even as they are joined. They are disjunctively united and made different in being made same. To borrow a phrase from Michelle Fine, this dynamic of "working the hyphen" of the self-other relationship is one which "both separates and merges personal identities with our inventions of Others" (1994: 70). One could half-jokingly suggest that in the phrase "self-organization" there exists a graphic illustration, namely the emergence and development of a self in relation and conjunction, but simultaneously separated from and through, the development of forms of organization. It is a process that unifies, conjoins, transforms and separates the various social elements involved: a grammar of social antagonism mirrored and mired within a grammatical marking.

The task at hand is not trying to express and communicate these varied forms of struggle, because there is always something fundamentally nontransferable about expressing an experience that would frustrate such efforts. I do not attempt to transparently represent these struggles or communicate them, that would be to transmit preformed subjectivities and methods that can be adapted in other situations, because there are no procedures and methods outside out of the situation. Rather, following the ideas of *Colectivo Situaciones*, this is a project and a question of research militancy, of finding patterns of resonance between these different projects and forms of organization. Research militancy does not represent or communicate struggles, but is useful for extending experimentation and exploring the forms of composition found within the situation, or in the various processes of interaction, collective valorization and productive compatibilities found between different projects:

> Research militancy does not extract its commitment from a model of the future, from a search for power (potencia) in the present...the labor of research militancy is linked to the construction of a new perception, a new working style towards tuning up and empowering (potenciar) the elements of a new sociability (2005: 68).

But this is also not just a question of looking at present existing examples of alternative forms of labor organizing and insurgency, but also historical and previous examples that existed as part of what one might be tempted to think of in Sergio Bologna's framing as the tribe of moles, or the collective agglomeration of Marx's old mole; in other words, organizing based not upon an embrace of the dignity of labor, but rather on avoiding and refusing work. Historical examples, not in the sense of something that is fixed and that one can exist outside of for the purposes of study, but rather history as an example of living memories, that resonate and flow through forms of organization that exist in the present. Here we could talk about instances found in the history of autonomous Marxism and organizing in Italy, the IWW, forms of council communism and workers' parties against work, the efforts of the Situationists and the events of May 1968, of trainhopping hobos and migrant labor that merged with Surrealism's attempt to realize the marvelous and materialize the power of the imagination in everyday life. Unfolding in the nexus between the self-management of work and work refusal, these struggles articulate what might appear to be a contradictory position, a desire to have the cake and eat it too. But in many ways both struggles express a complimentary relation to organizing and political change. It is not that self-management and refusal are necessarily opposed, but rather that the refusal of work opens new ways and possibilities for exerting control over life and labor, and self-management potentially becomes a path through which it becomes increasingly possible to refuse work.

By teasing out the resonances and connections between existing forms of creative insurgency and attempting to find new paths for organizing the inherited wealth of knowledge and the experiences of previous struggles, these layers and textures of materials move across places, times and movements for continued subversion in the present. These moments, while often separated by time and space, are nonetheless connected by their mutual resonances in an overall movement toward abolishing the present conditions of their exploitation. Resonant connections do not mean that these diverse and varied moments of rupture are all the same, nor are they subsumed into one thing. As argued by Antonio Negri, "there is no linear continuity, but only a plurality of views which are endlessly solicited at each determinant moment of the antagonism, at each leap in the presentation, in the rhythm of the investigation" (1991: 13). The fracturing of daily life and attempts to create something else, tessellate and build upon each other, drawing discontinous lines of flight and creating an archipelago of insurrection and joy.

What then, might constitute the conceptual tools that would be useful in furthering a rhythm of investigation toward a form of autonomous self-organization adequate for addressing the current social and economic transformations? Concepts, as described by Deleuze and Guattari, whose creation it is the task of philosophy to form, invent and fabricate as combinations and multiplicities, defined by their elements to exist as fragmentary wholes. Autonomous self-organization, as both a diverse set of practices and ideas, comprises a history of becomings defined less by spatial characteristics than the intensive coordinates of embodied expression. The concept is "the contour, the configuration, the constellation of an event to come" (1994: 32-33). Self-organization is a point, acting as a center through which vibrations of energy flow and the desires of the working class are expressed. Concepts are embodied and animated through conceptual personae that *"show thought's territories"* (1994: 64). To find the right tools for this reconsideration implies creating the means to draw from and elaborate forms of practice and organizing that have congealed into autonomy and self-organization as defined terms, and to evaluate how they continue to shape the forms of practice from which they emerged.

Compositional Analysis

Class composition – power, class composition– transition, the articulation of these relations are based on the materiality of the behaviors, the needs, and the structures of self-valorization. – Antonio Negri (1991: 11)

Class composition analysis is most often associated with forms of heretical Marxism developed in Italy between the 1950s and 1970s. While it is difficult to treat class composition analysis as a coherent and unified whole, it is marked by several distinct characteristics. Notable among these is the consideration of class not as an immutable fixed identity, but as a constantly evolving form of social relations expressed through technical and political composition. Technical composition involves particular forms of labor that exist in a historical situation, while political composition expresses the formation of the working class as an evolving historical entity which develops through solidarity created during its struggle against capitalism. The focus on class struggle as a dynamic motor of changing class relations is an image that capital has strived to accommodate itself to in an attempt to convert class struggle into the driving force of its own development. This is often referred to as the "reversal of perspective."

The history of capitalism is all too often narrated in such a way that capital appears to be the principal, and sometimes the only, actor. At best, labor and social struggles merely react to the effects of a continuing pattern of development with little hope of exerting any real influence. Harry Cleaver describes this as narrating from capital's perspective where capital envisages the working class as "a spectator to the global waltz of capital's autonomous self-activating development" (1979: 27). By shifting our focus to the self-activity of the working class and its struggles against capitalism we pave the way for exploration of how transformations in capitalism are a product of responses to social struggles rather than simply an expression of the eternal dynamics of capitalist development. These ongoing struggles against capitalism and the attempt of capital to reabsorb their energies into its own workings create cycles of composition and decomposition. A cycle of decomposition is little more, although that is more than enough, than the struggle of capital against its subordinate position in relation the determination by the insurgencies against it. Struggles increase the political composition and unity of the working class, its ability to act increasingly as a self-determining force, which capital then responds to with a vast array of technologies of domination, from psychology to economics, machines and methods of labor discipline, monetary inflation and planned crises. One common example is the argument that the revolts and strikes against factory work in the 1960s and 1970s caused capital to respond through the creation of new forms of decentralized flexible production and organization, much like the forms that workers had created for themselves by resisting the factory lines. It is argued that this is what caused the transition from the factory line (characterized by standardized, repetitive labor) to forms of flexible and mobile production forming a diffuse social factory.

The historical goal of class composition was to assess the relation between social struggles and the changing dynamics of capitalist relations, with a view toward understanding these dynamics and better identifying how struggles could more effectively intervene to undermine and subvert the workings of capital. Class composition analysis then came to involve not only looking at struggles within the bounded factory and workplace, but also other forms of struggle that had not previously been considered as a component of class struggle, such as the unwaged, housewives, agrarian workers and students. This reconceptualization and recategorization of the working class in a broader sense allows one to sense the diversity and strength of anticapitalist resistance beyond the reactive struggles of factory workers in response to the latest dictates. As different moments and forms of struggle connect with one another and find ways to extend themselves in the creation of higher forms of social antagonism and resistance, they create a cycle of struggles.

Expanding these cycles of struggle depends on understanding how struggles are communicated through what Romano Alquati referred to as their vertical and horizontal articulations (1970). Struggles are articulated vertically in their location within existing circuits of capitalist production and reproduction, while their horizontal articulation is characterized by how they are embodied and linked spatially. Understanding the changing nature of capitalist relations demands an appreciation of the varied and connected layers through which struggles articulate themselves and operate within, otherwise it is all too easy to fall back into an analysis that sees the working of capital as being a closed and self-determining system. The Zerowork Collective, attempting to summarize how these ideas have developed and to find ways to adapt them to new circumstances, argued that the dynamics and cycles of struggle could be broken down to four interconnected levels:

(1) The analysis of struggles: their content, direction, how they develop and circulate, the ways in which workers find ways to bypass the technical constrictions of production and find ways to affirm their own power
(2) How different struggles within varied sectors of the working class affect and resonate with each other, how they affect the relations of different parts of the working class under capitalism with each other and how they attempt to redefine and subvert these enforced divisions
(3) The relation between working class struggles and their "official" institutions (trade unions, political parties, etc.), keeping in mind that struggles often do not originate from these organizations and may have to struggle against them as an obstacle to their own development
(4) How these aspects are related to capitalist responses and organization in terms of generalized social planning, technological development, patterns of employment, and the ongoing transformation of capitalist society (1992: 111-112).

Class composition in this sense, in the words of Negri, becomes an expression of the collective subjectivity of the struggles; it "restates the problem of power in a perspective where recomposition is not that of a unity, but that of a multiplicity of needs, and of liberty" (1991: 14).

But it would not be desirable to take these forms of analysis, however valuable and useful their origins and despite their apparent applicability, and directly transport them into usage in the current day. Similarly, the concept of worker self-management, developed over several hundred years, cannot be directly adapted to a contemporary setting without reappraisal. The world changes and class composition needs to be continually reappraised in its relation to the transformations of the social, political and economic world. In this sense, class composition – which was developed to understand the changing dynamics organizers found themselves in – can offer tools for deciding how such a form of analysis would need to be reworked in order to be useful. Class composition also developed within forms of politics and ideas that despite their value as tools also come with baggage that is somewhat less appealing. One of the main tasks of class composition was to identify the vanguard of emerging class sectors. It was argued that the vanguard held a privileged position that was essential to the workings of capital, and could be effectively subverted through intervention.

While many organizers employing such an analysis rejected the idea of the vanguardist party necessary to effectively lead the struggle, this method of looking for the emerging productive vanguard was in some ways held over in their form of latent, underlying assumptions, such as that certain sectors of the working class held a privileged position in their ability to resist capitalism. This emphasis, and the desire to identify positions of higher dependence for capital with a view to more effective subversion, also commonly led to the overemphasis of certain struggles at the expense of others, accompanied by a tendency to restate a stagist conception of capitalism, or the idea that capitalism needed to develop in certain ways before it could progress in a new form. Given these reasons it would be unacceptable to adapt the tools and framework of class composition analysis without also appreciating its limitations and pitfalls. One might wonder why it would even be desirable to adopt such a framework given its limitations. Monty Neill, in his reappraisal of class composition analysis in light of the Zapatista revolution, argues that moving beyond the workerist limitations and framework from which class composition emerged is useful "not in order to locate a new vanguard, but... also to help the many class sectors come together against capital" (2001: 122). To employ class composition analysis becomes a project of inheritance, not an attempt to replicate it as was employed originally, but rather to creatively rework with, transform, and update class composition analysis through using it in a different time, place, and location in a set of intensive coordinates (Jones 2002).

In particular, I want to expand the notion of compositional analysis by paying special attention to the overlap between aesthetic and class dynamics in cycles of struggle. To understand composition not just in terms of the quality and form an intervention or piece might take, but also as part of the aesthetic dynamics of political antagonism and organizing. In a similar manner to the way the dynamics of resistance are argued to determine the course of capitalist development, light may be shed on the way that resistant aesthetics, anti-art and the avant-garde have greatly shaped the development of capitalism to the degree that it relies on rejuvenation through new images and imagery along with other forms of social energies. This is an area that has been tentatively explored in the work of Jacques Attali (1985), based on his understanding of the prophetic role of music in forecasting changes in the composition of political economic power. Similarly, his understanding of a coming mode of compositional production as un-coerced creativity and collaboration that is not determined by eco-nomic imperatives is quite useful, even if he seems to neglect the political and social struggles that would bring about such a condition. It could be argued that mode of socialized production has been real-ized (in commodified form) in the hypercapitalist networked world. Nevertheless, this provides an important starting point for consider-ation of the relation between class and aesthetics within a composi-tional framework, one that is enriched, stretched, mutated, broken and reassembled by such a consideration.

The Fire Next Time

I have not managed to conceive you
and you have already occurred
please be so kind and tell me
who it is that imagined you
– Antanas Jonynas (2002: 47)

The task ahead then is necessarily doomed to failure, albeit hope-fully one of the more beautiful varieties. It is the task of finding tools for what p.m. calls "substructing the planetary work machine" (1995). He argues that simply finding new forms of subversion and decon-structing forms of labor is not enough, precisely because, as also ar-gued by many figures within the autonomist tradition, these gains can quickly come to be turned against themselves in new forms of self-discipline and capitalist power. Substruction is a process of combining construction and creation to open new possibilities for living in the spaces recomposed by subversion. The process of substruction is all the more tricky as it is important to realize that we are ourselves work-ing parts of the planetary work machine; we exist as part of capital, and thus cannot discuss subversion or construction as if it exists as an external enemy. This dynamic of being embedded within capital, as part of the machinery, also provides obstacles for developing forms of self-organization, since it would be naive to believe that we can completely avoid these dynamics and that spaces can magically be created 'outside' of capital.

Let us then give a brief overview of the chapters that will follow, perhaps as a bit of a teaser, as a bit of a warning, or to give some sense of coherence to an argument that will develop more in spastic fits and plateaus,[3] walking Spanish down the hall: a vitality of resistance all too aware of what its fate will be, sooner or later.

First, we wake up screaming in the horrors of the capitalist work-place and real subsumption of society that exists today. It is in the moment of horror, of shock, of the scream of being dislocated from the workings of the world around us, that the emergence of the radical imagination begins. Amongst the zombies and wreckage it all seems an incomprehensible mess at first. But the question of 'how did we get here' is not one of lament or defeat or a rhetorical cry, but rather, a necessary prerequisite for founding a compositional analysis adequate to the weight of the present. By examining the violence that underlies the foundations of capitalism (primitive accumulation), and understanding how this violence of separation is not an isolated event bur rather a dynamic that is constantly rearticulated in renewed rounds of capitalist discipline and expansion, we can attend to the question of the relation between social struggles and capitalist accumulation. The problematic and shocking revelation is that social struggles do not die, but rather are left in a zombified state of indeterminacy where their only desire is to turn against themselves and eat the brains of the living labor of resistance. That is to say, each renewed round of capitalist accumulation is based on the ability to turn the energies of insurgency against itself. This sets forth the questions to be walked, as the Zapatistas might say, and concepts to be explored throughout the book in various forms and examples.

Next, we explore the nature of the relation between revelation and revolution ("Revelation Vertigo") through the mythic core of politics that seems to unite many disparate strands of radical thought: the backwards projection of the existence of an autonomous subject, collectivity and capacity that is integral to creating the conditions for the possible realization of an autonomous existence in the present. The existence of an already present form of autonomy is part of a process of mythological self-creation and institution that needs to be assessed based on its ability to animate forms of autonomy and self-organization.

From there we go on to explore the process of minor composition, or how social struggles find ways to redirect the energies found within pop culture motifs (as well as employing humor and satire) to create forms of autonomous organization within the collective imagination, which is understood as a shared and collective capacity. Minor compositions are premised not on the creation of hegemonic or representative forms of politics, but rather on intense relations and the capacity to create social movement from within them. This is the process where the mythopoetic self-organization and self-institution, its revelation vertigo, starts and builds out from minor moments and ruptures. In particular, this chapter draws from the history of the Industrial Workers of the World (IWW) as a form of social struggle that creatively employs music as part of its labor organizing, as well as some examples from more recent times (such as collaborations between the IWW and Billionaires for Bush).

"Space is the (non)Place," explores the role of images and themes of outer space and extraterrestrial travel as a pole of imaginal recomposition. How do the forms of minor composition and rupture articulate beyond themselves to become more than a localized form of social creativity? Even when it seems that there is no physical space in which exodus is possible, an outer space of collective imagination can be created through the exteriority of the radical imagination. It is here one can find a diffuse cultural politics, from Sun Ra to the Association of Autonomous Astronauts, that creates spaces of exteriority through the usage of space imagery. Space themes operate through the creation of an imagined space of exteriority from which other realities are made possible even despite (and perhaps through) the literal impossibility of the motifs used in constructing this space.

From the outer space of the radical imagination as exteriority, we turn more specifically to consider the ongoing importance of the avant-garde in constructing imaginal machines, as well as the limitations that are contained within such approaches. In particular, the focus is on the constant drive within the avant-garde to put an end to art as a separated or reified activity and to reintegrate forms of socialized creativity throughout the social field. In contrast to an imaginal space as pure exteriority, the theme is how the avant-garde 're//fusal' of reification and separation works in two directions: both as a refusal of a separated sphere for aesthetic activity and a re-fusing of new creative energies entering the social field. This chapter elaborates the concept of affective composition within political aesthetics. Similar to Joseph Beuys' (2004) notion of "social sculpture," an approach to aesthetics based not upon considering the content of the work, but rather the kinds of relations and connections animated and made possible by it (that can be created or sustained through shared creation). This is a dynamic that is found within avant-garde currents, as well as zombified within the workings of similar phenomena in the focus on interactivity and participation within post-Fordism, the net economy and cultural industries.

In "The Labor of the Imagination" the task is to examine ways in which forms of collective creativity and politics can be made durable through organizational forms, particularly in the case of worker self-management. Is it possible to create a space and form for the organization of collective labor and creativity without it being turned against its own aims and intentions, or would this just be another example of turning avant-garde intentions and desires into a stabilized form that can be used by capital? Drawing from my own experience with Ever

Reviled Records (a worker owned and run record label) as well as some historical examples, we examine the potentiality for recomposing autonomy within the organizational form of the self-managed workplace. The chapter concludes that self-management is prone to evolve into forms of collective capital rather than its subversion. This is the tendency for anticapitalist vampire hunters, once bit by capital, to become vampires themselves, even if the scary looking castle on the hill is run as a cooperative. The question remains how to draw from and expand upon the potentials of self-managed forms of organization while undermining its tendency to become subsumed within the logic of capitalist valorization (even despite its intentions to escape from it).

Moving away from questions about self-managed labor and its exhaustion, we turn to "Questions for Aeffective Resistance" and consider the roles of affective relations and spaces within the labor of creating communities of resistance. Drawing from the history of struggles around domestic labor (in particular campaigns such as Wages for Housework and more recent organizing by groups like *Precarias a la Deriva*), this chapter considers questions of sustainability and collective joy within radical politics, especially when the sedimentation or ossification of the radical imagination in a particular or distorted form impedes the further development of collective movement. This concerns the necessary overlap between the affectivity and effectiveness of political organizing, or the ways in which relationships and interaction are not something external or supplementary to politics, but are very much the micro-level everyday organization and continuation of autonomous politics.

"Precarious Politics" draws from the debates and organizing that have occurred during recent years around the theme of precarious labor, and how this has acted as a pole of movement recomposition in the wake of the anti-globalization movement of the late 1990s. Although precarious labor is far from being new (if anything, it has always been the condition of labor in capitalism), it provides tools and methods for organizing within the current context. The grounds for radical politics constantly need to be recomposed, that is to say, the grounds for politics they are also precarious, and will continue to be so.

In the last chapter, "Dance, Dance Recomposition," we return almost exactly to where we began by reconsidering the nature of processes of recuperation and their relation to radical politics. Drawing from sources ranging from the Situationists and more recent elaborations on recuperation prompted by post-Situationist writings, we can see that the phenomenon of recuperation is not a cause for alarm, defeat or cynicism, but rather that radical politics must be continually recomposed on the shifting social sands created by the constant recuperation of social insurgency and energy into the workings of capital and the state. Zombies or no zombies, the logic of 'incorpse-oration' is not one that is likely to be done away with anytime soon. Rather it is a question of how it is dealt with, to ward off the bony hands of the old world that constantly grasp and claw at our feet just when we thought we had escaped. This is the defining task of any radical politics that seeks to remain so, to find ways to not be transformed into just another tool for capitalist valorization or state power. This requires the continual rebuilding and reformulation of imaginal machines capable of animating new forms of self-organization and autonomy in the revolutions of everyday life

Notes

1. In Wilson's work, the concept of an imaginal machine is said to be employed in the traditional sense, although strangely this is never fully explained. I sense consistent parallels in Wilson's themes with Ibn Arabi. This is particularly the case around the motifs of the power of the imagination, not as a site of fantasy, but as an active agent of a much larger process. This space of engagement formed by the imagination is referred to by Henry Corbin (1969) as the "imaginatrix." There are also interesting resonances between mystic streams of Islamic thought with that of Christian mysticism, Spinoza and notions of imagination developed by the Situationists. Wilson also uses the imaginal machine in his writings on entheogenics, cyberculture and the workings of monetary systems, all united in their functioning as some kind of Gnostic system or method of transmutation (1996a). The imaginal machine has been waiting for a fuller explication to occur. This book strives to leave the concept open to further elaboration and growth.

2. Conceptual reduction can be used to 'simplify' a question but this usually requires an increase in the complexity of the assumptions necessary for that operation, thereby rendering any discovery or conclusion irrelevant to the reality that was initially under investigation. Thanks to Emma Chung for pointing this out to me, phrasing in a concise and clear format what I had struggled to express.

3. In the same way that this text both theorizes the formation of imaginal machines and constitutes one in itself, each chapter can be thought of as both describing and enacting the formation of a particular kind of imaginal machine. The formation of the overall machine builds up from the synergistic interactions between the various chapter-machines, as they cross cut, overlap, and cross-pollinate with each other (although there is not necessarily a linear or teleological development in this progression).

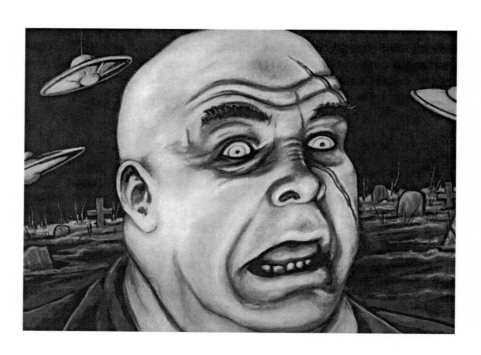

:: II :: Plan 9 from the Capitalist Workplace ::

Politics today is nothing more than the expression of the domination of dead structures over the entire range of living production. – Toni Negri and Felix Guattari (1990: 30)

Plan 9? Ah, yes. Plan 9 deals with the resurrection of the dead. Long distance electrodes shot into the pineal and pituitary gland of the recently dead. – The Ruler (1959)

The lights go off. Darkness fills the room as the curtain opens into the void of lost possibilities. Yes, indeed, it's time for the scary voiceover sequence filled with dire pronouncements: declarations that we today live an age of real subsumption, of the despotism of capital, inside an endless war on terror and global civil war, where all of our life energies have been colonized by capitalism in the unfolding of the social factory, where everything lived has passed over to representation in the infinite powers of recuperation of the all menacing spectacle.[1] Why, there have even been reports that low wage slaves have been replaced by brain eating zombies from outer space, or maybe it was the Third World. Anyway, the details are so hard to keep track of anymore.

But, fret not; after all, this is the theater of the radical imagination and not the defeatist after school special. One might expect, as with any good plot sequence, that it would also be foretold that the hero would salvage the situation from the appearance of total catastrophe at the moment when it seems that certain doom is nigh. But the hero, seemingly unable to stay with the script, seems to keep changing name and appearance – from what used to be that good ole' stand by, the working class (burly looking factory workers and what not); but nowadays seems to go by many different monikers, such as the multitude, the precariat, or dispersed networks and connections that have no names. Again, the details are so numerous, confusing, and easy to lose track of. And for all the dreams of liberation and escape from the many forms of bondage and social domination, these desires have more often than not been turned to other ends, to the becoming of something horrific, or sold back to us in neatly packaged forms. Or maybe all that at the same time.

But for now, let's step back from them for one second, put aside the veracity of these claims and forecasts and ask a few questions that might ruffle the feathers of the talking heads of revolutionary theory: Is this my beautiful social factory? How did we get here? Which way did the multitude go? How many precarious workers does it take to change a light bulb? How do we get out of here? Are we to rise up, an insurgency flowing from some mysterious underground of revolutionary fervor? Or, do we often find ourselves feeling defeated and isolated, proclaiming that things are just the same as they ever were?

Over recent years there has been a veritable explosion of interest in the political current of Italian workerism, *operaismo*, more commonly referred to as autonomist Marxist politics and philosophy, spurred mainly by the international success of the writings of Michael Hardt and Antonio Negri. Despite this, attention paid to this development has almost inverted the workings of the radical imagination of autonomist politics. While the theoretical vocabulary and language of autonomist politics has proliferated like so many Brooklyn hipsters, fittingly enough, it has done so in a superficial manner. Paradoxically, the radical intent underlying autonomism has seemingly vanished. Rather than understanding capitalist development as having been determined by the movement of working class resistance, autonomist concepts have been used in ways that make capitalist development seem like a hermetically closed, self-directing process. What I want to do is to get around this quagmire by returning to earlier phases of autonomist thought, drawing both from better-known *operaisti* theorists as well the work of the Midnight Notes Collective, Silvia Federici, Massimo De Angelis, and others, to reconsider the apocalyptic origins of capitalism. By understanding primitive accumulation not as a one-time event that underlies the formation of capitalism, but rather a process of violence and separation that persists and is expanded through the incorporation of the energies of social resistance, I hope to provide some new considerations for moving beyond capitalism.

Following the arguments of autonomous feminism and related currents, I am considering the working class not just as waged indus-

trial workers, but as all whose labor and social interactions are involved and necessary for the process of reproducing capitalism: students, farm workers, housewives, migrants, etc… The tactics of this
type of analysis should be accompanied not simply by a declaration
that such positions are involved in the production of surplus value
and therefore can contest its operations, but specifically of how they
are enmeshed in such. The value production specificities of each of
these positions, while clearly important, especially for considering
their submerged repertoire of practices of resistance (which far from
being spontaneous exist in the infrapolitical self-organization of the
undercommons), must be set aside for the moment.

Questions around how the nightmare of capitalism began, how
the horrors of capitalist accumulation were set in motion, are in many
ways a logical starting point for a consideration of the existing state
of affairs and how to escape from it. After all, without some understanding of the paths that led to our current location, how might it be
possible to find a way through the thicket of obfuscations and mystifications clouding how the world we live in is a mutually produced
social creation? And this is not to surmise that if only it were possible
to find some mystical trail of bread crumbs left by little red resistance
struggles along the path, then it would be possible to follow them back
to where things were before, to some idyllic pastoral fantasy of a pre-
capitalist past. Rather, it is by asking questions about the formation
of capitalism that one finds ways to tease out new ideas for moving
through and beyond it.

The Horrors of Accumulation

By a reversal of perspective, the life force of the body was
transformed into labor power; the body was now shadowed
by its double, an intangible soul that existed in a universe un-
connected with earthly survival, a universe accessible only
through death. – Raoul Vaneigem (1994: 26)

And so from here we begin, from a scream of terror formed in the
realization that the daily horrors and suffering around the world are
not props in some B-movie but are all too real. Dislocated by the un-
reality of this reality, the scream forms the basis of other vibrations,
other realities. As John Holloway observes, the scream is the basis of
critical reflection and radical social action:

When we talk or write, it is all too easy to forget that the beginning was not the word, but the scream… The starting
point of theoretical reflection is opposition, negativity,

struggle. The role of theory is to elaborate that scream, to express its strength and to contribute to its power, to show how the scream resonates through society and contribute to that resonance. (2003: 15).

This apocalypse necessary for the unfolding of capitalism, or primitive accumulation to use the parlance, is the process where the common lands and agricultural holdings are destroyed and people are forcibly removed from their lands and ways of life. It is necessary to start from an understanding of primitive accumulation as the origins of capitalism are tied closely to conditions for the realization of its dissolution. As argued by Massimo De Angelis: "the definition of primitive accumulation – of the *origin* of this *separation* – is linked to the heart of Marx's vision of a human society, as it mirrors a vision of its opposite: that the producers have *direct* access to the means of production" (2001: 14). Likewise, Silvia Federici argues (2004) that it is necessary for all those confronting the question of moving through and beyond capitalism to reconsider the nature of primitive accumulation.[2]

The forcible expropriation of agricultural populations from their land and homes, accomplished through forms of bloody discipline and state action had enormous and long lasting impacts that deeply influence the geopolitics of particular areas in different ways. Barrington Moore (1977) argues that the processes through which these enclosures occurred, the social relations embodied in them, had long-term consequences extending through and suspended within the world as we know it today. Deprived of any means of self-sustenance, populations found themselves "turned into vagabonds, and then whipped, branded, tortured by laws grotesquely terrible, into the discipline necessary for the wage system" (Marx 1973: 899). Capitalist discipline and social relations were formulated through experiments on worthless bodies, from factory discipline to the enactment of laws backed by vicious state violence. Marx uses the phrase *"experimenta in corpore vila"* (Latin for "experiments on a worthless body"), at several points through his work to describe the formation of new regimes of capitalist discipline in the factory system. The phrase also appears in several of Engels' letters and in *The Role of Force in History: A Study of Bismarck's Policy of Blood and Iron* (1968). States of exception, the creation of populations outside of measures of protection and law, were germinating within the operations of workhouses and bloody expropriations before they congealed into their now more commonly recognized forms of internment camps (or for that matter, 'illegal combatants'). *Vogelfrei*, workers and peasants indeed became "free as a bird," except that more often than not the freedom gained was that of losing the ability to live without dependency on the emerging capitalist social institutions. These forcible dispossessions and enclosures, the creation of populations with no rights and outside of human community and legal protection, were integral and necessary to the foundation of capitalism and the creation of conditions for "free workers" to "voluntarily" accept conditions of wage labor.

But primitive accumulation is not just a historical event, a period that precedes the formation of capitalism, although it is a necessary precondition. The continued separation between populations and their ability to sustain forms of social life and community that are not dependent on capitalist social relations is one that needs to be continually maintained and expanded and/or intensified. As capitalist production begins to come into its own, this separation is not only maintained, but is reproduced continually on an ever-expanding scale. Analyzing the likely trajectory and direction of capitalist development, or employing the "method of the tendency," to borrow Negri's conception (1991), is important precisely because it creates the possibility to understand and anticipate the nature of capital's reaction to forms of social resistance and constantly rethink them based upon this understanding. Indeed, while capitalism only existed in relatively discrete geographic areas at the time Marx began to describe and theorize its development, it soon stretched its greedy bloodstained hands far across the world through wars of conquest, subterfuge, economic sabotage, and other dodgy dealings. It is the foundation upon which the exploitation of labor rests, the very basis of capitalist social relations.

This is to say that while primitive accumulation is the historical process that constitutes and makes possible capitalist social relations, it persists as a constantly reproduced form. It is a form of continued and renewed separation of new populations from the means of production and the ability to support themselves through new forms of social production and cooperation. Primitive accumulation continues to exist as within the capital relation; it exists as what Werner Bonefeld refers to as its "constitutive pre-positing action." (2001: 7) Capital is the form of this separation, as are other forms of social domination, from racism to heterosexism, that all are interwoven with the workings of the economy and the state without necessarily being subsumed under a master logic. Hence, its permanence is not just in the uneven character of its development; but, rather, in its systemic nature.

One could say that primitive accumulation, which isn't very primitive at all, continues to exist suspended within and underpinning the continuing reproduction of capitalist social relations. It is the bloodsucking vampires, who unlike the mythical image of a cloaked figures in a castle, extract our vitality through a million tiny bites that siphon off energies all through our lives – not simply through what is usually thought of as the workplace, but through all areas of life (Godfrey et al: 2004). As Midnight Notes argues, any leap in proletarian power demands a dynamic capitalist response to maintain the conditions necessary for the continued existence of capital. Structural adjustment programs, devaluation of currencies, elimination of social spending and welfare programs, corporate subsidies and war profiteering, as well as many other drastic measures, all compose parts of this general process of creating new enclosures. Like the "old enclosures" that were necessary to separate agricultural populations from their land – as along with the processes of enclosing bodies and patterns of thought in corresponding forms – the new enclosures are essentially methods for ending communal control of the means of subsistence for populations, now accomplished over ever expanding geographic and intensive coordinates: "for every factory in a free trade zone in China privatized and sold to a New York commercial bank, for every acre enclosed by a World Bank development project in Africa or Asia as part of a 'debt for equity swap,' a corresponding enclosure must occur in the US and Western Europe" (1990: 2).

The difference between primitive accumulation, as the historical process necessary for the emergence of capitalism, and present accumulation, as a dynamic that is suspended, maintained, and reproduced within current capitalist social relations, is not a substantive difference but one that is rather located in the differing forms and conditions through which this separation is realized. During primitive accumulation this occurs as the production of a separation between populations and the means of production. This same dynamic is reproduced on greater extensive and intensive scales, encompassing ever-larger geographic and temporal spheres with the ultimate aim being the total subsumption of life into its workings. As new forms of social insurgency and political organizing seek to develop ways to autonomy and self-determination, they create new reservoirs of social cooperation and knowledge – that is, they create new commons. As argued by Massimo De Angelis: "This 'all-powerful social barrier' brought about by workers' struggles and which defines the extension of the working day, sets a limit to the extraction of absolute surplus value. The definition of a social barrier evokes the idea of a *social limit* beyond which capital cannot go in furthering the opposition of dead to living labor. In this sense, this social barrier is a form of 'social common' because it sets a limit to the extension, the scale of the separation between producers and means of production" (2001:18; 2007).

It is this process, the creation of new commons, that functions as a pole of political recomposition. And it is these commons, or the commons of resistance, that are expropriated through renewed rounds of primitive accumulation, and whose expropriation inaugurates a new stage in the nature of capitalist social relations. Indeed, as Marx noted, during the process of primitive accumulation, revolutions are "epoch-making that act as levers for the capitalist class in course of formation" (1973: 876). Primitive accumulation does not only occur as the rupture between modes of production during the period of transition to capitalism; primitive accumulation exists as the constantly reproduced separation between producers and the means of production, which persists within the social formation of capitalism and reemerges with greater intensities as new forms of social cooperation and production are created.

What can one make of this relation between insurgency and capitalist development? This relation between forms of social insurgency, upheaval, and modernization has been explored with clarity by Shmuel Eisenstadt (1966). Likewise, labor organizing and revolt is not something that appears with the flourishing of the waged industrial proletariat, but was also exhibited by chattel slaves and contract workers through informal verbal agreements, go-slows, sabotage, and strikes (Hart 1985; Turner 1995). It is here that one locates what has been described by Michael Burawoy as production politics, or the relation between processes of production and existing political forms, one that is built around a political apparatus "which reproduces those relations of the labor process through the regulation of struggles" (1983: 587). In other words, it is necessary for the workings of capital to constantly incorporate the social energies produced by worker's struggles as the motor of its own development.[3] The working class, which is what it does (i.e. labors), exists for itself before it exists as a class against capital. The task for emerging and constantly reemerging and morphing nodes of capitalist power is to harness these social forces and forms of cooperation into its own working. Capitalism exists as a snare, as an apparatus of capture that turns the vibrant flesh of life lived in resistance to the living dead humdrum of everyday banality.[4] For too long, the focus has been on the working of capital as the driving force of development and social transformation, existing as a force to which workers struggles are usually seen at best as resisting some inevitable tide that they barely hope to hold back. The style of analysis, by not taking into account the autonomous power of populations to resist and undermine forms of domination, tends to construct a narrative that treats the working class as "only a spectator to the global waltz of capital's autonomous self-activating development" (Cleaver 1979: 27). And that hardly seems like a fitting starting point for a radical political analysis as it builds in from the very beginning an implicit notion of the helplessness of the very people who are argued to be argents of social change.

It is the organization of workers' struggles and energies, rather than the autonomous and self-directed nature of capital, that has *determined* the course of development through its actions: as Mario Tronti argues, "the relationship between living labor and the constant part of capital is not a neutral process. Rather, it is determined, and often violently so, by the emerging class relationship between the collective worker and the whole of capital, *qua* social relations of production. We would then see that it is the specific moments of the class struggle which have determined every technological change in the mechanisms of industry" (1980). It is this thrust of working class struggle to escape from forms of bondage, (wage) slavery, control, and imposition, from feudalism to high tech surveillance, that necessitates the continuing economic development on the part of capital (Panzieri 1976; Sewell and Wilkinson 1992). The workings of capital are determined not by their own operations but by the necessity of responding to forms of social action that seem to undermine and destroy these relations of domination.

But as working class strategies for resistance and flight do not just occur within fixed moments and points, capital's strategies for responding to working class resistance also occur through ever expanding locations and social circuits. As working class cycles and spirals of struggles multiply themselves further over the expanding social fabric, they are met with recuperative responses at all those levels attempting to create new enclosures around the social wealth and co-operation they contain. But as the working class finds new ways to escape from confinement, enclosure, and servitude, the operations of capital likewise seek means to escape from being determined by the working class. The history of working class attempts to create means of exodus and withdrawal from relations of domination is mirrored by the history of capitalist development characterized by repeated attempts to withdraw from the class relationship determined by working class action, or as described by Tronti, "the history of the successive attempts of the capitalist class to emancipate itself from the working class, through the medium of the various forms of capital's political domination over the working class" (1980).

Tronti's argument is that as capitalism develops, social relations become a part of the process of production: "the whole of society becomes an articulation of production; in other words, the whole of society exists as a function of the factory and the factory extends its *exclusive* domination over the whole of society" (quoted in Wright 2002: 37-38). While there are legitimate concerns about the notion that the factory constitutes the exclusive mode of domination across the social field, this conception of the social factory, elaborated in the *operaisti* tradition, was greatly influential in moving away from an exclusive focus on struggles occurring within the bounded factory space to a plurality of struggles occurring across many different locations and modes. Class struggle, then, does not just occur only in the spaces most commonly understood as the workplace, but all through the various social fields that are increasingly subjected to the very forms of discipline, control, and regulation necessary to maintain the functioning of capitalism. It is important to stress this: for Tronti and those working within this tradition these struggles are not adjuncts to the "real class struggle" within the factory, rather they are the particular embodiment of class struggle within a socially and historically specific class composition and process of political recomposition of the class. Despite capitalism's drive to colonize, to realize the conditions of the social factory completely, there is always something that escapes: populations that find new ways out and methods to create an existence and forms of support for themselves to break free from these relations. The commoning found within resistance movements, the imaginaries and practices found within them, are the very substance that capital needs to co-opt and integrate into its own circuits of valorization. It is the new blood that entrepreneurial vampires crave, the brains sought by capital's zombie-like machinations as it stumbles forward. And it is here that primitive accumulation is constantly renewed and redeployed, formulating new experiments for extracting social wealth from populations.

During certain periods, primitive accumulation moves from a suspended and pre-positing element undergirding the reproduction of capitalist social relations to a level where the overall composition of capital changes, particularly during great periods of social upheaval. There is no one form of primitive accumulation; rather, there are technologies and techniques of constantly renewed primitive accumulation. Or perhaps, a more accurate name might not be primitive accumulation; but, rather, originary accumulation, or the social technologies and processes through which social insurgency and revolt are turned back against themselves and incorporated into founding and modifying regimes of accumulation and dispossession. This means that transformations in the logic and working of capital are not the plans of alien zombie invaders, a nefarious plot thrust upon us from some devious central command location; they are the refracted image of dead social struggles seeking to eat the brains of living labor. This is perhaps the key insight of autonomist analysis, which in this way can be understood somewhat as playing the Marxist LP backwards, starting with the potentiality of the working class as having existed before capitalism, continuing to exist through it, and functioning as the determinate motor of its development. By playing the record backwards, the demonic message discovered was that capital's narrative of triumphant self-directed development was little more than cover for the reality that all of capitalism is the recuperation of social energies not of its own being. It is, as Jacques Camatte frames, capital's necessary dependency on recuperating what is not of itself, for "capital is a form that always inflates itself on an alien content" (1995: 154). This argument and the politics of revelation enmeshed in it, the revealing of an already existing autonomy as a precondition for its creation in the present, will be explored in the next chapter.

The history of anticapitalist resistance is scattered with examples of *how* this process has occurred, from the revolts against feudalism that preceded the dawn of capitalism to current attempts to turn open source software and hacked technology into profitable commodities. For example, Keynesianism and the New Deal represents the moment where the dialectic of exploitation was socialized throughout every level and aspect of social life, where it became recognized that it would be necessary to focus on the balance of power and forces involved in class struggle not as something to be done away with; but, rather, to be integrated into an arrangement of connecting demands for higher wages to the functioning of the capitalist order itself. The working class, thus, comes to be recognized as the driving motor of development, although cloaked within the framing of this power as "effective demand." In other words, "capital's dynamism at this point only results from a continuous struggle, in which the thrust of the working class is accepted, and new weapons are forged in order to prevent the class from acting outside capital, and to make it act within a framework whose outlines are continually being drawn anew" (Negri 1988: 28-29; De Angelis 2000). Class struggle is resolved by its integration into the framework of capitalist development, resulting in a greater centralized and socialized planning of expenditure: the welfare state. The welfare state was then thrown into crisis by renewed forms of revolt against the factory line and social planning in the late 1960s and 1970s.[5] This process continues in various forms and incarnations, leading up the current form expressed as the simultaneous rise of post-Fordist economy and the intensification of those security measures through which working class struggles are integrated into the state through coercive force and restructuring (Hirsch 1991).

But, what is important here are not necessarily the details of the transformation itself, but the importance in realizing that these transitions in economic and political regimes (of forms of labor, forms of state) are not something that is actuated through the whims and actions of the autonomous power of capital. Instead, these transformations are determined by the efforts of state and capital to respond to the on-going and constantly changing forms of social insurgency that are occurring. Any attempt to periodize and understand this history of transformation and, from that, to understand how to formulate plans of action for today, finds at best that there is no coherent principle to do so in either case, and more likely finds itself based on a narrative of constant victimization and defeat (Clark 1992; Hardt 2002). This narrative of defeat is easily accompanied by social democratic or vanguardist politics precisely when one fails to recognize the autonomous capacities of people and the manner in which these capacities largely determine the course of history. The constant shifting of the relation between the form of state, labor, capital, and all other forms of social power dispersed through human relations, are constantly formed and re-formed in accordance with the ever accumulating and layering of forms of social struggle.

The process through which the relation of state-labor-politics changes is referred to by Sergio Bologna, as well as many others, as the form of the state. Bologna argues that the form of state, which emerges during certain historical moments (Italy in the 1970s, being a prime example), occurs when the crisis of one form of the relation state-labor-politics and the development of a new form of class composition risk escaping the dialectical relation between government and opposition. For Bologna, this leads to the development of a party system that "no longer aims to mediate or represent conflicts in civil society, but is increasingly compact and counterpoised against movements in civil society, and against the political program of the new composition of the class" (1980). That is to say, that electoral politics and unions develop in ways that increasingly are not expressions of these desires for radical political change and cannot mediate and work with them, but rather are opposed to their development. This seems to fit best with the development of the Italian Communist Party (well, communist parties in general). In fact, one could go as far as to argue that one should not be surprised that such parties "sell out," but rather that they could do anything else in such a position without fundamentally transforming the political situation they are embedded in. But the form of state cannot be reduced to just a strengthening of the repressive apparatus; rather, it is also expressed through a variety of political norms and values which are congealed around the ideology of crisis. In Italy, during the late 1960s and 70s, this was coordinated through what was referred to as the "strategy of tension," or where bombings and attacks were used as pretexts for increased militarization, security measures, detentions, and so forth. Typically attributed to anarchists and radical leftists (and only revealed later to often have been the work of right wing paramilitaries and often connected to government officials), this provided the pretext for increased security measures and for justifying these measures based upon people's fears and insecurities. This is not so different from the role that alleged 'terrorists' play today, or the constant search for heresy fulfilled for the medieval Catholic Church. But, the form of state is not in some ways a phenomenon that is opposed to the forms of social insurgency that have upset existing state-labor-union relations. The form of state expresses the changing nature of this relation and, therefore, is not a power that is as opposed to extraparliamentary movements as much as it is the inverse reflection of them.[6]

It is these moments and periods of rupture and social upheaval that are the pivots on which the continued development of capitalism and the state hinge. It would be a mistake to try and separate the economic and the political; as, while neither is subsumed within the other, they are so inextricably linked and bound together that trying to analyze one without the other inevitably leads to a deeply inadequate understanding. These founding acts of violence that underlie the creation of new forms of government and regimes of accumulation embody the mystical foundations of authority. Mystical here, as employed by Jacques Derrida, in the sense that a constitutional assembly, the process through which a new government is founded, rests on a legitimacy that does not exist until the founding act itself; which is created precisely by the constitutional assembly that purportedly rests on this "external" source of legitimation: "originary violence that must have established this authority and that itself could not have been authorized by anterior legitimacy, so that in this initial moment, it is neither legal nor illegal" (1992: 6). This founding violence provides the legitimation for animating whole sets of legal and juridical orders. It exists as a "moment of suspense" through which "this founding or revolutionary moment of law is, in law, an instance of non-law" which is paradoxically the whole history of law (1992: 35). The necessity and importance of revolutionary violence is widely acknowledged and celebrated in numerous national days of commemoration to mark the founding of their ruling government; although, more often than not, in the picnics and celebration that occur on such dates, notions of revolution are traded for those of patriotism and hot dogs with mustard. There exists, then, a close relation between the originary violence that underlies the founding of new forms of government and the originary accumulation and social dispossession that heralds the birth of a new regime of accumulation. But, if it is the process of integrating forms of social insurgency back into the workings of political and economic power, then it is in the space of suspension and indistinction that one must begin to find a way to go through and beyond it.

State(lessness) of Exception, Exceptions of State

To eradicate something, that very thing must be instituted in its most extreme, condensed, functionalized form... a quickening spiral of centrifugal waves of striation and centripetal smooth flows... the spiral of capture is converted into a line of fluid attack sent out in pulses. The aim is to accelerate the process to the point where the spiral melts with the line, and the pulse becomes continuous attack. – Brian Massumi and Kenneth Dean (1992: 41-42)

At the heat of the interlocking and overlapping relations between insurgency, accumulation, revolution, and recuperation is a curious relationship, an almost mirror imaging, between constituent power and states of exception.[7] This may seem to be a strange proposition to advance, but it would be a mistake to advance the idea that it is simply a question of revolutionary violence as opposed to reactionary violence, of our violence as opposed to theirs.[8] The social eruptions of constituent power during revolutionary times and the horrors of violence committed during suspension of law are linked in strange ways through similar social dynamics and processes which underlie them both. Constituent power and exception are not wholly other than each other; rather, there is a very close relation between them that is over-mistaken through the reversal of the image. Terrorist or freedom fighter? Patriot or traitor? Very often, the difference is only one of perspective, of temporal distance, rather than anything substantively different in the action involved. It is the reversal of the image. A reversal of perspective antagonistically turned back on itself again and again.[9]

Constituent power exists as the force underlying and connecting, through hidden and subterranean passages, in the outbreaks of revolutionary times and ruptures. It is what makes possible the creation and animation of new social relations and juridical arrangements. Embodied in the forms of social insurgency and fervor, it determines new regimes of accumulation, state forms, and dispersions of power as they are reintegrated into their workings. Constituent power, while existing as a force that breaks apart, interrupts, and shatters current arrangements of power in a violent and expansive manner, creates the possibilities for forming new relations. It is "an exceptional power that radically renovates the law in force through the radical modification of its social conditions" by rupturing the arrangements of power that exist as the boundaries of social action that have previously coalesced through the continuous interaction and conflict of these forces (Negri 1999: 115). Constituent power, thus, is exactly going beyond any limit imposed by current social constraints, the creating of possibility through the transgression of these limits.

But, one might ask, how does this relate to the creation of states of exception, a concept used more often to describe the workings of prison camps and other situations that are quite the opposite of any positive revolutionary developments? It is not that these are the same, as they are not; but, rather, there is a similar dynamic operating within both, one that connects and clarifies how it is that forms of social struggle and creativity end up becoming turned against themselves and become the basis of new forms of exploitation and enclosure.

This parallel process exists in that the camp, the state of exception as most famously theorized by Giorgio Agamben, is a space outside of current configurations of law that alters the condition of law itself: "It is only because the camps constitute a space of exception – a space in which the law is completely suspended – that everything is truly possible in them" (2000: 40). It is the role of the sovereign, who exists in a position that is paradoxically both inside and outside of the rule of law by being able to suspend the rule of law, that founds and modifies the rule of law. Both the camp and the role of the sovereign are included in the operations of the law and change regimes of law and power by this process of inclusions through exclusion. That is, because they are both outside but within it, the law is preserved through its suspension. It is in these moments and processes, this mystical foundation of authority where it is impossible to differentiate between transgression of the law and its execution, that we find the pivot on which such transformations turn. Negri comments on how the concepts of constituent power and states of exception can seem to embody much the same process and dynamic, particularly as employed in the work of Agamben. However, Negri argues (2003) that the difference and mistake which leads to Agamben's understanding is his failure to see that constituent power is that which creates life and the violence found in states of exception destroys it. While this is, to a large degree, true; it still does not take into account the similarities in their nature, in a common process, between these two phenomena, even if acting in different ways.

It is here that the two dynamics meet. Constituent power attempts to create a space beyond the law and the operation of current regimes of power from which it is possible to create new relations, forms of governance, and law – and, hopefully, to possibly escape from the machinations of statecraft and governance altogether. But constituent power through this process becomes constituted power, it is dispersed through the workings of government: it exists as precisely the mystical foundations of authority upon which new structures and relations of domination attempt to base their legitimacy through references to these founding moments.

The actual transition from constituent power to constituted power can seem rather hazy. Mystical, mystified, or perhaps zombified? If they are totally separate from each other, how do they relate? In some ways, it seems like the equivalent in radical politics of the problem in the philosophy of Rene Descartes, but this time as a question of "revolution in the state" rather than as a "ghost in the machine." The pineal gland that Descartes thought would solve this problem (by creating the possibility for a totally physical substance to interact and influence a totally mental one) is the same pineal gland that when shot full of electrons brings the recently dead back to an indistinct zone of the semi-living (at least in the film version). One would be the mystical social pineal gland that would function as the interface between the totally constituent power of revolutionary fervor and the constituted power of state sovereignty? It remains unclear, perhaps because it tries to solve a problem almost a ridiculous as that of Descartes. It seems more useful to answer this question in much the same way that Spinoza replies to Descartes: that minds are ideas of the body, not two substances, but one substance expressed into two different ways. Similarly, constituent and constituted power are not separate substances, but rather that constituted power is the state's idea of constituent power; another example of an apparatus of capture, an attempt to incorporate the functioning of the smooth space traversed by the imaginal machine into a governmental apparatus. It might seem logical for someone like Negri to follow this type of argument – to see constituted power as constituent power expressed differently – but, he seems reluctant to do so.[10]

Likewise, states of emergency, exception, the suspension of law and the creation of camps are most often responses by existing state structures to attempts made to destabilize, undermine, and then reincorporate these embodiments of the radical imagination. But one must be clear that these processes appear in sharper and most obvious form during attempts to create revolutionary social change, because these attempts are themselves involved in the dynamics of power and exception (either during their gestation or later on); yet, these processes are much more widely dispersed through time and daily life. As Angela Mitropolous argues, "the state of emergency is not the exception which suddenly takes shape under the geopoliticised heading of 'war has come home'; rather, it is the norm and the experience of the world, whose functioning is laid bare in moments of crisis" (2006: 98).

The problem is less that of finding a form of constituent power that does not exhaust itself in a new form of constituted power; but, rather, what Agamben describes as finding how to "clearly differentiate constituting from constituent power" (1998: 41). And, to a large degree, this is indeed a good part of the question, especially given the dynamic of how revolutionary fervor has been constantly used as the base and determining factor of formulating new forms of exploitation. It is, one might say, the right question to the wrong answer. The problem is that constituent power doesn't exhaust itself but becomes undead. Differentiating constituent from constituting power is not, then, a question of being able to tell the difference between totally different phenomena; but, rather, the difference between a living social struggle and one that has become undead, an inversion of the cycle of struggles. Constituent power does not turn into something else; rather, it is multiplied and expanded by horrific proportions, becoming menacing and all encompassing. Insurgencies and attempts to escape from previously existing fields of power become the means through their reflection, resurrected as zombies that eat the brains of the living labor of resistance.

Thus, what connects this hidden history of struggles and rebellion are not just the forms of constituent power underlying them, but also the constant process of recuperation, redeployment, and resurrection of the very successes of revolutionary movements as tools used against them. Through a dynamic of crisis and exception, the exception to the rulers becomes an exception justifying, at various times, new martial measures and forms of governance. The circuits of capital, labor, state power, and social control become increasingly integrated, connected through logics of crisis, emergency, and exception that spread out and are connected with each other until they are no longer exceptions but the rule themselves. What one sees, then, is an increasing subsumption of life: the incorporation of the ongoing flow of social existence brought more and more into the working of capitalism, the state, and social domination by a continued series of social insurgencies that have been turned against themselves and incorporated into the logic of capitalism. This pattern and dynamic repeats itself at increasing scales, intensities, and durations, moving away from bursts of exception and towards attempting to meld itself into a continuous pattern of attack and the spiraling of new desires into methods of control.[11]

Indeed, as Negri argues, "crisis is to be seen as a possibility for rejigging those free and independently acting elements of a system which lie outside of the possibility of control… Crisis becomes a fundamental stimulus within the system" (1988: 54).[12] The crisis of the radical imagination is the inability or refusal to see the ways in which many of the horrors we rage against today are precisely the dreams of yesterday's revolutionaries turned upside down.

Whose Zombies, Our Zombies!

Force is the body – and we want to construct the movement outside of the dead body which tradition has left us; we want to reinvent a living, real, body, to live and experience a physiology of collective liberation. – Antonio Negri and Felix Guattari (1990: 91)

It is important to emphasize that this is not a one-way process. There is no mad scientist genius, a malevolent cabal of cigar-smoking wrongdoers sitting in a room plotting all of this out. There is no alien spacecraft that has landed, unleashing hordes of little green men who are gnawing away at the revolutionary imagination. In the same way that it would be a mistake (tactically, analytically, and ethically) to take on board a reified, ahistorical repetition of a Leninist vanguard structure mirroring the mind-body split (where the party develops ideas that are used to impose and determine the actions of living bodies of resistance), so it would be to assume that there is some centralized structure where our best efforts to create a new world all end up frustrated and turned against themselves (Eden 2005).

The Plan 9 from the capitalist workplace is the process through which recently dead struggles, by having electrons shot into their pineal gland, become resurrected as horrifying and monstrous creations.[13] The London hanged of the eighteenth century didn't just die as part of instituting a regime of bourgeois property rights over and upon what was the commons, as Peter Linebaugh has shown (1999). In a way the structure of bourgeois law and property rights is just as much the body of the hanged made into law, the flesh made word, as the corpses that adorned the gallows. Struggles don't die in this sense, but, rather, are brought back into a semi-living state, a zone of indistinction, between living resistance and undead nightmare. We, too, participate in the process of constantly trying to revive the body of dead struggles, trying to repeat the same ideas, slogans, tactics, or plans in hopes that they will have the desired effect. They simply don't. Or even worse, they are resurrected into forms that are turned against living struggles. But even that process is not one way, and it might be in finding ways to reclaim struggles that have been zombified that a new radical politics can be explored. Such as the way, to strike a whimsical note for a second, one might recall the gravediggers who during 1968, inspired by the calls for self-management and worker's control by so many other sectors in Paris and throughout France, decided to occupy the cemeteries. Perhaps, taking the slogan "all power to the imagination" quite seriously (as one should), they imagined that the voice of the dead could take part in the worker's council through the regrettable but seemingly necessary mediation of the Ouija board (Vienet 1992: 74).

This is the nature of what Martin Parker (2005) calls the 'organizational gothic,' or the critique of the horrors of what is through their exploration in representation. It shows that the dystopian imaginary is fueled by a desire to escape that haunts it: in other words, that dystopianism is fueled by a utopian desire for escape. But, likewise, it stresses the important point that the haunted house allows no easy escape, for the vampire never gets dispatched quite that easily, and there's always a skeletal hand to reach its way from the earth when you think that you have gotten away. It's silly to think that by repeating the right words, reciting the magic incantations, we can bring back the days and struggles of 1525, 1871, 1968, etc. Indeed, by continuing to yearn for this kind of reincarnation, we might end up missing the liberatory possibilities of the unwritten present and the future flowing from it, or creating a pet cemetery of previously radical ideas which no longer are. As inspiring as events such as the Battle of Seattle, the Zapatista uprising, the organizing of the Black Panthers, the rise of punk and so forth are, it becomes harmful to simply keep repeating those things to ourselves as if by some magic incantation it will bring them back.[14] Perhaps it might. But if it did, it would be as a corpse, a remnant of its former vitality, a dead body. And dead bodies have rigor mortis set in, losing their former flexibility and vivacity, and soon begin to smell quite awful.

To start from this perspective means realizing that the forms of oppression and exploitation that we face in our daily lives are not something that is totally foreign and other to the very fervor we are taking part in by desiring to create a better and more just world. Reaction and revolution are undergirded by similar dynamics and social forces, constituent power turning in other directions and morphing into other forms that are no longer recognizable as desirable or liberatory. But that is not necessarily a lament, a realization that any attempt to create radical social rupture is doomed to become a totalitarian nightmare. It also means that the forms of social domination that seem to encompass and control us are also to a large extent fused and formed out of the very same constituent power and capacities that can be used to do otherwise. The question is how to work with this dynamic, how to act otherwise within it, rather than pretending that it is totally other than the process we are trying to create. Matteo Mandarini, drawing from the later work of Mario Tronti (none of which has been translated), describes this as the good fortune to act within the state of exception. The state of exception is not the negation of politics but rather the possibility of reopening the terrain of the political: "Outside the state of exception, there is no politics, we are left – instead – with the fate ordained by technical-economic rationality" (2008: 181). Thus it is possible to find not fear, but hope, in the apocalypse: to turn the process of the subsumption against itself and to create a new basis for radical politics from the reclaiming of the flesh of zombified struggles. To take these zombie-categories and institutions in all their ambivalence as the flesh of recomposition, reclaiming these zombies as our zombies.[15]

Once, during an interview at a film festival, Subcomandante Marcos was asked why it is that the Zapatistas rebelled. He answered, quite fittingly for the occasion, that he dreamed of a day where it would be possible to live a different cinema program everyday. The Zapatistas rebelled because they had been forced to watch the same film for the past five hundred years, to live an existence of unending indistinction between mere survival and truly living (Holloway 2004). We can no longer go on continuing to watch the same movies, to continue acting out the same script and lines provided for us, even if those very lines are the ones provided by comrades in an independent media project. And besides, for all the horror of zombies and alien invaders, they embody a certain charm that perhaps, if we are creative and imaginative, might be redirected to other uses. The everyday life of revolution – the ceaseless movement of the radical imagination–is premised not only upon creating and embodying new desires for liberation, but also working from the social energies unleashed all around us (sometimes far from where we might like to go), and redirecting their course. To recuperate the recuperators – as none will be free until the last formerly useful notion of every B-movie revolutionary is hung with the pretensions of the insurgent who thinks that the methods of insurgency have been solved once and for all, or will ever be.

Curiouser and curiouser and curiouser still
Some present you gave me, the bitterest pill.
– Alien Sex Fiend, "Now I'm Feeling Zombified"

Notes

1. For an exploration of the concept of real subsumption, see Negri (2003); despotism of capital, see Camatte (1995); and spectacle, see Debord (1983). For a recent attempt to connect these various lines of thought around current events, see Retort (2005) as well as, the "In Times, In as Global Conflict" issue of *ephemera* (2006) Volume 6 Number 1.

2. This discussion of primitive accumulation and its importance is heavily inspired by the writing of the Midnight Notes Collective (1990) around their concept of the "new enclosures" (1990) and the debates that it inspired in a special issue of the commoner (2001).

3. Mario Tronti, among others, was very important in developing this line of argument, which came to be identified as the main core of that heretical form of Marxism known as *operaismo*, or autonomist Marxism. Unfortunately, very little of Tronti's writing has been translated into English. For more information and contextualization of the development of such ideas, see Steve Wright (2003) *Storming Heaven: Class Composition and Struggle in Italian Autonomist Marxism*. For some recent writing on Tronti's ideas and their implication for radical politics today, see *the commoner* Number 11 (Spring 2006) as well as Mandarini (2008). Available at www.commoner.org.uk; and an electronic symposium on Tronti held by Long Sunday, which is available at www.longsunday.net. Tronti's most important book was recently republished by DeriveApprodi, and MayFly Books plan to publish the first English translation in the near future

4. For very insightful and provocative writing on capitalist reproduction and everyday, see the work of the Situationists as well as Lefebvre (2002/2006) and Aronowitz (2007).

5. For more information on the work refusal and social insurgency during this period, see Zerzan (1999) *Wildcat Dodge Truck Strike 1974* (1996), and Wright (2003).

6. For a consideration of forms of labor in the state, see Harney (2002) and Bratsis (2006).

7. This formulation was first suggested to me by Anthony Iles from Mute Magazine.

8. It would be a mistake either to uncritically support or decry all forms of violence in revolutionary politics; perhaps all the more so, given the slipperiness of definitions and given who is the one doing the defining. But one can definitely say that such questions and judgments are wrapped up in a whole host of ethical, political, and strategic questions. For some reflections on these questions and how they have played themselves out in radical politics, see Berger (2006), Churchill (1998), Rubenstein (1970), Vague (2005), and www.germanguerilla.com.

9. Or maybe, a more accurate metaphor might be the kind of after image that one experiences after looking at a particular object, for instance a flag, for several minutes, then followed by looking directly at a white sheet of paper. The image of the object is retained briefly and is thus experience in an inverted form. For instance, if one would stare at an American flag and then a sheet of paper, the colors red, white, and blue would be replaced by black, yellow, and neon green.

10. The description of Descartes' thought functioning as a "ghost in a machine" was coined by Gilbert Ryle (2000 [1949]). Negri's writing on Descartes has recently been published (2007).

11.For instance, one could consider that Hardt and Negri's theorization of the formation of Empire, rather than being any sort of break or rupture in the formation of imperial power, to be another incarnation and continuing development of these very forms of power. It has also been argued that their analysis of Empire was a bit of a misstep, that Negri's previous writing on this area (where he argued that the form of state most fitting for the current era was that of the "nuclear state") was more accurate.

12.For more on crisis and disaster in the regeneration and reformulation of capitalism, see Cleaver (1988), Caffentzis (2006), Van Meter (2006), and Klein (2007).

13.For more on living dead struggles, see Dauvé (n.d.), who argues: "Power does not come any more from the barrel of a gun than it comes from a ballot box. No revolution is peaceful, but its 'military' dimension is never central. The question is not whether the proles finally decide to break into the armories, but whether they unleash what they are: commodified beings who no longer can and no longer want to exist as commodities, and whose revolt explodes capitalist logic. Barricades and machine guns flow from this 'weapon.' The greater the change in social life, the less guns will be needed, and the less casualties there will be. A communist revolution will never resemble a slaughter: not from any non-violent principle, but because revolution subverts more (soldiers included) than it actually destroys."

14.For a critique of the Black Bloc, see "Maggie" in Kendra and Lauren (2003), as well as Rock Bloc Collective (n.d.).

15.The notion of the zombie-category and institution is borrowed from Beck (1999).

:: III :: Revelation Vertigo ::

Autonomy is both the goal sought after and that whose presence – virtual – let us say, has to be supposed at the outset of an analysis or a political movement. This virtual presence is the will to autonomy, the will to be free. – Cornelius Castoriadis (1997: 192)

There exists a tendency, shared across different strains of radical political thought, to see the horrors of our present as comprising a false totality, that when torn asunder, will reveal a more liberatory existence hidden beneath. This is to understand revolution as revelation; as the dispelling of the conditions of false consciousness, and a reclamation of an autonomous existence that continues to live on, albeit deformed, within this world we must leave behind.

For the autonomist, this comes in the form of the working class for itself whose existence was disrupted, not destroyed, by the violent upheavals that formed the economic basis of capitalism (a process which Marx observes [973: 873] plays the same role in political economy that "original sin" does in theology). In primitivist thought, this becomes a reclaiming of a mythical ancestral past crushed, but never fully destroyed, by the weight of technological development and the machinations of alienation. As powerful as such lines of argument can be, one danger in the politics of revelation is that every act of revealing not only illuminates the existence of certain processes and phenomena, but also effectively conceals others that do not fit within the structure of the revelation. It is when revelations become dogmatic, when they become "churchly," one might say, that they blind the true believer to all that falls outside the blinkers they have placed on their intellectual vision.

To question the process of questioning is to return to the etymological root of the concept of revolt, one based on a process of returning, discovering, uncovering, and renovating; one that is a state of

permanent questioning, of transformation, of change, an endless probing of appearances. This is exactly the line of argument pursued by
Julia Kristeva (2000, 2002), who argues for an understanding of revolt as the transgression of an order coupled with the promise of other
possibilities. But this transgression does not only take the form of contestation, which revolt has been reduced to, but also many embodied
forms of movement and transformation not recognized as revolt. It is
this multiplicity of revolt as (self-)questioning, psychic, analytic, and
artistic, that must be kept continually open, or else what seems like
revolt is rather its pantomime. Revolt becomes reduced to reproducing constituted image rather than renewing itself through new constituent possibilities and reconfigurations.

For it must be remembered that every act of revelation is not simply a discovery of what is, but also a construction of that which is,
through a process of shared perception and understanding. Thus, to
speak of an autonomous self-determining capacity that existed before
the advent of capitalism providing the seeds and routes going through
and beyond it, is not simply to uncover its existence, but also to take
part in its collective construction. It is the presupposition of this autonomy, based on a perhaps mystical foundation, which enables the
struggle for its realization. The danger, or at least one of them, contained within such a style of argument, is the risk of projecting back
into history some sort of prelapsarian subject that only needs to be
reclaimed to bring about the end of alienation and the failings of our
current existence. Fetishizing this sort of imagined past contains very
real risks, as nearly none who proclaim the benefits of such an existence have ever experienced it themselves (except those who have
racked up a good bit of frequent time traveler miles). But this is not
to discount what can be learned from these attempts to understand
what has come before. As David Watson argues, no affirmation of
aboriginal lifeways can provide unambiguous answers to the multidimensional difficulties facing humanity today, but "their lifeways, their
histories, remind us that other modes of being are possible," which
offers one possible way, although certainly not the only one, for discussions about forms of social life and organization other than the
misery of the present (1996: 240-241).[1]

Perhaps there is a different dynamic at work here – a process that
seeks to avoid the pitfalls of creating and projecting forth static
utopias of imagined futures with no methods for attaining them in the
here and now – although clearly this is not the only meaning of utopianism (Shukaitis 2004; Parker 2002). But this is rather a process
based on what Antonio Negri calls a "constitutive dystopia" (1999:
322). In other words, a process based on the constituent power of the

dystopic nature of the present. A dream of a different future through the rejection of current constraints, and an implicit understanding of a life lived without those dynamics. After all, what is really so negative about this kind of backwards projection anyway? Yes, there might be pitfalls involved in that kind of mental process – but there are far worse things that could develop. One could argue that this sort of process involves a form of what postcolonial theorist Gayatri Spivak calls "strategic essentialism," or to stipulate an essence in a way that is useful to those engaged in a social struggle, regardless of whether it is necessarily a true statement or not (1996).[2]

The danger of creating totalizing concepts, narrations, and frameworks isn't necessarily the totalization itself. There is no need to be followed by a *Lost in Space* style robot that obediently intones. "Totality, Will Robinson, totality!" at the first sign of one's appearance. For all attempts to understand the social world and its transformations, to participate in trying to pull this shaping in a particular direction, necessarily relate to some conception of totality, even if only implicitly stated. The level and scope of this totality, however, varies widely – from the often and unfortunately assumed frames of the nation-state and political revolution premised upon seizing power at this level – to a broader and more encompassing notion of social space that can vary from a very local to a global (or beyond) scale. Richard Day (2005) calls this assumption of the nation-state framework in revolutionary politics the "hegemony of hegemony," which he opposes to a politics based of creating lines of connection, alliance, and collaboration that do not seek to become totalizing, which he refers to as being based on the "affinity for affinity."

The concepts of the temporary autonomous zone and the intergalactic *encuentro*, associated with Hakim Bey and the Zapatistas, are extremely valuable especially in how they expand the breadth and range of the radical imagination. From fleeting and temporary moments perhaps taking place between only two people (in the midst of a riot or in each other's arms), to possible relations with beings from other galaxies we are not even aware of yet, are all part of an expanding and open totality of possibilities. The same can be said for the Situationist idea of the society of the spectacle and the autonomist notion of the social factory, except that these operate based upon the rhetorical force of a constituent dystopia to work their expansion of the radical imagination.

These lines of thought employ a visceral argument about the total colonization of the present as a means to ferment a scream against existing conditions, very much in the way that philosopher John Holloway (2002) describes "the scream" as a moment of dislocation, critical reflection, and the building of vibrating intensities with the potential to undermine the conditions that cause the scream in the first place. The difficulty of such an argument is, if all of everyday life has been totally colonized, as Guy Debord and others often argued, then how would there be any grounds for resistance? Who would resist and how could they possibly resist if they had been completely colonized by the logic of capitalism? Similarly, if the existence of the social factory is totalizing (where there is a unifying logic of command in which relations of the factory have extended all throughout society in one unifying logic of domination), from where would it be possible to contest this logic?

What exists is a *rhetorical strategy* where force is given to the screaming calls for resistance to forms of domination by *presenting* them as contesting totalizing systems of control. That is to say that the argument is not really that everything has been totally colonized, because if that were so it would make putting forth strategies for contesting capitalism to stand on rather shaky ground precisely because it is quite difficult to make arguments for forms of resistance based on an analysis that stipulates the existence of total control while at the same organizing in ways that are based upon existing cracks and spaces where this control is not totalizing, or at the very least not to the degree that the analysis tends to imply. It is this imaginative move – which might indeed sometimes be one of the necessary delusions of resistance – which is described by cultural theorist Gavin Grindon as the breath of the possible: making a certain leap of faith, one whose history one can trace as it evolves through interconnected movements (2007).

The danger of totalities is not that we construct or employ them, but rather that we take them for the world itself, as it actually exists, rather than as conceptual tools to understand the world. The risk is that we, to borrow from Situationist phraseology, take our totalities for reality. Revelations can induce a sense of conceptual vertigo, as we dangle far from the Earth, precisely because of the distance introduced and enlarged by taking ideas for the things themselves. The world, after all, is always messier than the concepts we create to understand it. The danger is when such concepts, which are a part of the reality they attempt to describe and take part in shaping, leave us blind to existing dynamics that do not fit into the conceptual scheme; when it constitutes a misstep that forecloses other possibilities that could exist outside of these conceptions.

Concepts are products of the imagination. That is, they result from the body's interaction with the world around it. Affective traces of these interactions compose the body and what it can do through the imagination. Thus, understanding them is absolutely essential as a basis for any adequate understanding of the world, our place within it, and attempts to increase our collective capacities and forms of self-determination: to spread forth lived joy and abundance of life. In this way, perhaps the similarities in dynamics of thought between strands of Marxism and Christianity is not so surprising. Both involve the creation of a totalizing scheme useful in making sense of the everyday experiences and affects upon the bodies of those involved, and explaining them within this conceptual scheme. For the Christian, the suffering of the present, this "veil of tears," is explained as a result of a fall from grace eventually to be overcome through ascension into heaven.

For Marxism, the transformation of the pre-capitalist world by the bloody expropriation of primitive accumulation is a condition to be destroyed and overcome by the eventual proletarian revolution. Both are premised upon what the Christian Marxist Ernst Bloch, a clever synthesizer of the two lines of argument, refers to as the "not-yet," which indeed operates as a principle of hope for those enmeshed within such a framework, but often does precious little for those alive in the here and now. And, just as it doesn't take a weatherman to tell you which way the wind is blowing, it doesn't take a Keynesian to remind you where we all end up in the long run (i.e., dead). Opposed to these worldviews that promise a brighter future "someday" to excuse the misery of the present one also finds bursts and outbreaks of demands for the creation and realization of liberated life in the here and now: from the English radical Christian visionaries, the Diggers, Ranters, and the brethren of the ever-renewing free spirit,[3] those clamoring for the creation of heaven on earth now, to those who working toward creating spaces of insurrection, insurgency, and autonomy in the present. The totality and march of historical time is broken,[4] ripped away to reveal modes of collective experience and joy inscribed on the bodies of those rising up.

And, as one of Flannery O'Connor's mad, wandering prophet outcasts might correct her (emerging from the warped realm created by her gothic Southern Christian imagination), all that rises up does not necessarily converge, even if the patterns of strange attraction of the gravity of Eros to tend to warp time and space around them. *Everything That Rises Must Converge* (1956); that rather Hegelian sounding titling of her work, which was published posthumously, is taken from the work of anthropologist and Catholic theologian, Teilhard de Chardin, in his description of the omega point, or the point where everything converges in the glory of god. While Flannery's writing is perhaps torn between similar tensions, in her case between her strong

Catholicism and how this is manifested in her work through marginal and off-kilter characters that come off as if they would fit better in a Tom Waits song than what is usually expected in any sort of moral parable. Her characters, and writing in general, tend more to divergence and heresy, apocalypse and tragedy, as means of revelation, as opposed to anything that seems like de Chardin's omega point. This makes the choice of the title for her book, which after all was not chosen by her, a bit odd, since it seems to take part in a process of imposing a point of convergence in Flannery's writing that is not really there. It is almost as someone felt that there needed to be this convergence point for her work, a working out of dialectical tensions now finally reconciled. But Flannery's work has no omega point. Perhaps this serves as a warning for all those whose work try to avoid such truly grand totalizations only to have them fitted over one's work after you can't do anything about it: sometimes the weight of Hegel weighs on the bodies of both the living and the dead.

A total and unitary frame of reference, time or experience – whether the spectacular time of the commodity or the spectral time of religion – is shattered and begins to become replaced by what Debord describes as the mutual federation of freely reversible forms of time (1983: 167). It is striving towards creating conditions for the realization of autonomy, in Bifo's phrasing, as the "independence of social time from the temporality of capitalism" (2009: 54). This is the movement of *movements*, or the movement of movement itself; the constantly shifting and transforming of the radical imagination, social relations, compositions, and affections. And, this is not just the movement of what are usually considered as forms of social movement (which tends to give too much emphasis to the technicians and specialists of political action, the seeds of tomorrow's bureaucratic class) and their recognized forms of visibility, but social movement as just that: the movement of the social. Transformations occur constantly and in often-imperceptible shifts, minor revolts and mutinies that disguise their importance beneath their seemingly insignificant forms. This process of minor composition, often connected and articulated through aesthetic forms and cultural motifs, will be explored in the next chapter.

This movement of an infinite totality, composed of many elements and machinations of desire that in many ways can be regarded as totalities in their own right (this is the exact point made by Hakim Bey when he argues that we begin as the sovereigns of our own bodies, but that this is a sovereignty which is socially constituted in a relation between bodies), is described with great skill by none other than Spinoza. Beneath the veneer of what seems to be an overwhelming religiosity, the framing of his argument that nothing is possible without god, is his heretical view of what that means. For Spinoza, god or nature is this infinite totality of which we are all parts. The foundation of his argument is an understanding of our position within and in relation to this all-encompassing and infinite totality. From this he proceeds to describe the joyous and happy life, the blessed life of liberation, which is founded upon such an understanding of what is possible for the free individual. This sort of argument finds great resonance with the ideas of someone like Raoul Vaneigem (as well as Deleuze, Guattari, Negri, Castoriadas, and many others), who, like Spinoza, see desire as the essence of humanity. Whether understood as the living of happy life or increasing affective capacities through the liberation of desire, the unfolding of the everyday life of revolution, of liberation, is built upon how the everyday connects and relates to, as well as embodies, the totality of social relations and processes.

Whether a statement or conception is in itself true or false does not mean that cannot be useful to ongoing struggles. There are times where a claim of an argument being false, particularly in relation to core notions, what one might call the myths we live by, is not even necessarily an objection to it. Indeed, for false judgments themselves often are still life advancing and necessary. As that old German malcontent Nietzsche argued, "To recognize untruth as a condition of life: that is, to be sure, means to resist customary value-sentiments in a dangerous fashion, and a philosophy which ventures to do so places itself, by that act alone, beyond good and evil" (1990:36).

To live the everyday life of revolution is certainly a dangerous task, one fraught sometimes with very necessary illusions, allusions, and delusions. The presumption of an already existing form of autonomy that Castoriadis describes in the quote that opens this chapter might indeed not have existed until those acting based upon it already existing by their actions take part in creating it. Whether this autonomy really existed is not necessarily important compared to how this presumption, resting on a virtual and undetermined capacity for autonomy, takes part in the process of its actualization. Such a process is not necessarily positive or negative, but depends on other processes and dynamics involved, and from whose perspective this judgment is being made. The task then is to work through how these formations occur, and whether they tend to move in directions we want them to go, or whether they come to be objectified and turned against us, where the tools and notions that once were helpful are nothing more than baggage at best, and phantoms and specters which continue to haunt us.

You and I return to the scene of the crime
Let's go out and wash our sins away
Everyone's an actor in this play
Trading lines with broken phantoms
– Mission of Burma, "Fever Moon"

Notes

1. For more on the use of anthropological studies and information in radical political thought see Graeber (2004) and Clastres (1977).
2. See also Jones (2005).
3. For more on this see Vaneigem (1994), Norman Cohn (1993), Wilson (1988). It is interesting to note that Hakim Bey / Peter Lamborn Wilson's focus on fleeting moments of insurgency and autonomy, which he develops into the notion of temporary autonomous zones (TAZs), originate in his study of various strands of heretical religious thought within Sufism and Taoism.
4. For an exploration of this theme, see Holloway (2006). For more on collectivity, insurgency, and time, Negri (2003). For a useful, albeit if flawed, typology of different kinds of movement imaginaries in relation to conceptions of time, see Mannheim (1936).

:: IV :: Dancing Amidst the Flames ::

Dance-time is here, folks, the artistic ballet of fucking it up, and shaking the old world to the ground. – Raoul Vaneigem (n.d.: 12)

In the autobiography of James Carr, one-time Black Panther and cofounder of the "Wolf Pack" with George Jackson in Soledad Prison, it is related that upon hearing the song "Dancin in the Streets" by Martha and the Vandellas, he knew that his political philosophy had changed. He wanted to overcome the duality between Martha and the Vandellas and the ruthless ends-justifies-the-means militancy of Sergei Nechayev: to find a way to "make the revolution a dance in the street" (2002: 214). During the mid-1960s in Chicago there emerged a crossover between the militant syndicalist labor organizing of the Industrial Workers of the World (IWW) and Surrealist in-spired flights of fancy, embodied and circulated in publications such as the *Rebel Worker*. But rather than the somber and austere images of labor struggle that one often finds, this section of the IWW embraced youth revolt, free jazz and artistic experimentation, and rock n' roll in their pursuit of developing "critical theory at it Bugs Bunniest Best" and "dialectics in the spirit of the Incredible Hulk."

Taking their inspiration from the growing tides of political unrest expressed increasingly through forms of pop culture they would come to write about the political potential for developing social struggle drawing from these social energies, arguing in pamphlets like *Mods, Rockers, and Revolution* that songs like "Dancin in the Streets" show that the yearning for freedom and refusal to submit to bureaucratic pressures are not just the desires of small bands of militants but rather "almost *instinctive* attitudes of most of our fellow workers" (Rosemont and Radcliffe 2005: 131). From this they would conclude that their task was not to "bring" awareness of the problems of capitalism, racism, and social injustice to people who for the most part were already quite aware of them. Rather, taking more inspiration from Lennon than Lenin, they sought to connect the multitude of forms of rebellion and discontent that already existed involving all sorts of social subjects whose actions were not often assumed to have a political character:

> Long live the Incredible Hulk, wildcat strikes, the Nat Turner Insurrection, high-school dropouts, draft-dodgers, deserters, delinquents, saboteurs, and all those soul-brothers, wild-eyed dreamers, real and imaginary heroes of defiance and rebellion who pool their collective resources in the exquisite, material transformation of the world according to desire! (Rosemont and Radcliffe 2005: 434)

But how are these moments and revolts and insubordination, bridged tenuously through the semiotic scaffolding of this pop song, connected? Is there something particular about this song? While such a question could easily raise the concern that such is a mere coincidence, it is illustrative of a larger process of the politics of minor composition: a politics based on using whatever materials are available in the social milieu to formulate new relations, forms of self-organization, and embodiments of the radical imagination.

Indeed, everywhere that Martha and the Vandellas played in the late 1960s they seemed to be accompanied by the occurrence of a riot – people "dancing amidst the flames" (Smith 2001; Reeves and Bego 1994). While touring they were constantly questioned by the press if their music was a call to riot and if they were the leaders of militant movements in the United States. Music here can be seen as constituting a key part of daily life rather than a distraction from it, as crystallizing and bringing together social energies and political passions through a tune that one could easily claim is "just a party song." Through the circulation of particular musical compositions people found a means to organize and articulate their desires for escaping from the daily grind of the workday, to develop a critique in culture (rather than of culture) of the dystopian nature of work that people sought to escape from (Lafargue 1989; Rhodes 2007). A form of political composition materializes around the form of an artistic composition, articulated through the distributed workings of an emergent social imaginary – another incarnation of the carnivalesque energies that have "displayed a power and ability to challenge traditional hierarchies unseen for centuries" (Kohl 1993: 146). It is through these kinds of circulations, connections, and relays that the revolution of everyday life is fermented and realized – that is, it is embodied and evolves through a constantly morphing everyday life of revolution.

The Politics of Minor Composition

Make do with what you have
Take what you can get
Pay no mind to us
We're just a minor threat
    – Minor Threat

Insurgencies are the incubators of new ideas and knowledges: places where hopes and energies that there could exist other forms of social arrangements different from that what exists today, that there are alternatives, are cultivated. It is not, as it sometimes assumed, that there is an unbridgeable chasm between such forms of cultural politics and what might more commonly be understood as class issues (organizing around directly economic issues, work conditions, etc). They are not merely symbolic struggles or superstructural issues, but a key part of how people order, understand, orient, and change their lives. Collective capacities and compositions are built up not only through the more obvious and visible forms of political organizing, but also through a myriad of channels and interactions unfolding across and through all spheres of social life. After 1968 it was common for figures such as Mario Tronti, one of the key figures in autonomist thought, to declare that there was a movement from the era of the grand politics of class struggle and communism to an age of small politics. As Ida Dominijanni (2006) observes, while figures such as Tronti tended to overlook that which was subversive and radical about this transition, not necessarily in relation to a conception of class politics that had been lost, but in themselves, figures such as Antonio Negri often made just the opposite mistake. That is, in celebrating the subversive character of these new minor forms of politics and struggle many tended to overlook the way in which they inherited and took on many of the same problems and troubles which had plagued the "old" politics.

Social and political ideas are circulated in ways that are both enunciated publicly and coded in ways that are not readily obvious to the gaze of existing political authorities. Through these infrapolitics of resistance, woven through the hidden transcripts of everyday life, songs, stories, and social interactions come to congeal and coalesce radical political desires (Scott 1990; Kelley 2002; Grossberg 1992). It is this usage of cultural symbolism, as embodied in the example of the

Martha and the Vandellas song, that expresses a doubly articulated seen and unseen aesthetics of organization – the continual morphing of the radical imagination – the importance of which is not necessarily the content of the composition itself but rather the energies in sets in motion for its listeners (Linstead and Hopfl 2004; Buchanan 1997). Rather than affirming an identity posited and defended through political organizing, there operates a form of politics which draws from existing social energies and ideas in circulation while using them to other means, to introduce new meanings and relations by circulating them to other uses and creating "chain links of singularities all oriented toward their self-production and multiplication" (Negri and Guattari 1990: 109-110): the politics of minor composition.

The concept of minor composition takes its cue from Deleuze and Guattari's (1986) notion of a minor literature, Nick Thoburn's (2003) expansion of this idea into a minor politics, and the elaboration of the autonomist notion of class composition into a broader analytical framework. Deleuze and Guattari develop the concept of a minor literature through their analysis of the work of Franz Kafka. Although this work is focused specifically on writing of Kafka it is oriented to drawing out the processes and dynamics embodied in his writing. This process is not something particular to Kafka as a master author (as that would contradict their entire line of argument) or the particular media form in which he worked. In other words, they are interested in how Kafka uses the German language to strange and unforeseen ends, how he uses German to become a stranger within the language itself and attaches himself to lines of flight and draws paths of escape characterized by a strange joy. This is the same process Alice Becker-Ho (2004) describes in her work on gypsy slang and argot, or how the criminalized migrant underclass created space for semi-veiled communication through their mutation of French. A minor literature, which for Deleuze and Guattari emerges not from the existence of a distinct minor language but rather how a minority constructs within a major language, has three main characteristics:

1) Its language is affected by a high degree of deterritorialization.
2) Everything within a minor literature is political. The concerns of the individual connect immediately to other individual concerns. The social environment no longer exists as a mere background against which these dynamics emerge.
3) Everything takes on a collective value; exists as a form of collective enunciation.

The notion of the minor is quite an important one for Deleuze and Guattari and connects and underlies their work not only on literature, but also language, territorial configurations, the workings and becomings of minorities, and so forth. It comes along with an entire social ontology. And while there is a rich history and good deal to be learned from a full presentation of their views (as well as some very real limitations), what is more interesting for the purposes here is the way this describes a process of collective composition through the reworking of forms within a dominant, or major form, without seeking to become the hegemonic form.

This minor process of becoming, of intensive reworking and productive mutation, connects with much longer traditions of refusal, exodus, and escape: it is the tunnel burrowed through by a discontinuous but intensive non-tradition of mutant workers and migrants, one that connects maroons and hidden enclaves with the desires for exodus from the factory and the cubicle (Thoburn 2006). As a process of creative subtraction from the dynamics of capitalist valorization and the workings of governance, it draws thin tenuous lines from those who have 'gone to Croatan' (Koehline and Sakolsky 1994; Wilson 2003) in the colonial area (as an era of extensive expansion and imperial conquest) with those who while 'reclaiming the streets' bring back reworked notions of otherness and indigeneity into the heart of metropolis (in an era of intensive domination and endocolonization), whether as metropolitan Indians or dancing-fiends-*cum*-political activists. What is important in the terrain of minor composition, one which can serve to connect the particular aesthetic composition which the larger social composition, is that this is a politics not based on the representation of a people, but rather of their creation, and more particularly on a creation which attempts to elude being fixed within a major form. As argued by Nick Thoburn:

> The conditions of this creative composition are not the subjective and material resources (legally sanctioned and autonomous subjectivities, recognized histories, cultural consistencies) that one would conventionally associate with self-creation; these are molar forms. Rather, the creativity of minor politics is a condition of those who lack these resources, or who experience them as oppressive or inadequate (Thoburn 2003: 10)

The history of the IWW is formed by a discontinuous series of minor compositions formed around ebbs and flows of social resistance. Historically, with their organizing work rooted deeply in the

culture and practices of migrant laborers, train hoppers, hoboes, bo-
hemians, and traveling populations, the IWW used humor, irreverence, and wit, often adapting popular songs and religious hymns to
rework with anticapitalist motifs (Renshaw 1999; Shaffer 1985;
Bekken and Thompson 2006; Bird, et al. 1985). The reworking of
Christian hymns itself began not as a clever ploy, but out of necessity.
During the IWW's early days of soapboxing and labor organizing on
the streets through speech making often times they would find themselves confronted by attempts to literally 'drown them out' by over-
powering with noise, often in the form of the Salvation Army Band.
Writing labor-oriented reworkings of Christian hymns created a way
for IWW organizers to turn the attempt to swamp their union message into something else, to turn attempts to silence them into an op-
portunity. By carving out a space for this form of minor
communication within this format it worked on multiple levels because their ideas were presented in a format that was more memorable
(song) based on melodies people already knew.

Songs such as "The Preacher and the Slave" and "Dump the Boss
Off Your Back," while most commonly associated with the better
known IWW songwriters and re-workers such as Joe Hill, they have
been in continuous circulation since the initial publication of the *Little
Red Song Book* in 1904. And this process of constant circulation has
continually expanded itself as new organizing campaigns and events
of collective significance are added to this evolving history and reservoir of shared knowledge and experience. Through the medium of
song the earliest IWW campaigns connect to the most recent, tracing
a tenuous but unbroken line from T-Bone Slim to current musicians
who are working within and expanding the tradition of labor song
writing such as David Rovics, the various members of the Riot Folk
collective, Shannon Murray, and New York based hip hop group
Kontrast, as well as the work of various artists who have explored the
legacy of the IWW through comic art. In this way the IWW serves
as an important bridge between an older labor militancy and working
class culture and countercultural politics, as Franklin Rosemont
(2002) examines with great detail and flair in his biography of Joe
Hill. The old time wobbly and the freshest batch of hipster rebels meet
in the figure of Kerouac's Japhy Ryder (*Dharma Bums*, 1958), or in
hobo-esque paean of the escape to the 'Big Rock Candy Mountain'
where 'they hung the jerk that invented work.'

Thus the particulars of events, campaigns, and actions become enmeshed within the evolving collective assemblage of minor cultural
politics. It is not that the various individual concerns and interests become subsumed within a collective homogenous general interest (for

the sake of the movement and so forth), but rather than individual in-
trigues are connected to other concerns; each connection and concern,
"thus becomes all the more necessary, indispensable, magnified, because a whole other story is vibrating within it" (Deleuze and Guattari
1986: 17). This dynamic can also be noted in the ongoing development
of countercultural politics and organizing associated with punk rock
and forms of collective authorship that have been employed from
Dada to the shared names of Karen Eliot, Monty Cantsin, and Luther
Blissett (Home 1991; Blissett 2005). In other words it is not a process
of forming a new collective subject that will act towards achieving
certain political goals (the punk community will do this or that), but
rather that it operates as an assemblage for developing and articulating ideas through intensive forms of social relations created through
the emergence and continuation of a dispersed and fluid community
– for instance in relations to various concerns about war, poverty,
ecology, gender, gentrification, and any other host of issues. In other
words, there "isn't a subject; *there are only collective assemblages of enunciation*" (Deleuze and Guattari 1986: 18). The self-organization of the
punk community, which at face value is often seen to only reflect a
kind of youthful nihilism of no political content, is in many ways directly political through how the use of music and artistic expressions,
the intensive usage of language, becomes an integral part of formulating non-alienating and often post-capitalist social relations in the
present and connecting these emerging relations to what is more commonly recognized as politics (Holtzman, Hughes, and Van Meter
2004; McKay 1998; Lauraine 1999).

It is this form of politics based not upon projecting an already
agreed upon political solution or calling upon an existing social subject
(the people, the workers), but rather developing a mode of collective,
continual and intensive engagement with the social world that embodies the politics of minor composition. It is a mode that rather than
relying upon notions of already understood subjective positions works
from within particular sets of identities, relations, and flows of power
to develop continually open and renewing intersubjective positions to
organize from. These processes of minor composition are articulated
through forms of collective enunciation. For instance, in the mid
1960s, the UK Diggers, a British group of radicals inspired by the
17th century radicals from whom they took their name, put forth a
conception of politics they argued was not based on representing the
people but rather on electing them, that is to find a form of concerted
political action through which a subjective position of the people is
created (Stansill and Zane 1999). It is a process of minor composition
that connects together apparently distinct moments of revolutionary

subjectivation in linking together hippie culture, the free festival scene, punk, ravers, and both the anti-roads and anti-globalization movements (Stone 1996).

In many ways the organizing of the IWW (as well as many other examples that can be grouped under the conceptual framework of minor composition) continue in longstanding dynamics of class formation and contestation that have been described by sociologists such as Charles Tilly, Sidney Tarrow, and social historians such as E.P. Thompson, Peter Linebaugh, Christopher Hill, and Silvia Federici. Arguably, by recovering such stories and histories of contestation and antagonism without needing to write them into an overarching linear progression of a grand historical narrative, social history written from below can inscribe these minor instances and protagonisms in a way fitting to their form. This is very much the case for the history of a formation like the IWW, which is comprised more of stories told round the fire in the hobo jungle and in songs than the formats often recognized as the key points of historical development. As Ricardo Blaug (1998) argued some ten years ago, there is a certain "tyranny of the visible" that persists in social analysis and particularly in organizational research which has the effect of blinding one to much which is of interest. While these histories and movements have not received as much attention within organization studies as they merit, there have been some important contributions that have begun such an inquiry.

The politics of minor composition is concerned with developing a form of politics not based upon fixed identities, a consequent emphasis on the social relations formed with political organizing, and the intensive mode of engagement through which these emerge. The politics of minor composition are formed around particular situations and convergences of social forces intensively engaged with and complicated. As described by Nick Thoburn (2003: 44-45), "The particular thus becomes the site of innovation (not identity) as minorities rework their territory and multiply their borders. It is this form of engagement, a constantly open and intensive engagement self-organized through redirecting the social energies of everyday life, which comprises the processes of minor composition.

You Want a Union with that Latte?

One example can be found in the working of the Starbucks Workers Campaign, an effort of the New York City IWW that has been operating for the past several years. While the main demands advanced by the organizing campaign and unionization drives (increased pay, guaranteed hours and full time positions, the end of understaffing, and various workplace health and safety issues) are not particularly striking themselves, what is more interesting is the methods that have been employed in the organizing, particularly the use of humor, irreverence, and an engagement with cultural politics growing out of the IWW tradition of employing these, a politics of class that Nick Thoburn (2003a) describes as based not on hegemomic, monolithic conception, but rather as a mode of creating and elaborating difference. The campaign is also significant in that is it trying to develop ways to organize in retail chain stores, a sector that due to high turnover and the often short-term nature of employment in such locations has not been an area of focus for larger and better established labor unions in the United States (or, for the most part, anywhere else). It is also notable that the Starbucks Workers Campaign is not seeking to become the bargaining representative for all Starbucks workers (to become the major, or representative form), but to participate in and organize protests and actions focusing on the collective demands enunciated through their organizing. The campaign, which has began to spread throughout the US and to the UK, has also attracted the attention of the business press, such as the *Wall Street Journal*, and there have been motions passed in city councils, such as Cambridge, affirming the IWW's right to organize and condemning Starbucks' union busting. The campaign has also been integral (although it is hard to tell to what degree) in obtaining the recent wage increases for workers in New York City stores. Wages have been increased for new employees from $7.50 to $7.80, rising to $8.58 after 6 months (and $9.63 in New York City locations). While this clearly isn't a living wage, it is a real material benefit and contributes to the growing self-awareness of those involved of their ability to affect the conditions of their employment.

The operation of a company like Starbucks, much like the workings of any corporation in the highly mediated post-Fordist economy, is increasingly dependent on the forms of symbolic labor and communication involved in creating an image and corporate persona (Marchand 1998). This, however, is not to imply that these processes of symbolic mediation in the creation of the imaginary of the corporation are something new that has occurred in the post-Fordist economy, as they are indeed part of a much larger and on-going social processes. It is rather that in the changing nature of the post-Fordist economy they have come to play a more central role in the productive process. Thus, it is a change in the composition of economic forces rather than anything resembling a sharp break in regimes of production, as is sometimes claimed. Starbucks' operations, as one can see by looking through any of the company's literature and at the *way* that it presents itself, is largely based upon creating an image and aura of the coffee drinking experience – one that appeals to its customers as somehow embodying a sort of "Italian café excursion," including finely ground and roasted coffees and wistfully referring to its employees as baristas (Elliot 2001).

Starbucks needs to create and maintain its image as an appealing company, but one that is different from what might expect from a large corporation now ubiquitous in the sub/urban landscape. This is done through the cultivation of imagery portraying the company as placing high importance on ecological sustainability, treating its workers well, and buying into what might be described as generally progressive political values. This is accomplished through the well-placed display of Fair Trade coffees, support of tsunami relief efforts, forming a Citizen's Healthcare Working Group, general layout and design of the store, and carrying coffees from around the world evoking an "exotic" multicultural appeal. Starbucks has also began to release albums by various well-known artists (Elvis Costello, Bob Dylan, Ben Harper, Paul McCartney, etc) designed for exclusive release at its stores, which have taken measures to integrate listening to various genres and styles (jazz, folk, rock) as part of the particular Coffee Drinking Experience Starbucks vigorously hawks. One must be clear, however, about the way that Starbucks goes about hawking its wares. It is not the old direct sell, which at times almost takes on a carnivalesque atmosphere of its own, but rather something that is more subtle and insidious – what might described more as a tactic of immersion and spreading: becoming the background, becoming the context in which activities and interactions take place.

When campaigns like the Starbucks Workers union drive questions the image that Starbucks has built up for itself about being a different kind of company with an overall progressive agenda, one that respects and cares for its workers, and provokes the company to take measures to try and undercut the union organizing drive, it becomes increasingly difficult to maintain this image. In a sense then when the Starbucks Workers Campaign finds ways to intervene and disrupt the symbolic labor and processes integral to the continued recreation of the Starbucks image that is so important to their operations, they are developing ways to directly intervene in the workings of Starbucks, even if it is occurring not directly inside what one might usually think of as the labor process. A perfect example of this is the joint picket action staged between the Starbucks Workers Campaign and Billionaires for Bush in August 2005, although for the purposes of the demonstration it was necessary to make it appear that they were opposing forces. At different points during the day a group of campily

dressed *Great Gatsby*-esque billionaires appear at the Starbucks situated on 1st Avenue and 8th Street and in Manhattan and proceeded
to thank customers within the stores for "keeping the bucks within
Starbucks" and to praise the company for its union busting efforts.
They then proceeded to present a mock award of the "Better Billionaires Business Bureau Award for Outstanding Unfair Labor Practices" (which regrettably was declined as management decided to call
the regional manager to ask for advice of how to deal with this unforeseen set of circumstances).

When the Starbucks Workers and various allies arrived there resulted a mock confrontation, with the IWW picket line marching back
and forth next to the line of Billionaires pretending that they were defending their cherished enterprise from the devious actions of the das-
tardly pro-union forces and their attempts to enforce rigidities in the
labor market, thus potentially lowering the profits of Starbucks. One
of the Billionaires obtained a pamphlet that the IWW was passing out
and brought it inside the store, reading out loud with dramatic indig-
nation the "absurd" demands of the workers for things like livable
wages, a decent number of hours, bathroom breaks, and "similar clap-
trap that you might often hear the indentured class complain about"
(Denz 2005). Brandishing forth signs with slogans humorously twist-
ing well known slogans such as "Think Globally, Oppress Locally"
and "Let Them Work for Beans" the two allegedly opposing sides proceeded to chant and glare at each other, trying desperately to stop
from laughing at the humor and surrealness of the situation. The
chants used by the Billionaires included "Sarah Bender [IWW member fired for her union organizing], don't defend her / Get in there
and work the blender!" and "Starbucks workers, get a clue / Living
wages aren't for you!" This serves to create new ways of articulating
the demands of the campaign, but not simply through stating them:
the Billionaires take what is often the logic and claims that they are
arguing against and by ostensibly embracing and celebrating them,
push them forward in a way that reveals their absurdity. Similar tactics have been employed by the media stunt duo The Yes Men as well
as those involved in the London-based Laboratory for Insurrectionary
Imagination who, in 2004, organized a "March for Capitalism" during
the European Social Forum and a "Police Victory Party" during May
Day. This tactic of over-identifying with a set of claims (rather than
directly contesting or disputing them) can then work in novel ways
to draw out their questionable effects and consequences, and by this
different approach throw off the expected direction and course of conflict (Monroe 2005). A good part of the success of these actions are
based upon the fact that while there are most definitely forms of

protest action and politics that are easily recognized as such (and often ignored precisely because of this recognition), these actions have found ways that scramble the expectations and normal flow of social life, and thus at least for a second open a possibility for some other form of communication and interaction to occur. They create the conditions for the emergence of what Ben Shepard (2007) describes as a ludic counterpublic, where play opens up a spaces for non-expert forms of organizing and convivial politics.

The humor, play, and tactical frivolity are here not something that is external to the organizing, but rather are a part of it. The mock confrontation with the Billionaires for Bush as part of what otherwise might be a rather standard picketing and protest becomes a space where intensive forms of social engagement occurs as a integral part of the developing the collective self of the organizing campaign as well as an intervention within the symbolic labor process that Starbucks requires to maintain its image and profit margins. These forms of tactical absurdity have played a large role in the workings of the global justice movement, from the Clandestine Insurgent Revolutionary Clown Army to the fairy dances of the Pink Bloc, and also have a long history behind them (Harvie et al. 2005). They are another embodiment of what Gavin Grindon (2007) describes as a long-standing tradition of the festival as a form of political action and engagement, which at some times provides a safety valve for social discontent and at another operates as a catalyst leading to a generalized insurrection. Or, to put it another way, the politics of carnival do not have any particular set direction *a priori*, whether radicalizing or stabilizing, but are only determined within particular historical conjunctions (Stallybrass and White 1986).

Imaginaries, Composition, Regulation

The work of the radical imagination is, vis-à-vis reflection, fundamental in the contribution it makes to the content of reflection and of theory. This contribution consists of *figures* (or of *models*) of the thinkable...the imagination gives rise to the newly thinkable. – Cornelius Castoriadis (1997: 269)

This is not to say that a process of a minor engagement and use of pop culture motifs is purely a positive thing. For every time that the energies of a pop culture motif can be used in another way, détourned to other ends, there are attempts to use this subversion against itself, to recuperate it back into the spectacle, as the Situationists would say. As Brian Holmes argues, the social imaginary functions "simultaneously as a seductive capture device for popular culture, and as a productive discipline for mid-ranking symbolic analysts... to stimulate our interest, attention, passions – that is, to exercise the contemporary function of control, through the modulations of subjective energies" (2004: 152). These symbolic analysts, or the creative class of marketers and all those involved in various cultural fields, maintains a fluid relation (often borrowing from and bringing into its own operations) with those who are attempting to subvert its functioning (Florida, 2002). The question is not one of reasserting a pure space of the outside as much as finding tools and devices for the fermenting of forms of antagonism and struggle from within this dialectical relation of the movement toward exodus and its reterritorialization. In other words, to develop means to ferment what Matteo Pasquinelli (2007) refers to as "immaterial civil war." Thus one should not look to these various attempts of cultural subversion, minor engagement, and self-organization as cases to be emulated and reused as is. Rather through understanding the process of composition of social relations and connections that emerges through and as a part of them the most valuable lessons are learned. This is what Stephen Duncombe (2007) has identified as the most important task in rebuilding a progressive politics in an age of fantasy: engaging with the desires and imagery that crisscrosses the horizon of collective consciousness, and to build one's politics drawing from these social energies. But to do so with caution, always aware of the pitfalls of such an endeavor. But it is important to not allow the giddiness of line of flight and seemingly endless deterritorialization to obscure the very real line of command of appropriation that capitalist valorization uses precisely in these networks of coding, decoding, and overcoding (Mandarini 2006). Wayne Spencer (2007) emphasized this point in a recent article, pointing out that while autonomous currents have gained much from a creative engagement with pop culture motifs and imagery, they have also often become caught within that terrain, within a consumerist terrain. The difficulty remains one of whether one can use capitalism's tools to take apart capitalism. His response to this difficulty is continually back to the idea that whatever global capitalism can offer will never be enough.

At such a juncture, to borrow Stefano Harney's (2005) argument, management itself has become a cliché. That is to say rather than necessarily directing the labor process within a bounded workspace, it becomes more about the ability to capture and valorize the social energies and ideas already existing within circulation. Management then is reduced to the manic invocation and repetition of its stated goal and purpose, for it has already to a large degree lost its object of organization through the diffusion of value production across the social. To say that management has become a cliché, however, is not to say that it does not still fill a function. Rather, it is the function of harvesting out of the diffuse and productive basin of immaterial labor, from within the deployment of the cliché as a form of strategy. Immaterial labor, a much debated and confused term, is a concept developed, starting from within socialist feminist debates around the productivity of housework and reproductive labor for capital as well as questions and a consideration of the role of students, the unwaged, an other positions as they are involved in forms of tertiary labor and value production. As these debates continued they broadened into a general consideration of how forms of social interaction and labor not taking place within the bounds of the generally recognized workplace. The many forms of inquiry and research into these questions (unfortunately very little of which has been translated into English), which could perhaps be seen as a more sophisticated analysis of the same questions considered within the analysis of 'knowledge work' and other considerations of cultural labor, has generally come to be understood as formulated by Maurizio Lazzarato (1996): as the forms of labor which produce the cultural content of the commodity. Immaterial labor represents not a complete break in terms of productive relationships (it did not one day appear), but rather a change in their composition as certain forms of relationships and value producing practices were brought into and subsumed within a logic of capitalist command (Fortunati 2007). This deployment becomes the way in which immaterial labor is programmed, or made productive within the requirements of capitalist valorization (Harney 2006). And just as management has had to go beyond the bounds of the workplace in its quest for the valorization of capital, this breakdown and blurring has been met with forms of labor organizing and disruption along these multidirectional line of accumulation, generally through a greater emphasis of cultural politics and organizing.

This turn toward cultural politics as a means to create common positions to organize and work from, positions that while formerly based around the community and constant contact of the bounded workplace and interactions within it, have become less available as people are engaged in part time, short term, and variable patterns of work where such longer term relationships and contact no longer exists – or at least not in the same form it did before. These concerns and conditions have been addressed increasingly over the past few years throughout Europe through organizing around the concept of precarity, or the forms of non-standard and variable jobs that have emerged as a result of the neoliberal restructuring and roll back of the various gains of social democracy over the past 60 years. This motif, originated by the Milan-based labor organizing and media activist group the Chainworkers, has spread quickly across the continent, particularly through the increasingly large EuroMayDay demonstrations held each year on May 1st which have taken up the concerns of precarious workers as a key area of focus. In particular this focus on precarious workers has spread effectively through the creation of seductive and creative imagery to embody the organizing process that it emerges out of. A particularly striking instance of this is the creation of a new saint, San Precario, to represent the needs and demands (housing, transportation, communication) of the precariously employed. By using the motif of a saint the Chainworkers have created an image which draws from the social energies and imagery of Catholicism in Italy while finding ways to enunciate their social demands, arguing for a new form of flexible security, or flexicurity, for those adrift in the workings of today's post-Fordist economy.

This tactic has also been used by projects such as Yo Mango. Yo Mango, which is colloquial Spanish for "I steal" plays on the name of the trendy fashion company Mango, to coordinate organized shoplifting actions replete with singing, dancing, and other forms of planned absurdity. Similarly in New Zealand the "Supersize My Pay" campaign playfully uses the McDonald's phrase as a motif for its demands around higher wages, the end of the youth rate pay scale, and attempts to organize those working in chainstores and precarious jobs such as Starbucks, Wellington, Burger King, and related call centers. The use of digital and communication technologies have also been used to create various forms of technopranks ranging from the creation of a mock website for various international financial institutions to the creation of political video games such as the "McDonald's Videogame" and "Tamatipico Your Virtual Flexworker," all of which exist along the more commonly expected uses of such technologies for communication and organizing in the electronic factory of struggle (Drew 2004; Cleaver 1998). As examples of a general process of minor composition the energies of pop culture phraseology and imagery are used to expand the workings of what Cornelius Castoriadis (1997) calls the social imaginary, or the endless process of social self-creation enacted through a multitude of symbolic forms and channels. The movement of the social imaginary, which are developed here not at a society wide level but through various organizing campaigns that attempt to proliferate and spread anticapitalist ideas through their operations, create what Castoriadis describes as figure of the thinkable, or frames in which forms of social interaction and relations become possible. The workings and expansion of the social imaginary, through these

intensively engaged minor compositions, operate across three deter-
minations: intention (the goals of the movements), affect (the social
bonds and relations formed through them), and representation (the
development and deployment of symbols used in these processes) as
part of the "unlimited... representational flux and representational
spontaneity without any assignable end" that is the work of the shared
imaginary of resistance (Castoriadis 1997: 178). Thus there exists a
constantly shifting relationship between the workings of the social
imaginary, forms of self-organization, and the intensive relations and
interactions that both express and develop through these compositions.

Dance, Dance Recomposition

I had no problem with what they were saying, but the writing
was lame. It had nothing to inspire or arouse the passions.
And the round man's speech was just as bad – the same old
tune with different words. The true enemy of this bunch was
not State Power but Lack of Imagination. – Haruki
Marukami (2003: 74-75)

Often it is through subtle moments, movements and gestures that
the formation and reformulation of the social imaginary can shift in
unexpected minor directions, pushing social energies and relations in
different directions. The social imaginary is not usually expressed in
specifically theoretical terms, but in forms of collective understandings
found between people in everyday life – embodied in images, stories,
and myth making: it is how people imagine their social existence and
how they understand and relate to each other. In the words, it is what
Charles Taylor describes as "that common understanding that makes
possible common practices and a widely shared sense of legitimacy"
(2004: 23). These shared imaginaries and understandings may be the
result of what might seem like insignificant acts, but ones that
nonetheless change the definition of the situation and the relation of
those involved in it in substantial ways. Such gestures obviously do
not mean the same for all those who witness them. For instance, activists who have moved a march on to the streets frequently are heard
to chant "this is what democracy looks like," sometimes drawing
queries of whether a street demonstration is really an embodiment of
democracy – and perhaps more often the ambivalently curious,
slightly disdainful stares of those nearby who try to figure out just
what the protest is about (for often this is not readily apparent). But
this overlooks that the chant about democracy also refers to the
process of formulating and organizing that led to the action in ques-

tion, through a series of consultas, gatherings, and planning. It is this process of creating new forms of horizontal organizing and participation distinct from the often alienating realm of electoral politics which is often the most difficult to communicate, but that which is referred to by chants, leaflets, and the information circulated (Graeber 2007). Paradoxically this constantly refers to experiences that are integral to the overall organizing but nonetheless never seen within its most visible manifestations.

To give a particular example of this form of social movement, one can look to yet another example of this phenomenon in the organizing of the IWW, one that I observed when I was in Sydney for the May Day protests in 2005. Upon arriving in the designated park where the march was announced to begin, it seemed at first glance to be shaping up as quite an uninspiring event. Despite all of the larger, more mainstream liberal and social democratic trade unions urging their members to come out for the march (easy enough since May Day happened to fall on a Sunday), the number of people was quite small. Protest marshals were busy scurrying about handing out information sheets indicating the march route and the order that the unions involved were to march, making sure that everyone has been neatly coded and arranged by their easily identifiable union affiliation (what color is your t-shirt, comrade?). Spots at the end were arranged for the less well politically connected groups involved and those unaffiliated with the ranks of recognized political formations. The planned trade route amounted to walking a not so large circle through Sydney's financial district, which given the day of the week meant that it would be a march seen and heard by virtually no one. Self-marginalization seemed not to be an unfortunate side effect of the situation, but rather was seemingly built into the very planning and framework that had been created.

As the event kicked off this initial impression was not dispelled. It was opened by a clichéd older bearded male who sang various songs about solidarity, the dignity of the working class, and other such motifs all trapped within an imaginary and aesthetic framework that seemed to have not moved since the 1920s. This was followed by a seemingly endless array of speakers who droned on about fighting the proposed cuts to various social welfare programs and changes in labor legislation. One topic for the speakers was the introduction of "Voluntary Student Unionism," a proposed change in legislation which would alter the framework of student support and funding across Australia and which was also the target of a national day of action that had occurred several days before (Brewer 2005). If one thinks about rallies and actions as manifestations of the creative potentiality and possibilities of creating a new world out of the fabric of the present, this event seemed more like extending the mundanity of the present into an infinite future, focusing only upon maintaining the meager gains that had been won by previous organizing rather than putting forth anything new or inspiring. As Murakami's narrator notes, commenting on the predictability of student politics and organizing in late 1960s Japan, a problem not of confronting state power, but of a lack in the imagination.

Thankfully it was not all that bad. Members of the Sydney IWW had rigged up speakers and a sound system contained within a plastic garbage can on wheels, replete with a backing rhythm composed of various pieces of kitchenware and buckets. As the procession trickled on to the street the makeshift sound system was used to play songs like "9 to 5" by Dolly Parton and "We Gotta Get Out of This Place" by the Animals. Contrasted to the somewhat uninspiring surrounding milieu, the rag tag drumming, improvised dancing, and off key singing along with the songs gave forth a feeling of joyous celebration and exuberance that seemed to be lacking elsewhere. Various individuals who did not seem to give the march any notice looked up and smiled when greeted by the admittedly amateurish but striking gaggle of singing, dancing people. Perhaps they recognized the songs in question and connected to the idea that indeed working 9 to 5 ain't no way to make a living and that we have to get out of this place – connected to in a way that for all the good intentions invoking the dignity of labor and solidarity just didn't seem possible.

But whatever one may speculate about how this was received by those watching the events, it certainly did create an affectively richer composition of relations for those involved. At one point during the dancing and merry making "Darth Vader's Theme" from *Star Wars* was played, leading to a heated debate about whether the Rebel Alliance in the film represented a progressive force trying to overthrow an empire, or rather embodied a reactionary attempt to reinstall a previously existing monarchy. The arguments about the politics of the film mingled freely in conversation with the experiences of several IWW members about their attempts to organize various parts of the crew involved during the filming of the latest installments of the series. These debates continued during the march and spilled over through many beers during the after-party. Each of these moments of taking an element from the realm of pop culture, whether a song, movie, or anything else, to other ends, could be argued to take up and extend the Situationist idea of détournement, where combinations of social elements and practices are diverted to new ends, to create situations where the unleashing and realization of collective social energies can bring about a new world and social relations. It is not that a song like "Working 9 to 5" or "Dancin' in the Streets," anymore than Star Wars or camped up imagery of wealth and disdain, are in themselves revolutionary, but rather that they are used in these situations to vibrate with new intensities and meanings. And, it is this vibration and social resonance, around which the workings of the social imaginary are constantly renewed and self-organized, that embodies the process of minor composition.

The everyday life of revolution, spreading out through songs, stories, snickers, rants, and mocking laughs, spares no sacred cows. Cycles of struggle multiply and form spirals not only through forms of politics usually recognized as such, but through all the facets of everyday life. Scrawled on the city walls, whispered in hush tones, related over a drink – the flow of ideas and the desire for liberation move according to the needs of the social terrain, constantly changing and reforming. Oh, a sigh for the poor tyrants, how their power crumbles when no one takes it seriously anymore, when everybody laughs as them. As the absurdity of spectacle and spectacle of absurdity, it reveals in full clarity the absurdity of the world around us – from the workings of capitalism and state craft to the lesser bunglings of union bureaucrats and other minions of the old world. This contains the wonderful, ambivalent paradox of minor politics: they do not seek to put themselves forward as a set model and plan for a new world, but yet in their joy contain the very seeds to build a new world. The capacity to imagine a space outside this world, perhaps in the form of dreaming of exodus to outer space (a topic to be explored in the next chapter), becomes an imaginal space from which it becomes possible to begin building it in the present. Organizing to undermine the state, capitalism, and all forms of social domination does not mean that one is faced with a choice between the joys of dancing and reveling and the serious work of class struggle. Far from it. Indeed, if one wants to be a revolutionary, perhaps it is the dancing that one should take more seriously.

Notes

1. *Rebel Worker* had a sister publication in the UK called *Heatwave*. For more information on Heatwave see King Mob Echo (2000).
2. While one could have a quite interesting debate as to whether there are particular aesthetic elements within a composition that make the process of minor composition explored possible, this is beyond the current scope of this chapter. Rather than explore the aesthetics of a given composition and how they relate to a process of minor composition, this chapter focuses more generally on the framework and operation of minor composition. In other words, it

starts from the position that social actors have taken up certain aesthetic compositions to rework for their own ends rather than exploring why they choose any particular composition.

3. For more on the artists mentioned, see David Rovics (www.davidrovics.com), members of the Riot Folk collective (www.riotfolk.org), Shannon Murray (www.shannonmurray.com), and Kontrast (www.myspace.com/kontrast). Also see Buhle (2004).

4. See also the issue of *Fifth Estate* (2005) celebrating the 100th anniversary of the IWW and explores in detail the history of this song and its role in radical labor culture.

5. See, for instance, O'Hara (1999), Haeffler (2006), Hurchalla (2005), and Andersen (2000).

6. See, for instance, Tilly (2004), Tarrow (1994), Thompson (1966), Hill (1972), Federici (2004), and Linebaugh (2008), as well as the recent issue of *Management & Organizational History* (Fleming, et al. 2007).

7. For instance see Parker, et al. (2007), Böhm (2005), Fleming and Spicer (2007), as well more generally writing found in journals such as *ephemera: theory & politics in organization*.

8. For some examples, see Maher (2006) and Fisher and Nicholas Tabor (2006).

9. For more on this development see www.starbucksunion.org/node/1082 and Krauthamer (2007), as well as *Together We Win*, the documentary on the Starbucks campaign (www.starbucksunion.org/documentary). For more about this dynamic of empowerment through direct action see Gross and Tessone (2006).

10. Information about the Starbucks Workers Campaign (www.starbucksunion.org) and Billionaires for Bush (www.billionairesforbush.com). For more on other related forms of culture jamming, see Dery (1993), Lasn (2000), and Reverend Billy (2003).

11. For more on the Laboratory for Insurrectionary Imagination: www.labofii.net. The Yes Men: www.theyesmen.org.

12. For more on immaterial labor see the *ephemera: theory and politics in organization* issue on "Immaterial and Affective Labor: Explored," Volume 7 Number 1 (2007), Ed. Emma Dowling, Rodrigo Nunes and Ben Trott

13. Information on the Chainworkers (www.ecn.org/chainworkers), EuroMayDay (www.euromayday.org), and San Precario (www.sanprecario.info). Also see the precarity themed issue of *Greenpepper Magazine* (Number 31, Fall 2004) and *Mute Magazine* (Issue 29 Spring 2005) as well *fibreculture* Issue 5 (2005), "Multitudes, Creative Organisation and the Precarious Condition of New Media Labour." Available at journal.fibreculture.org/issue5/.

14. Fore information on these various examples please see Yo Mango (www.yomango.net), Super Size My Pay (www.supersizemypay.com), and Molle Industria (www.molleindustria.org.

:: V :: Space is the (non)Place ::

I'm looking for my first trip up into space. Whatever training needs doing count me in. Wages can be negotiated. Any job considered. Oh and one more thing I don't have the uniform and a little scared of heights, hope this isn't a problem. – Anonymous, "Freelance Astronaut" advertisement on Gumtree.com London, April 24th, 2008

Joe Hill, in a letter he wrote the day before his execution, said that the following day he expected to take a trip to Mars during which, upon his arrival, he would begin to organize Martian canal workers into the Industrial Workers of World. Why did he do this? After all, it might seem a bit odd that Hill, famous in his song writing and reworking for consistently mocking the promises and deceits of religious reformers offering "pie in the sky" (and that's a lie) to oppressed and exploited migrant workers more concerned about getting some bread in the belly (and maybe some roses, i.e., dignity, too). Hill continues to say that with the canal worker he'll sing Wobbly songs "so loud the learned star gazers on Earth will for once and all get positive proof that the planet Mars is really inhabited" (Smith 1984: 164). So why the reference to some form of other worldly-ness, one in which rather than promising salvation or escape from the trials and tribulations of this world, Hill rather imagines himself as extending and continuing the very same social antagonism that brought him to the day before his execution in the first place?[1] Aside from the personal characteristics of Hill's immense wit and humor, this chapter will argue that there is something more than that, something about the particular role outer space and extraterrestrial voyage play within the radical imagination. It will explore the idea of voyages out of the world as an imaginal machine for thinking and organizing to get out of this world that we want to leave behind, to borrow Jacque Camatte's phrasing (1995). For if utopia has "no place" in this world, no spatiality on our maps, the dream to leave this Earth can hold quite a seductive sway for those who desire to found a new Earth upon escape from this one.

Within the imaginal space created through the imagery of space travel one can find an outer space of social movement, a smooth space and exteriority made inhabitable through a labor of collective imagination. It is this labor of the imagination that draws together such diverse phenomena as the Misfits' suburban New Jersey punk anthems ("Teenagers from Mars," "I Turned into a Martian," etc.) with Sun Ra's cosmic madness and mythopoetic self-institution, that ties together the Association of Autonomous Astronauts' call for a worldwide network of community-based spaceship construction with Red Pilot / Noordung Cosmokinetic Theater's usage of retrofuturist Soviet space design as fodder for their collective imaginings.[2] In these spaces of collective creativity outer space operates as an effective meme[3] because it creates a space for engagement with weighty issues (exodus, escape, racial politics, otherness, militarization, global catastrophe, etc.) while allowing an enticing playfulness to be employed. Indeed, one could argue that through much of leftist politics runs the notion of an apocalyptic moment, of some magical event (usually revolution), followed by the creation of a new and better world. The event, or the visitation, can both act as a pole of imaginal recomposition, or a projected hope that provides an excuse for acting in the world as it is, even if to find ways to escape from it.[4] It is the process of negotiating these ambivalences in social movements, making contact with the other to come, where it becomes possible to build, in Bifo's words, "spaceships capable of navigating upon the ocean of chaos: rafts for all the refugees that depart from the bellicose and arid lands of late-modern capitalism" (2008: 174).

To Infinity and Beyond!

Mannoch drivels on with mindfucking stupidity about "visiting agitators from Handsworth," what a load of fucking bullshit! No, as EVERYONE knows, the riots were started by Communist Alien Stormtroopers from the red planet Bolleaux who landed on the roof of the fucking Ritzy. – Peter from the Class War Federation explaining the true cause of the 1981 Brixton Riots (Quoted in Bone, 2006: 270)

Perhaps an interesting question, or one of them, is not so much a question of whether there is a presence of outer space imagery and extraterrestrial travel residing within the workings of the social imaginary, but of their function. Their presence is felt both when the poet and songwriter Gil Scott-Heron complains that can't pay his doctor bills or rent and wonders what could be done with all the resources that would be available if they weren't being spent on getting "Whitey on the Moon" (1971), and when Stevie Wonder contrasts the utopian conditions of "Saturn" (1976), which are peaceful and free from capitalist exchange, with conditions and problems of the urban ghettos. The persistence of space imagery in the social imaginary seems relatively straightforward and easy to demonstrate (and could easily turn this chapter into an extended list of examples, which would be a condition better avoided),[5] perhaps because to some degree the unknown and the mysterious are almost by definition of particular fascination to those crafting mythopoetic narratives and imagery. There's simply not enough mystery in the familiar, banal and well-known. One can try to evoke a mythos from a faceless man in a grey flannel suit, or any other kind of everyday-everyman type figure, but tend to lead in a completely different imaginal direction. The curious question is why has there been an increase in forms of space imagery and narratives during a period of time roughly corresponding to the end of the end of the second world war, which since then have gone through peaks and spurts in their usage within various political milieus.

One way to approach this question, which might seem odd at first, although hopefully will ultimately become clear, can be found within a recent collection on the history of artistic collectivism and practices of social imagination since 1945 edited by Blake Stimson and Greg Sholette (2007). In their introduction they argue that there was a transformation in artistic collectivism in the post-war era, which they identify as a change in the composition of avant-garde artistic practice. The main reason for this is a movement away from communism as an ideological backdrop (although admittedly the relation between the avant-garde artistic practice and communism had been fraught with tension for some time), with there also existing connections and relations of affinity almost as strong if not stronger with various currents of anarchist thought and politics.[6] Putting aside the particular details, this argument is made of part of a broader observation of the forced removal of forms of collectivism from political, economic, and social life of various forms. This can be seen in the blatant attacks on all forms of collectivism through political witch hunts, the purging of more radical organizers from unions, and the general rise of McCarthyism in the US. Paradoxically the destruction of forms of working class collectivism from political life is directly connected to the rise of ingenious forms of capitalist collectivism, such as mortgages, stock options, retirement plans, and so forth, which are then employed in dual capacities as means of discipline and social support for populations enmeshed in them.

What is of interest here is the relation between the disappearance and destruction of certain forms of collectivism, and their reappearance in others. As Stimson and Sholette observe, the disappearance of collectivism from the political realm lead to these forms returning in a "mutated and often contradictory form within the cultural realm" (2007: 8). It means that the rise of science fiction films in the 1950s with their imagery of bizarre alien races functioning by some sort of incomprehensible totalitarian collectivism, in many ways reflect the recoded and redirected imagery of communism.[7] The specter of communism reappears as a UFO. This is perhaps not a new argument in itself, for the imagery used in genre science fiction has been interpreted as coded for communism before, with *Invasion of the Body Snatchers* (1956) as the most commonly used example.[8] But what is interesting about the Stimson and Sholette spin is their argument for a displacement of energies from the economic and political sphere embodied in working class resistance into mutated forms in the cultural sphere. This can be read as a form of recuperation or co-option in some senses, but it is not so straightforward. As I have previously argued in the first chapter, the Plan 9 from the capitalist workplace is not a clear-cut case of the integration of energies of social resistance into the workings of capitalism, not one that is irreversible. The mutated and contradictory forms of collectivism that appear might start with imagery of an alleged collectivist communist-totalitarianism, but their ambivalence is also a space of possibility, one that can be turned to other uses. The despised other is often also the secretly desired other, a dynamic that can be viewed as imaginal forms, held out as examples of an Other to be rejected, start to be drawn back into other forms of politics, other forms of usage, and the pleasure of these usages. This is a dynamic that emerges more clearly in the 1960s and 1970s, as the utopian traces of a repressed communism congealed within the imaginal form of outer space imagery, are slowly reclaimed and brought to other uses.

This is not to say that outer space memes and images of technological development have always played a totally progressive role. Indeed, aside from space exploration and technology, there is a longer history of the relation between scientific innovation and discovery and their connection with right wing and conservative politics (Federici and Caffentzis 1982). Richard Barbrook (2007) has shown quite convincingly that the imaginary futures formed around space and technology animated collective imaginaries across the entire political spectrum,[9] with both the diffuse spectacle of Western capitalism clamoring towards supremacy through technology, while the concentrated spectacle of bureaucratic collectivist capitalism in the East trying to do much the same, albeit framing it in different terms. While early efforts toward cybernetic communism were initially developed within the Soviet Union (until they were crushed by the party who rightly feared they could not control it), Barbrook notes ironically that the first working model of communism as social cooperation through technology was developed by the US military in the form of DARPA Net, which would later become the internet. Despite apparent vast differences across a communist-capitalist divide, there existed a more profound underlying agreement on technological development as a road to liberation of human potential, one that was shared by autonomist currents who argued that movement toward increased automation of the labor process would reduce necessary labor to almost zero, thus freeing up great amounts of time for activities other than repetitive labor.

Outer space, far from being a pure space that is always available for recomposing imaginal machines, also connects areas of political thought that veer off in strange and bizarre directions, showing, as Deleuze and Guattari would concur in their more sober moments, that absolute deterritorialization can easily end in death, insanity, or absurdity. The mere mention of alien invasion, coupled with anxiety about the worsening conditions of world affairs, famously led to outbursts of panic during the 1938 Mercury Theatre Halloween broadcast of a radio version of *War of the Worlds* that Orson Welles directed. And why is it that alien visitations seem to always happen in small, rural towns where the residents seem more likely to greet the visitors with shotguns rather than curiosity? Among the classic examples of space related impaired-judgment one can find the Heaven's Gate cult led by Marshall Applewhite and Bonnie Nettles. In 1997, 39 members of the cult committed suicide to coincide with the Hale-Bopp comet passing the Earth, an act they believed would allow them to be transported to a spaceship following the comet, thus averting the impending total cleansing and recycling of the planet.[10]

Further back in the history of the diffuse wonders of the wingnut international one can find the baffling case of Juan Posadas and the Fourth International. Posadas was an Argentinean Trotskyist and, at one point, a relatively well-known football player. During the 1940s and 1950s he came to the leadership of Fourth International affiliates in Latin America, which later became well known for their role in the Cuban revolution. Beginning in the late 1960s Posadas also become quite renown, or more likely infamous, for his views on UFOs. Posadas' logic flows in a quite simple way: as Marx tells us, more technologically advanced societies are more socially advanced. Because of this, the existence of space aliens demonstrates the existence of

intergalactic socialism, as the level of technology and social cooperation necessary to advance interstellar travel could only be produced
by a communist society. The goal of the party, therefore, should be to
establish contact with the communist space aliens, who would take
part in furthering revolution on this planet. While Trotsky argued
against the possibility of communism in one country, Posadas took
the technological fetish along to its logical conclusion, that there could
not be communism on one planet.[11] While this was met with great
derision by much of the left, as China Miéville explored in a recent
article (2007), the derision was for entirely the wrong reasons. Putting
aside the existence or non-existence of aliens, the problem was rather
the conclusions that Posadas made from their existence. If the long-
standing problem of authoritarian communist and socialist political
organizing is the contradiction of their implementation from above,
Posadas transfers this problem to another level, literally. Posadas' politics necessitate socialism from above, *way* above, an outer space that
can only be hoped to intervene in the earthly realm and obeyed. The
imaginal machine animated by outer space in Posadas' politics therefore contributes almost nothing to the further development of collective composition in social movements, and through its vanguardist
nature, if anything tends to act against the development of autonomy
and self-organization. It is, however, rather amusing.

Due to this, as well as other reasons, outer space travel and imagery has not always figured positively in the workings of the radical
imagination, which is not so surprising given the ways that the
dystopian future narrative often plays just as prominent a role (although often it is technological development enmeshed in an authoritarian social arrangement that is the problem rather than the
technology itself). A notable exception to this is found within anar-
cho-primitivism, which does not find much thought to be redeemable
within space travel and imagery. This is not surprising given that
many primitivist thinkers find nothing redeemable in any technological development, including agriculture itself, which is sometimes argued to contain implicit all forms of subsequent technological
development, and therefore forms of domination based on them. This
gives an almost mystical, autonomous power of self-development and
organization to the forms of technology themselves, one that does
more to reify and mystify technological development than actually explain its workings in any way constructive to a radical politics. Asking
a primitivist about technological development is like asking a neoliberal economist about the economy: they both weave tales of mystification. In this case the imaginal exteriority of space travel has been
internalized as a dystopian feature and attributed to forms of technol-

ogy themselves, rather than the imaginal processes flowing through and animating the particular assemblages in question.

Mythopoetics & Imaginal Space

Do you find Earth boring? Just the same old same thing? Come and sign up with Outer Spaceways Incorporated – Sun Ra, "Outer Spaceways Incorporated" (1968)

Oh we were brought up on the space race, now they expect you to clean toilets.
When you have seen how big the world is how can you make do with this? – Pulp, "Glory Days" (1998)

All the efforts expended on technological development and innovation, alas, largely failed to deliver on many of the promises on offer, including unlimited energy, artificial intelligence, robots that cleaned the home and eliminated the need for most manual labor, and so forth. To put it crudely, one could say that while most of the forms of technological achievement anticipated by people living in the early 20th century (cars, radio, rockets, television) were largely achieved by midway through the century, for the second half of the century this was not the case. In the second half of the century much more was promised than actually delivered. People thought that soon they would be engaging in outer space travel, driving flying cars, and other such wonderful things that never appeared. If anything, it seems that the main technologies developed during the second half of the century were mainly premised on their ability to simulate things rather than actually do them. Perhaps Baudrillard was waiting with great anticipation for anti-gravity boots and upon their non-arrival decided his only recourse was to conclude that only simulation was possible now? This does not mean that the imaginary future held out by the seductive sway of the promised future did not continue to have powerful effects. If anything that served to diminish the fascination of outer space and the techno-fetish, it is perhaps, as Barbrook points out, when people actually began to acquire personally ownable forms of these wonder technologies (personal computers, allegedly programmable VCRs), only to discover that they were far less intelligent and sensible than the mythology surrounding them would like to suggest. The actual technology delivered was somewhat less impressive than a menacing HAL 9000, now reprogrammed for beneficent purposes, for every household.

But more than just the disappointment of not receiving those anti-gravity boots for Christmas, techno-utopian space dreams often came with less desired attributes. It often was a case of desiring a transformative war machine, in Deleuze and Guattari's sense of the potentiality of exteriority and its transformation, and instead getting an actual war. To find oneself caught playing a bait and switch game of dreaming of space travel and getting Star Wars as a missile defense system instead. After all, this trick only worked for Reagan precisely because of his ability to tap into and draw from the utopian trace of space imagery in order to justify and narrate a nationalist-militarist project. Reagan very well might have been making policy decisions based on movies he remembered seeing (or acted in), but this was as much a source of ridicule as a certain kind of populist appeal derived out of his confusion. To some degree there is a large population out there that wishes it was living in a movie set, and these desires congealed in Reagan's confusion and rhetorical bombast.[12] And yet again, one premised on having to confront the all-menacing threat of the communist other and the evil empire. All this is to say that the imaginal space attached to technological development and dreams of space is highly ambivalent, dragging along with it a post-apocalyptic bad-new future.

This makes the role of outer space as a theme for imaginal recomposition much more complicated than might be otherwise, and also more directly politically relevant, to the degree the provision of imaginal energies, imagery, and resources are necessary to the continued existence of capital and the state. To put it simply, they function a lot better when people have some reason and justification for their actions. Often it is the dreams of escape from the drudgery of wage labor and the banality of the everyday that creates spaces for fermenting these "new spirits of capitalism," to borrow Boltankski and Chaipello's argument (2005). Why then might outer space emerge more prominently as a theme for imaginal recomposition in the period of the 1960s and 1970s? Aside from the previously mentioned point of mutation of collectivist energies from working class resistance, one could also say that there was a shift in the nature of imagined exodus. While previously it might have seemed possible that exodus could take an immediately physical form (go westward young man, or take to the high seas, or escape to Croatan, or find a promised land), this no longer appeared possible as the borders of global frontiers vanished. The world seemed to have most of its territories mapped and at least somewhat known, even if not totally. Outer space provided another avenue of possible exit for those desiring an exodus from the world as we know it, or at least a route to be imagined for this purpose.

In a way, while the map is not the territory, an imaginal landscape is a precondition for actually finding a northwest passage in the physical world. A shift to imaginal recomposition around outer space themes is part of the shift from a conception of exodus in physical terms to one in terms of intensive coordinates. In other words a shift towards a form of exodus that does not to leave while attempting to subtract itself from forms of state domination and capitalist valorization. This is perhaps seen most clearly in the development of late 1960s so-called "drop out culture," even more so the case of places like Italy where it is organized in terms of collective and development of other forms of sociality and collectivity rather than a sort of individualized notion of withdrawal (which became much more the case in places like the US). This is part of an overall transformation of political antagonism towards forms inhabiting a mythic territory and space of composition and are involved in forms of semiotic warfare and conflict.

A shift toward a mythic terrain of conflict and image generation can be seen in Afrofuturism, which as a literary and cultural movement is based on of exploring the black experience through the relation between technology, science fiction, and racialization.[13] While Afrofuturism is a wide-ranging area of cultural production, what is most of interest for the purposes here is the way it provided a space for going "black to the future," to borrow Mark Dery's phrasing (1995): in other words, to fuse together an engagement with historical themes and experiences and the ways that they play out within a contemporary racialized experience. In Paul Miller's Afrofuturist manifesto he framed it as a "a place where the issues that have come to be defined as core aspects of African-American ethnicity and its unfolding... [are] replaced by a zone of electromagnetic interactions" (1999). In other words, as the space of publicness for the exploration of these dynamics has faded or withered, or has become transformed into a paradoxical form of publicity without publicness through hypervisibility, Afrofuturism exists as an imaginal for this exploration, coded within forms that are perhaps not instantly recognizable as dealing with the political content they actually work through.

Afrofuturism was first elaborated by Sun Ra in the 1950s.[14] The Sun Ra Arkestra continues to play to the present day, fusing together hard bop, experimental jazz and electronic music with outer space imagery and Egyptian themes. The Sun Ra Arkestra was one of the first ensembles to make extensive use of electronic musical equipment, synthesizers, and instruments in their performances. They directly combined a continued engagement with new forms of technology and experimentation at a time when most jazz performers who were trying to be taken seriously avoided them (but then again they also avoided appearing on stage in Egyptian garb, claiming that they were from another planet). Perhaps more importantly for the discussion here, Sun Ra elaborates a sort of mythological performance and cosmogony based around fusing together ancient Egyptian imagery and scientific themes. This is clearly expressed a scene from the 1974 film *Space is the Place* (in which Sun Ra engages in a cosmic duel over the fate of the black race, who Sun Ra hopes to transport to another planet in a form of space age Marcus Garvey-esque exodus). In a discussion with some youth in a community, Sun Ra, when asked if he is real, responds

> How do you know I'm real? I'm not real. I'm just like you. You don't exist in this society. If you did your people wouldn't be struggling for equal rights. If you were, you would have some status among the nations of the world. So we're both myths. I do not come to you as the reality, I come to you as the myth, because that's what black people are, myths. I came from a dream that the black man dreamed long ago. I am a present sent to you by your ancestors (1974).

As we can see from this quote, Sun Ra used this as a means to formulate and develop a politics based around this mythological self-institution. Over five decades the Arkestra released almost seventy albums and gave countless performances while living communally and elaborating forms of mythic narrative and imagery as part of the process of creating a philosophical system, or equation, as Sun Ra referred to it (Wolf and Geerken 2006). The potentiality in the creation of such imagery does not depend on whether or not Sun Ra is really from Saturn, but rather on social energies and desires that flow through the creation of these images. The Sun Ra Arkestra were also among the first ensembles to experiment in a serious way with collective improvisation, which can be understood in some way as an emergent model for a self-organized communist mode of production and social organization.

These themes have been picked up and elaborated since then by artists such Parliament-Funkadelic and George Clinton in the 1970s, whose work contained frequent references to the mothership and other-worldly exodus, fusing together space themes with cultural black nationalism. This can also be seen more recently in the work of the hip hop project Deltron 3030, with its descriptions of intergalactic rap battles and strategizing industrial collapse through computer viruses (2002). Similar themes can be found in the work of artists including Octavia Butler, Samuel Delany, Colson Whitehead, and in films such as *The Brother from Another Planet*, and most famously in *The*

Matrix. Across the many particularities within the work of these various artists one can find what Fred Moten describes as the ontology of black performance, a performance primarily animated through a "blackness that exceeds itself; it bears the groundedness of an uncontainable outside" (2003: 26). At first this might sounds rather strange, but it makes precisely my core point: that it is not necessarily the feasibility of space travel or literal other-worldly exodus, but it is possibly even the case that the imaginal machine based around space imagery is made possible by its impossibility in a literal sense. In the sense that this possibility cannot be contained or limited it becomes an assemblage for the grounding of a political reality that is not contained, but opens up to other possible futures that are not foreclosed through their pre-given definition.

It is in this sense that outer space plays its most powerful role in the building of imaginal machines, despite and through the ambivalent roles that it has and continues to play in some regards. This is the very point made by Eduardo Rothe in an article he wrote in 1969 for the journal of the Situationists in which he argued that science, scientific exploration and discovery had come to play the role formerly played by religion in maintaining spectacular class domination. The heavens, formerly the province of priests, were now to be seized by uniformed astronauts, for those in power have never forgiven the celestial regions for being territories left open to the imagination. Space then becomes the possibility of escaping the contradictions of an earthly existence, which Rothe frames in ways that makes him sound much closer to the priestly caste he claims to despise so much:

> Humanity will enter into space to make the universe the playground of the last revolt: that which will go against the limitations imposed by nature. Once the walls have been smashed that now separate people from science, the conquest of space will no longer be an economic or military "promotional" gimmick, but the blossoming of human freedoms and fulfillments, attained by a race of gods. We will not enter into space as employees of an astronautic administration or as "volunteers" of a state project, but as masters without slaves reviewing their domains: the entire universe pillaged for the workers councils (1969).

The messianism bubbles palpably within his rhetoric, seductively so. For many within autonomous movements of the 1960s and 1970s (as well as for many before and after that), what was previously conceived of as the inevitable march of dialectical progress towards a communist future, propelled along by the laws and motion of historical progress, seemed at best something antique or a myth. But it was that imaginal machine that provided a great deal in terms of nourishing the resistant imaginary. It was this narrative that provided an outside from which critical thought and interventions were possible. In the same way that the narrative of progress towards a communist future was based around a forward projection of an outside to capitalism enabling a space of possibility in the present, here one can see outer space functioning in much the same way: a moment where a unity is reclaimed within the wealth of social knowledge and production (in this case in terms of the alienation of science and from state usage) which then enables a communist future in the present, one that overcomes the master-slave dialectic and an outburst of creativity in the organized form of workers councils.[15] A mythopoetic creation indeed, but that is exactly the point, for the capacity to structure an imaginal machine is not necessarily based on the feasibility of enacting the ideas contained within it, but rather in acting as a compositional point for collective social desires. And if today we live, as Stephen Duncombe argues, in an age of fantasy, our developing ability to understand, intervene, and work within the flows of imaginal desires and flows is precisely the ability to think through a collective radical politics despite and because of the ambivalence that the desires of the multitude contains.

A more recent example of space as a pole of imaginal recomposition comes in the form of the Association of Autonomous Astronauts (AAA), which formed in 1995 as a response to the continued militarization of space through programs such as Star Wars. The AAA operated as an umbrella organization, or as a collective name for the autonomous activities of many different groups operating across numerous cities. While the AAA initially emerged very much out of the mail art and pscyhogeography scene, their efforts were intended to take the practice of the collective name and extend it from being an artistic practice to a wider form of organizing and political action.[16] For the AAA the collective name opened the possibility of creating a collective phantom, one that "operates within the wider context of popular culture, and is used as a tool for class war" (Anonymous 2004).[17] Thus they, in a diffuse sense, proceeded to formulate a five year plan to boldly establish a planetary network to end the monopoly of corporations, governments and the military over travel in space. Although in a certain sense one might say that the AAA 'failed' in that they did not actually establish any sort of autonomous network of space exploration, that would be to mistake their stated goals for actual goals rather than as points of imaginal recomposition, a sense in which they were much more successful. Or, as Neil Starman frames

it, the AAA was an attempt to turn nostalgia for the future into an avenue for political action, to "make good some of the unkept promises
of our childhoods" (2005). People dreamed they would explore space
only to discover themselves not floating amongst the heavens, but
rather as the Pulp song intones, stuck in dead end precarious jobs
cleaning toilets or something equally uninteresting.

Among the AAA's most noted actions was a protest outside the
London headquarters of Lockheed Martin against the militarization
of space held in 1999 as part of the J18 "Carnival Against Capitalism."
It featured the strange site of police blocking men in space suits from
entering the building. This also marked the beginning of the "Space
1999 – Ten Days that Shook the Universe" festival. Given the then
waxing expansion of the anti-globalization movement one might think
that this would be an opportune moment for the expansion and proliferation of the AAA. Rather, it became the moment when the AAA
decided that it was time, according to their own previously charted
five-year plan, to move towards self-dissolution. This might seem a
bit odd, but as explained by Neil Disconaut:

> So why stop now? Well even the wildest of adventures can
> become routine, startling ideas clichés and the most radical
> gestures a source of light entertainment. Space imagery has
> become increasingly banal and retro, featuring in numerous
> adverts and pop videos. We don't want to be the space indus-
> try's court jesters when capitalism itself is being openly con-
> tested, as seen in Seattle and the City of London in the last
> year (2000: 13)

The point made here by Disconaut is quite clear. While the AAA
was intended to, and did, act as a pole of imaginal recomposition, it
was not intended to be an end in itself.[18] To act as an end in itself
would all too easily slip into a form of aesthetic escapism that might
be said to characterize many forms of science fiction not particularly
concerned with its politics. But the AAA did not want to fall into such
a trap, not to end up generating more imaginal fodder for the capitalist
image machine, and thus chose to dissolve in 2000. ET sold out to a
capitalist communication company, but the AAA had no intention of
doing so. In other words, the members of AAA sensed the potentiality
of space imagery as a point of recomposition at one point, and also
realized that such was not permanent and that would it would strategically better to move to something else.

Outers Space & the Communist Other to Come

We really don't think it's worth going through all the effort of getting into space just to live by the same rules as on Earth. What attracts us to space exploration is the possibility of doing things differently. We are not interested in finding out what's its like to work in space, to find new ways of killing. We want to find out what dancing or sex feels like in zero gravity. – Association of Autonomous Astronauts flyer for J18 Anticapitalist Carnival, 1999

Lastly, let us turn to the lovely example of the recently created Martian Museum of Terrestrial Art, which existed at the Barbican in London from March 6th through May 18th, 2008. The museum was coordinated by Martian anthropologists visiting Earth for reconnaissance purposes, sent on a mission to reconsider whether the previous classification of Earthlings as an unsophisticated and backwards population amongst the cosmos is as accurate as previously thought. This particular section of the Martian Museum took on multiple functions, including both playfully engaging with the commonly felt near incomprehensibility of contemporary art as well as the othering and alienating effects contained within unreconstructed uses of traditional anthropological methods (ethnography, fieldwork, living amongst the primitives). To put it bluntly, it was clear from the arrangement that the Martian ethnographers were quite baffled, although they tried with great valor, to understand the function and purpose of contemporary art. Agent 083TOM33McC5THY, one of the more astute among their team, commented the following in a red paper[19] that accompanied the creation of the museum:

> The fact that art occupies a symbolic stratum – and, moreover, does so with a rationale whose key or legend seems to elude both Martian *and* Terrestrial observers – has led to a suspicion that it forms an encryption that among Terrestrial codes has hitherto eluded deciphering. That it serves both as repository and index of the population's desires, fantasies, and so on suggests it as potential field for mind control activities – yet one that must be mastered, or alternatively, neutralized by Martians lest it be directed against us. (2008: ∞)

This is quite an astute observation. Here we find mingled together an observation of the large degree of incomprehensibility of the artistic world with some vague premonitions that there could be something dangerous happening. Art could lead to mind control, which could be potentially used against the Martian forces. Quickly, let us do away with the incomprehensible other for there could be something dangerous here. This is not far from the attitude of many secret service organizations or colonial regimes, although it is one that would tend to dispute that previously argued for inherently progressive politics required for cooperative space exploration.

But, again, there is an ambivalence that is also a possibility. When you think about it the emergence of a radical future, communist, anarchist, or otherwise, is almost always necessarily defined by its very otherness from the world as is. It is the other future that emerges through struggle and to some degree necessarily seems alien from the world as is, because otherwise it would not be (an)other world at all, but merely a rearrangement of the present. While Juan Posadas and the Fourth International may have argued that space aliens would inherently be communist, maintaining an open relation to encountering the other means having to confront the realization that despite all our wishes, space aliens might in fact not be communists at all! The becoming-other of the communist future can be found in the becoming-other and abjection of the present as well as the past, an abjection which brings together the twin dynamics of rejection and desire in an otherness already in the process of becoming. This is perhaps why the Zapatistas, when they call for an encuentro, often frame it as being an intergalactic encuentro. Not that they actually believe a delegation from another universe will arrive, but in the sense of maintaining an open relation to the actually existing not-yet other, the other of the future. It is in these spaces where, among many others, one finds cracks in the imaginary of a present that is often not nearly as hegemonic as thought: imaginal breaks and tesseract through which other voyages and transformations become possible. A communist future is not an uncritical celebration of this otherness but rather an ethics of engagement with an Other that is truly other, and a politics founded through that. The question is not really whether there are little green men or communist partisans on the red planet Bolleaux, but what can be gained through the imaginal gymnastics of imagining our relation to them. In other words, how the imaginal outside created through space motifs ferments social and cultural energies that rejuvenate the body of social movement, which will be explored in the following chapter through the twin dynamics of the refusal of aesthetics as a separated sphere and the re-fusing of social creativity into aesthetic politics. As the Association of Autonomous Astronauts always say, "Above the paving stones, the stars." What to be found beyond the stars is an open question, an unidentified future, and that is precisely the reason why it is the only one worth living. Out there, somewhere, Joe Hill is still singing.

Notes

1. This is perhaps somewhat of a misstatement in the sense that what brings Hill to the day before his execution is not really so much his political engagement and organizing as much as the trumped-up charges and biased justice system, most likely trying dispense with him precisely because of the role he played in articulating IWW politics and organizing in creative ways that resonated greatly with people at the time. In this sense what brings Hill to such a position is not his politics but the response of the state and business interests to them. For more on Hill's life and the politics of the IWW that Hill embodied and articulated through songs, see Rosemont (2002).
2. For more on the activities of Red Pilot / Noordung Cosmokinetic Theater, and the NSK Collective more generally, see Dubravka and Suvakovic (2003) and Monroe (2005).
3. For more on the use of memes in political organizing see the SmartMeme project, www.smartmeme.com
4. Thanks to Thomas Seay for this argument and for his cautionary take on outer space as an imaginal machine. It would be quite sensible to analyze the way that outer space has operated in a similar fashion for the radical right, such as in the alchemic and occult thought of someone like René A. Schwaller de Lubicz (Vandenbroeck 1990), but this will have to be put aside for the moment.
5. At the risk of hypocrisy, having just announced a desire to avoid lists, some of my personal favorite examples of cultural production using space themes include: the music of Deltron 3030, Devo, Failure, space rock (Pink Floyd, David Bowie, Monster Magnet, Spacemen 3, Mars Volta), space music more generally (as a form of ambient and texturally oriented music, including, for instance, Stockhausen, Brian Eno, Radio Qualia's "Radio Astronomy" project, and Tangerine Dream), feminist science fiction (Ursula Le Guin, Marge Piercy) and some of the better highlights of science fiction more generally (Philip K Dick, Stanislaw Lem), and of course one must not forget the outbursts of cheese which are too bad to be anything but good, such as Doctor Who, Space Balls, and Mutant Enemy Production's Firefly merging of science fiction and the western.
6. For more on these tensions as well the connections between avant-garde arts and anarchism, see Lewis (1990), Weir (1997), and Antliff 2001/2007.
7. For a consideration of science fiction in relation to organization see Parker, et al. (2001), particularly the chapters on Star Trek, Philip K. Dick, and cyberpunk. Also of interest in a similar vein but coming from further left field is the *Semiotext(e) SF* science fiction collection, which brings together a selection of politically motivated science fiction writing by notable weirdos as Burroughs, Gibson, Anton Wilson, and Ballard (Rucker, et al., 1991). Also quite interesting is the inclusion of "Visit Port Watson," an unsigned fake travel pamphlet written by Hakim Bey / Peter Lamborn Wilson. When Wilson received mail and questions about actually visiting the utopian destination of Port Watson described in the pamphlet he responded by saying that that Port Watson is that place where one actually is in the moment when you believe that Port Watson could exist. The task of making that actually starts from the space of possibility opened in the imagination. At its best outer space utopia operates in the same opening, opening a space of possibility within the

present through which other realities become possible.

8. For analysis of this film (as well as other closely related ones), see Brosnan (1978), McCarthy and Gorman (1999), and Von Gunden and Stock (1982).

9. The retrofuturist artwork created for the book by Alex Vaness is quite striking as a good illustration of the fascination of outer space imagery in the workings of the radical imagination. Full color versions of the images can be viewed here: www.imaginaryfutures.net/gallery.

10. For more on Heaven's Gate see Theroux (2005: 207-221).

11. For the best overview of Posadism available in English, see Salusbury (2003). Although Posadas died in 1981 Posadist sections of the Fourth International have been able to continue to produce apparently new material from him for some time since then due to what seems to be a very large reservoir of taped materials he left behind. Among the more interesting rumored aspects about the Posadaists of the Fourth International, although very difficult to verify (except by some members of the Marxist Ufologist Group), Posadaists have been known to appear at CND rallies passing out flyers demanding that China launch a pre-emptive nuclear strike against the US as a first step toward creating socialism. While one of the main subtexts of this essay is the idea that even the most bizarre sounding ideas often contain some sort of merit, this, along with Posadas' fondness for dolphins based on the belief that they were a highly sentient alien race, cannot held but to lead to at least some chuckling, if not a belly laugh or two. For an interesting and useful approach to such issues and their form, see Bratich (2008).

12. An excellent analysis of this dynamic can be found in the work of Dean and Massumi (1992), who explore the relation between the role of the Emperor's body in the first Chinese empire and the mass mediated role of Reagan's body in the workings of the US Empire. Dean and Massumi argue that President Bush (the first one) attempted to engage in a similar kind of populist media politics, but failed. Extrapolating from this it seems arguable that the second President Bush attempted much the same, even attempting to revive the Star Wars missile defense system. Likewise this has been of mixed success. Many children, including the author, at one point during the 1980s wished to grow up to be the president like Reagan. It is likely that there are far fewer children making the same wish in regards to President Bush at the moment.

13. For more on Afrofuturism see Eshun (2003), Nelson (2000), Williams (2001), Weiner (2008), Yaszek (2005). Also, see the special issue of *Social Text* on Afrofuturism (Nelson 2001), the *Journal of the Society for American Music* special issue of technology and black music in the Americas (2008), and www.afrofuturism.net.

14. For more on Sun Ra, see Szwed (1998), Cutler (1992), and Elms et al (2007).

15. This is in sharp contrast to the arguments of Amadeo Bordiga, the Italian left communist, who declared moon landings a hoax and space travel impossible. Thanks for this information and several other references used here are owed to Alberto Toscano, who continues to insist that Karl Marx was not a space alien.

16. For more on space art see the Leonardo Space Art Project group site (spaceart.org/leonardo). Leonardo is quite interesting for the work they've published over the past forty years exploring the links and overlaps between science, technology, and the arts.

17. For more on the first few years of the AAA and its emergence from the mail art scene see Home (1997). For more elaboration on the concept of the

collective phantom, see Brian Holmes (2007).

18. One can find somewhat of a parallel to the AAA in the Men in Red radical ufology group, which grew out of the student movement in Italy in the early 1990s. For Men in Red radical ufology starts from a politics founded from disputing the proposition that the universe is made in man's image, and proceeds to think of ways to autonomously engage in contacting extraterrestrial life forms. In a parallel to the AAA as collective phantom, Men in Red state that they themselves wish to remain at a level that is the same as what they study, namely unidentified. For more on them, see www.kyuzz.org/mir.

19. Bizarrely, despite being called a red paper, it is printed on paper that is most definitively green. Special thanks to Agent Stephanie Schreven for providing me with access to these dangerous, secret intergalactic documents.

:: VI :: An//aesthetics & Re\\fusal ::

Today the avant-garde is not moral commitment, beautiful soul, ideological militancy, etc.; the new realism is rather the testimony of a desperate epoch, constructive punk realism, expressive violence and shaking the techniques of mystification of communication... a hope incarnated by that which we know can no longer sustain it – is the line of flight for our world. The violence of our experience abstract, directed against us and against others, is the only possibility for producing catharsis, but a continually frustrated catharsis... The avant-garde does not lead time, but rather is that which constitutes it radically; it is the definition of the beautiful that we have given and that becomes the conscious motor of production itself. – Antonio Negri (2002)

First there was a scream. A shattering of an understanding of the world, dislocated by the shock of the real. Suspended between that rupture in perception and the realization that it need not be this way something happened. The chance spotting of a marker, a beacon marking the travels of others who no longer wished to be involved in the bloody machinations of the world as is, but who struggled against it not with a sense of stoic ardor but rather of insurgent joy. Do you remember it? Maybe it was the rhythms of a marching band lingering over streets, or an absurd slogan scrawled on an alley wall, or the appearance of a revolutionary army of clowns. In a passing, fleeting, ephemeral moment, perhaps not even realized at the time: a minor motion, internal movement traced along the contours of an emerging collective time. And in that moment, everything changes. Not that everything actually changed, but the disruption from the usual rhythms of life allows the emergence of something else, the emergence

of a form of sociality, animated by temporary overlapping and con-
joining of aesthetics, politics, and life. In this point occurs the conjunction of artistic and revolutionary machines in the formation of
new imaginal machines, a space where Gerald Raunig argues they
"both overlap, not to incorporate one another, but to enter to into a
concrete exchange relationship for a time" (2007: 18).[1]

Perhaps we can call this the an//aesthetics of re-fusal: not the refusal of the aesthetic domain, not a call to realize art by transcending
it. It embodies, rather, the refusal to separate aesthetics from flux of
the on-going social domain, and through that, the re-fusing and con-
joining of aesthetics in the construction of an imaginal machine. If in
the previous chapter we discussed the outer space of the radical imagination as exteriority, now we are turning to the point of reentry of
the imaginal machine: where new forms of creativity are thus spread
through the social field. An art of intense relations, not as anaesthetic
to reduce pain, maintain stability in the face of precarious existence,
for the anaesthetic, as David Levi Strauss tells us, "only masks symp-
toms; it does not treat the root causes of pain, to trace it back to its
source, give it meaning, or counter it with pleasure" – but a much
older radical practices of aesthetics as immediacy and affective composition (1999:12).

But what kind of imaginal machines is it possible to produce
within an artistic framework, if, as Brian Holmes has argued, to talk
about politics in an artistic frame is necessarily to be lying (2007: 81)?
Perhaps a politics of joyous mythopoetic creation then, one that does
not concern itself with the truth or falsity of creation as much as what
it affectively animates: an aesthetics that whistles past the graveyard
of undead imaginaries, agreeing with Tom Waits that since it never
told the truth it can never tell a lie. From these fleeting ephemera and
moments the movement and self-institution of the radical imagination
are born, unfolding in a process of affective composition in aesthetic
politics. At this nexus unfolds a conception of an aesthetics based on
focusing on the relations and intensities emerging within the process
of collective creation rather than the content of the artistic composition. A sense of aesthetics focused on the relations of production not
as a concern secondary to the content of what is produced, but rather
as the explicit process of self-institution and creation of a space where
the art of politics is possible. That is, rather than assuming the existence of a forum where politics, the creation of intersubjective understandings that make collective life possible, can be articulated through
art. Here we see the creation of an affective space: a common space
and connection that is the necessary precondition for connections,
discussion, and communities to emerge. This is political art – not nec-

essarily because of the directly expressed content of the work – but because of the role this plays in drawing lines of flight away from staggering weight of everyday life, in hybridizing sounds and experience to create space where other relations and possibilities can emerge.

There has long existed both an intense and troubled connection between avant-garde arts and autonomous politics. That a composition is aesthetically innovative does not necessarily mean that its particularly progressive politically, either in its content or the relations animated through its creation and circulation. The Futurists do not just represent the point where, as Stewart Home explores, utopian currents based around the integration of all aspects of life, which were viewed primarily as religious during medieval times, moved over to be considered part of the artistic sphere (1991). The Futurists are perhaps the clearest indication that interesting aesthetics do not necessarily correspond to progressive politics, as their intense fascination with war, speed, patriotism, and eventual movement towards fascism display. There are countless more examples less dramatic but all the more complex, ranging from Surrealism's turbulent relation to the institutional communist movement (and eventual severing and usage by US state propaganda efforts and fronts) to debates about the role of street art in gentrification (Anonymous 2006).

The point here is not to attempt to reopen and revisit the entire history of the avant-garde and its relations to politics, for that would be far too vast.[2] Rather, it is to revisit and draw from this history is a specific way, namely to consider ways through which the conjunction of artistic and revolutionary machines enables the building of imaginal machines, or the possibility for forms composition drawing from aesthetic politics. This question becomes all the more pressing when the legacy of the historical avant-garde is far beyond simply being dead, it is rather undead, become monstrous, reemployed, and turned into all sorts of zombies bent on devouring the brains of living creativity. The avant-garde has played much the role that Jacques Attali attributes to music, a prophetic one where changes in aesthetic production precede and foretell changes in the overall modes of economic relations and social power (1985). The problem is that in much the same way that the determining role of anticapitalist resistance on capitalist development has often turned liberatory movements into mechanisms then turned against themselves, the compositional modes created within avant-garde arts have also been turned against themselves and zombified. Innovative modes of aesthetic production have become, as Negri hints at in the quotation above, the conscious motor of production to the degree that capitalism relies upon the production of new imagery and creativity for its continued existence.

The question becomes how to go about the production of imaginal machines and a compositional politics in ways where aesthetics do not become separated from the body of social movement or congealed into a specialist role within it. An aesthetics that avoids the charms of an aesthetic Leninism, or as imagery of state function (artistic production will act as the vanguard of social transformation or sediment the imaginary of the clearly understood national realm), and the separation of aesthetics from collective movement into the decoded flows of capital. How to subtract from being a conscious motor of production into a role of becoming a mechanism of anti-productivity, a machine against work. All forms of social separation which in the distance between continued aesthetic production and the body of social movement create conditions where this is no longer experienced as production self-directed through social movement, but at best a kind of anaesthetic treating the continued forms of separation existing within capitalist social reality. The an//aesthetics of re-fusal is precisely this, the continued struggle against the separation of aesthetic production and politics from the body of social movement, one that through it constantly re-infuses the social wealth and creativity of aesthetic production into the body of social movement.

Avant What?

Why talk about autonomy when the major thrust of experimental art in the 1960s and 1970s was to undermine the autonomous work?... But one sometimes wonders if the members of the art establishment, while seemingly obsessed with these transgressions of a very old status quo, are in fact not afraid to draw the most basic conclusions from their own ideas. For if you truly abandon the notion that an object, by its distinction from all others, can serve as a mirror for an equally unique and independent subject, then the issue of autonomy becomes a deep existential problem. – Brian Holmes (2007: 100)

A sensible, although perhaps somewhat predictable, place to begin inquiry into the nature of the avant-garde is Peter Burger's seminal text on the subject. Burger's theory of the avant-garde is one that is not directly a history of particular movements (although they are clearly involved in underpinning the formulation), but an understanding of the changing social position and institution of art within society. Theories of art and its social role, not surprisingly like all forms of knowledge, are situated within and influenced by the historical period and social processes occurring at the time of their writing. For Burger the avant-garde is defined by a turning away from criticism of previous periods, movements, or styles into a critique and attempt to detonate the institution of art itself, and to reintegrate artistic practice back in and through the praxis of life itself. The avant-garde is thus a reaction against the idea of the autonomy of art, or aesthetics in itself, in the understanding that to the degree there is any truth to this it is founded on the essential irrelevance of artistic practice at best, and a worst a form of reification and the separation of the "aesthetic experience" into a disassociated and meaningless realm. For Kristeva the avant-garde, in the history of signifying systems (including the arts, religion, forms of ritual, and so forth) is composed of fragmentary phenomena that "underscore the limits of socially useful discourse and attest to what it represses: the *process* that exceeds the subject and his communicative structures" (1984: 16).

The questioning and attack on the autonomous role attributed to art attempts to undermine its institutionalization and the attribution of innovation and creativity to individual genius, not just to pose the collective as the subject of production, but tending towards, in Burger's framing, "the radical negation of the category of individual creation" (1984: 51). Burger argues that this leads toward an attempt to negate the perceived unity of the work of art, a task it fails at, and rather negates a specific kind of unity, the relationship between the part and the whole. Paradoxically, this leads to the avant-garde assault on art as separated production and an institutionalized sphere to be realized within the overall composition of the continued institutionalization of art as a separate sphere: "the intention to revolutionize life by returning art to its praxis turns into a revolutionizing of art" (1984: 72). In other words, the avant-garde aim to end the separate realm of art as a specialized role itself becomes a specialized role within artistic institutions. This can be seen clearly in the way that the history of contemporary art is narrated, where the assault of the avant-garde on the institutional realm becomes an almost obsessive point of reference and locus to draw ideas from, although not too surprisingly done so in a way that cleverly strips away the critique of institutionalization and separation, or perhaps renders them in a way that is more copasetic to the continued existence of this separation is a slightly more amenable form. A lovely and fitting comment on this dynamic is David Hammons 2004 piece "The Holy Bible: Old Testament," which at face value is just a well made leather bound bible, except that the only words contained in the book are "The Complete Works of Marcel Duchamp."[3] The irony is that this makes the point even clearer. The avant-garde attempt to disarticulate the institutionalized space of artistic production becomes the point for the continued inscription of the borders of institutionalization, to the point where it is known to be an almost holy text and history to be referred to, even the more effective as a sly joke. The patterns of circulation become all the more closed even in the appearance of being open.

Constituent Spirals

A singularity, a rupture of sense, a cut, a fragmentation, the detachment of semiotic content – in a dadaist or surrealist manner – can originate mutant nuclei of subjectivation... [these] assemblages of aesthetic desire... are not entities which can easily circumscribed within the logic of discursive sets... One gets to know them not through representation but through affective contamination.   – Félix Guattari (1995: 18/92)

One recurring challenge for political art is to circumvent the assumption, implicitly contained within a didactic composition, that the work's arguments can take place in an already existing public sphere – the common ground and frame of reference – that preexists the particular expression. Unaware of this challenge, much political artwork strives to create interesting and compelling arguments, flourishes of speech, in hopes that the message will reach the listener with little interference. In order for political speech to cause affective resonance, conditions need to exist for the constituted audience to be able to identify with those who are expressing them, to possess a capacity to affect and be affected. This process of affective composition so often begins from minor moments and interactions: yet through them spaces of commonality, where new relations and interactions are possible, emerge. Deleuze and Guattari's observation that "the people are missing" is not a lament, but a realization that the task of politics is precisely the composition of common space through processes of intensive engagement not bound by the closure of already understood identities and positions (1986: 216; Thoburn 2003). This is precisely the point explored by Randy Martin in his work on the role of theater in the producing and forming of publics, acting as a means for the production of socialist ensembles: "publics must continue to be generated if a revolutionary project is to maintain its resonance" (1994: 197). For Martin autonomy is not something granted, but rather a critical presence existing through and despite networks of governance. The continual generation of new publics, of new forms of the resonance of ideas and relations, is the process of affective composition, whether through the forming of publics through theater or any other of the possible means.

But what is meant by affective composition? At the risk of launching yet another trendy neologism, the concept of affective composition is formed by the bringing together of notions of affect with the autonomist notion of class composition. The concept of affect was developed in a submerged history of philosophy, stretching from Spinoza to Deleuze and Guattari (and having been developed further by figures such as Antonio Negri and Genevieve Lloyd), to indicate an increase in capacity to affect or to be affected by the world. For Deleuze and Guattari, artistic creation is the domain of affective resonance, where imagination shifts through the interacting bodies. Composition is used here, borrowing from the autonomist Marxist notion of class composition, indicating the autonomous and collective capacities to change the world created through social resistance. As forms of collective capacity and self-organization are increased, composed by the circulation of struggles and ideas, the workings of the state and capitalism attempt to find ways to disperse them or to integrate these social energies into their own workings. Thus there are formed cycles of the composition, decomposition, and recomposition of struggles. A key insight of autonomist thought was the argument that the nature of struggles and the forms of social cooperation created within in them determine the direction of capitalist development, rather than the autonomous self-directed power of capital. Considering affective composition through forms of street art and performance is to look at the ways that the capacities they create contribute to the development of affective capacities and forms of self-organization. It is the ways in which street arts can take place in what the Infernal Noise Brigade mission statement describes as "facilit[ating] the self-actualization of the mob" (Whitney 2003: 219). This self-actualization is not something which ever reaches a final or finished point, but continually doubles over and immanently above itself, turning cycles of struggles into spirals of movement composition.

The affective composition of relations and intensities in aesthetic politics is a pressing question because of ways that the possibilities for the existence of public and common space have changed over recent years. The increasingly drastic commercialization of public space, corporate domination of media outlets, and predominance of fear mongering in all areas of life, has created a condition where there are immense flows of information and data available for discussion, but precious little public sphere in which this data can resonate. Paolo Virno argues that where forms of collective intelligence do not find expression in a public sphere where common affairs can be attended to it produces terrifying effects and proliferations of unchecked and groundless hierarchies. These are areas of "publicness without a public sphere" (2004: 40-41) There are flows of information and images constantly surrounding and immersing us that allow for new possibilities for communication and the formation of subjectivities, but which can also be quite overwhelming and go in directions that are not necessarily liberatory. Chat rooms and blogs meld seamlessly with the commercial landscapes of gentrified cities and the 24-hour a day flow of "news" that may excite the libido or intone the constant reminder of "be afraid," but do not constitute a common place of collective engagement. More than anything they tend to pro-actively prevent the emergence of shared space in ways that have not been overcoded by the workings of state or capital.

One cannot assume that there is an already existing public sphere, an existing arrangements of bodies, ready to receive information conveyed through an artistic composition. Relying on the expected aesthetics of propaganda means circumscribing possible patterns of resonance more limited than might be wished. Political art derives its politics not just by its content, but also by the ways in which it is designed to work with or against the predetermined forms of circulation of ideas, images, and relations. In other words, to appreciate that forms of street art do not derive their subversiveness simply from the fact that they occur on the street (which can also include a whole range of viral marketing and quotidian forms of spectacular recuperation), but rather from unfolding the relations that avoid the overcoding operations of the art institution and commodity production. It is this focus on patterns of circulation and relations as a politico-aesthetic activity, what George Katsiaficas describes as "engaging aesthetic rationality in the process of political transformation, of turning politics into art, everyday life into an aesthetically governed domain," that comprises the process of affective composition (2001: 310).

One approach to understanding relationships and the construction of community in an artistic framework recently has been Nicholas Bourriaud's notion of "relational aesthetics," which he developed during the mid-1990s coming out of his curatorial work. Relational aesthetics, which Bourriaud frames as part of a materialist tradition, is argued to represent not a theory of art, but of form, namely one where "intersubjectivity does not only represent the social setting for the reception of art... but also becomes the quintessence of artistic practice" (2002: 22). Collective understandings, experiences, and interactions then are not something that is added on the work afterwards but rather compose the starting point and substance of the work itself. While any artwork can be thought of as a relational object through the kinds of interactions it animates (often times a gentle stare with a determined air of trying to appear clever), the difference here is that these relations are the core of the work itself. Bourriaud argues that today the designation of art seems to be little more than a "semantic leftover" which should be replaced by a definition like "art is an activity consisting in producing relationships with the world with the help of signs, forms, actions, and objects" (2002: 107).

From this Bourriaud tries to recast the critical function of aesthetic intervention, arguing that rather than being based on forming imaginary and utopian realities, artistic intervention is aimed at forming living models of action and being within the existing world. The artistic composition exists then as "a *social interstice* within these experiments and these new 'life possibilties' appear as possible" (2002: 45). A piece's aura no longer lies in another projected world, nor in the form itself, but rather in the temporary collectives and communities that coalesce for the purposes of producing the exhibition or the space itself (although for Bourriaud clearly this is all about the exhibition rather than any diffuse process of creation going beyond the gallery walls). For Bourriaud the subversive and critical function of artistic creation is the invention of individual and collective vanishing lines, lines of flight, in the creation of temporary nomadic constructions.

At first this seems reasonable enough, and relatively close to what I'm describing as the process of affective composition, the movement from artistic creation based around objects to the creation of relations and modulations of affect. But slowly the situation becomes more problematic. For instance, there's no necessary dichotomy between forming imaginary and utopian realities and micro-practices of intervention. Utopian dreams and models, rather than being stated and fixed models to impose, have often acted as inspirations for finding micropolitical modes of intervention, which is to say that they have often been connected rather than mutually exclusive. Likewise one can build an overall vision drawing from and extending micro-practices. But what might at first appear to be a relatively minor difference not worth quibbling about that much becomes more pronounced, especially when Bourriaud makes the argument that today "social utopias and revolutionary hopes have given way to everyday micro-utopias and imitative strategies, any stance that is directly 'critical' of society is futile" (2002: 31). Rather than there being just a distinction between imaginary and utopian projects, here it is argued that these projects in so far as they are directly critical of the social world (the state, capitalism, war, exploitation) are futile. In other words, dear artist, give up any hopes of having anything to say about social conditions on any large scale and make yourself content with micro-interventions and practices. This sounds quite similar to approaches ascribed to politics and thought coming in the wake of 1968 and post-structuralism, and so called "identity politics." In other words a shift in politics, from grand to minor, in a way that micro-practices and interventions are divorced from large questions and social structures.

This does not mean that all practices and questions have to be directly oriented to addressing large scale social and historical projects, as might be argued by the looming clichéd image of the overly zealous Trotskyite who insists that everything must be about directly contesting capitalism from the perspective of the working class or it is "objectively reactionary." There are many ways to congeal and conjoin minor articulations informed by and relating to large social questions, that are fundamentally concerned with an overall social critique, without having that critique determine and overly confine these practices. The difference here is while the ascription of a move to withdrawal through micro-practice ignoring larger social questions was typically one that was ascribed to these practices as a criticism of them (and more often than not that was not really the case at all), here Bourriaud can be seen to almost be taking on the accusations and embracing them as a positive condition, for as he specifically states, to do otherwise would be futile. Perhaps he is confused about words and really meant to say fertile. Sadly this does not seem to be the case.[4]

What makes this even stranger is his claim that relational aesthetic production, because the art produced is made of the same material as social exchange (after all here sociality is the artistic composition itself), has a special role in collective production processes, in the production of a presence in space that goes beyond itself (2002: 41). This seems fair enough and sounds much like Attali's argument about the prophetic role of music production in terms of foretelling changes in production. But then it becomes even more bizarre when Bourriaud argues that relational art is "well removed from the administrative rationality that underpins it" (2002: 47). This seems bizarrely contradictory. How can relational art both occupy a special place in the process of collective production but also be removed from administrative rationality? If *only* subtracting oneself from capitalist imperatives were that simple! This occurs through two moves. The first is that Bourriaud basically is raiding the history of practices and arguments about the disarticulation of the borders of artistic production and institutionalization of artistic production from the history of the avant-garde and reinscribing them very much in a capital A artistic world. This becomes very clear if one catalogs the names of artists that are referenced through the text, which are exclusively gallery artists, and totally exclude all forms of artistic practice and invention going beyond this world. As Marina Vismidt points out, the dematerialization of the art object in conceptual art production during the 1960s, in that it involved a shifting towards symbolic mediation and the production of events (rather than objects), "is actually information, as it is subject to the same forms of proprietary relations" (2004). Which is to say that shifts of performance in artistic production developed practices that brought artistic production *more* under the control of various forms of administrative rationality, not less. Just as Peter Burger observed the avant-garde critique of the art institutionalization was realized within the artistic institution itself, it is in this sense that Bourriaud can say that relational art is free from administrative rationality in that it has carved out a space of autonomy within the process of institutionalization. A space of autonomy created by its appearance of not being directly tied to larger economic considerations and no doubt helped along by his fostering of its as a model of artistic production in his curatorial and authorial role.

But Bourriaud, in the construction of his procrustean bed of relational art, both stretches it to bring new forms of life back to the institutional space, and also systematically amputates concerns about larger social and economic concerns. He does not just actively counsel against artistic interventions that concern themselves with larger critical functions (which he even regards as being regressive), but also systemically neglects and pushes aside the economic function of the institutional art space and production. While the production of relational art within the institutional might be argued to attain a status where it is relatively free from administrative rationality, one would need to be delusional to say that artistic production has magically freed itself from the much broader provider of an administrative rationality, namely capitalism and the imperatives produced within capitalist social relations. For Bourriaud you can have your micro-intervention and eat it too, provided of course that you have mastered the alchemical art of transmuting creativity into the materials needed for social reproduction. This is exactly the sort of magical / mythical process that is alleged to animate the formation of creative clusters, the net economy, and the post-Fordist economy more generally, all things which we weren't supposed to worry our silly little artistic heads with while we were busy micro-intervening. Bourriaud plays the Mickey Mouse sorcerer's apprentice to Richard Florida's symphonic arrangement, while many are left running around with buckets trying to bail out a rising tide of gentrification (or perhaps that is just another piece of relational art where the eviction becomes a compositional form).

Bourriaud, however, is not a totally exceptional case or drastic shift in thought. Rather, what he is arguing here is the logical shift of an overall nature of collective practice within some strains of artistic practice coming out of the historical avant-garde. The best exploration of the trend is the recent edited volume by Blake Stimson and Gregory Sholette on the history of artistic collectivism since 1945, or as they call it, the art of social imagination. As discussed in the previous chapter, they argue that the post-war attacks on collectivism within working class politics are connected to the rise of capitalist forms of collectivism, acting both as benevolent and disciplinary mechanisms. This leads to the returning of collectivism in the cultural realm in mutated and contradictory forms. Although this is a somewhat circuitous argument to make, it is in the decades following this, particularly in the process of recuperating the social energies unleashed by the struggles of the 1960 and 1970s, that sees the rise of one might call a entrepreneurial artistic collectivism, the depoliticization of art collectives, and the rise art grouplettes as the embodiment of enterprise culture.[5] The somewhat primordial, mystical reunification of art through life that typically been the province of the avant-garde was exchanged for a DIY, hyper-capitalist collectivism. In other words, for the collectivism of the new economy. And this is precisely the point drawn out by Paul Helliwell (2007), who sees in the net economy obsession with interaction and collaboration the ghost of relational aesthetics, which is the lingering spirit of the avant-garde. As Helliwell quips, is relational aesthetics a critical practice or an art and aesthetics for the service economy? It is perhaps both. Or perhaps it can be the former because it used to be the latter. Similar to the way that in Volume 3 of *Capital* Marx describes joint stock companies and other forms of capitalist cooperation as a strange form of "socialism founded on the grounds of private property," paradoxically one could say that this is the process going the other way, or capitalism founded on the grounds of artistic collectivism. Or more fittingly, a capitalist rejuvenated through its ability to decompose and recuperate the energies of the avant-garde, to transmute them into a more readily usable form.

It is for such reasons that the relation between avant-garde artistic production and anticapitalist politics, even when thought of through a compositional framework, still exist in some degree of tension to each other. The prophetic role ascribed to changes in artistic production can be seen to operate in a fashion similar to how practices and ideas found within forms of social resistance and labor insubordination influence and determine the direction of capitalism. But there are differences which also explain some of the tensions. The recuperation and reterritorialization of labor insurgencies results in outcomes that are fairly easy to understand as positive advances despite the partial neutralization of their critical energies. For instance, the creation of the welfare state, higher wages, improved working conditions, and so forth; outcomes that are easy to appreciate despite the disciplinary role unions or other institutionalized forms can play in mediating roles. It's much harder to see such an appreciable gain as ideas and practices developed within and from an avant-garde tradition are utilized within a capitalist framework. Vaguely Surrealist advertising or viral marketing, relational and interaction design, and so forth, do not have the same appreciable benefits in their recuperated form. While one can see how the former tend to result, even in recuperation, in collectively positive outcomes, even if limited, the same process drawing from avant-garde aesthetics and practices tend more to individual benefits and collective costs, although this does not need to be the case. It is for this reason why Boltanski and Chiapello would make a differentiation between social and artistic critique (2005), but this would be an outcome of the failure to appreciate the compositional dynamics within specifically artistic movements, which is to say a dynamic that tends to occur more precisely because of the separation of aesthetic radicalism from the body of social movement. Because of these tensions it is perhaps not so surprising that there would be a tendency to dismiss forms of aesthetic radicalism and experimentation as not being part of the 'real' issues of struggle. Ironically this is part of the same process of separating radical aesthetics from social movements and the construction of imaginal machines more generally, a process facilitating their individuation and recuperation, which is then both the cause and the symptom in a self-reinforcing cycle.

By far the most well thought out attempt to elaborate a notion of political aesthetics based on the relations contained and enabled by them, one that could provide a way out of this conundrum, is Hakim Bey's notion of "immediatism." As a form of utopian poetics, immediatism describes creative collective activity designed to reduce the degree of mediation involved in artistic activity. It is based on forms of play and the free exchange of gifts (and performances) in a way intended to avoid the logic of commodification. There is no passive consumption: all who are spectators must also be participants. Immediatism strives not towards the production of art objects, but rather of immediately present experiences and connections for those who are participating in its creative realms of the clandestine institution of community through shared creation. Immediatist practices involve a wide variety of activities not typically thought of within the rubric of the arts. For instance the quilting bee, formed as a practice of spontaneous non-hierarchical patterning producing something useful and beautiful to be given to someone involved in the quilting circle, can be expanded to include parties, potlatches, banquets, and forms of artistic happenings and events. Whatever particular case may be, the key notion is to reduce as much as possible the presence of mediation in the construction of collectively experienced situations and the shared presence of them. Indeed, Bey suggests that the best immediatist agit-prop "will leave no trace at all, except in the souls of those who are *changed* by it" (1994: 26). As Bourriaud comments, "anything that cannot be marketed will inevitably vanish" (2002: 9), although in this case that is a rather positive dynamic, as the invisibility can act as guard against commodification and/or recuperation by the gallery system and the ways this is used for capitalist regeneration and renewal.

War Machines, Imaginal Machines

This is an invitation not to get up this morning, to stay in bed with someone, to make musical instruments and war machines for yourself. – Radio Alice, February 9th, 1976

But let us return for a second to a particular kind of moment of the breaking down of barriers through affective composition, namely through forming an affective space through and around the performance of radical marching bands. A moment where the passivity of the crowd perhaps is broken, and the nature of the space is transformed. Bodies milling about, held awkwardly at a distance, a space maintained and looks a little chilly. Not from malice or mistrust, but from not knowing. But in that instant borders fall. The first hit of the drum is the first crack in the wall of the objectifying, separating gaze, the space created by the passive stare of an audience towards a performance, an exhibition: a spectacle. As the melody pulses through the crowd we revel in the timbre of the horns. Arms, words, memory and noise tenuously connect through time and desire. Ideas, memories, histories, cultures and stories are crossbred. Rage blends with joy; dislocation replaced by emerging, momentary worlds.

It is in this sense that radical marching bands are of the most interest: in the ways they undercut the usual space (and sometimes relations) of performance and create mobile and affective spaces in the streets where it becomes possible for other forms of relations to emerge. Projects such as the Hungry March Band, the Infernal Noise Brigade, and Rhythms of Resistance, closely connected with the late 1990s upswing in streets protests and parties such as Reclaim the Streets, brought carnivalesque energies and excitement into the all too often ritualistic and stale mode of political protest. One could argue, perhaps paradoxically, that while in the upswing of organizing and summit protests that occurred in the post-99' realization there already were existing movements against the more egregious excesses of the state and capitalism, there was somewhat of a shift away from diffuse forms of cultural politics to more spectacular media friendly forms such as mass mobilizations and lock downs. Radical marching bands and other forms of tactical frivolity were important in keeping open space for the emergence of intensive and affective relations within such spaces, relations which hopefully would find their ways out on to all of the fabric of daily life.

Hakim Bey describes how marching bands were invented by Turkish Janissaries, members of the Ottoman Imperial Guard, who belonged to a heterodox Bektashi Sufi order. The marching band, developed for use in military campaigns, functioned as a form of psychological warfare through music that induced sheer terror in their opponents (1995: 31). Their effect on European armies, who had never experienced anything like that previously, must have been complete fear, most likely resulting in increased morale among the Turkish troops. Marching bands were adopted by European states for use in military campaigns and increasingly in symbolic and ceremonial functions as forms of amplified communications technologies became developed. Forms of marching band music moved with the migration of Roma people from the Ottoman Empire to the southern US, who brought along with them brass instruments that had a profound effect on the development of music in the area.

Not surprisingly then the repertoire of many marching bands is also a veritable melting pot of styles, cultures, and background, bringing together anything from jazz and big band tunes to klezmer, Moroccan music and Indian wedding tunes to calypso, salsa, reggae, and Sun Ra. There are also large degrees of inspiration from projects that

have merged together the energy of punk rock and street performance, such as Crash Worship and ¡TchKung! (who had members that
went on to form marching bands). There are large degrees of
crossover and mixing between political marching bands and other
forms of street and performance art and theater (such as Vermont's
Bread & Puppet Theatre, which provided a key source of inspiration
for many marching bands) as well as underground circus and vaude-
ville (such as the Bindlestiff Family Circus and Circus Contraption).

One of the best examples I can think of how a marching band altered the composition of a situation occurred at the Foo Festival in
Providence, Rhode Island in July 2006. The event, organized by people from AS220, a local arts space, filled the greater part of a city bloc
while literally thousands of people milled about attending various
talks and workshops, casually munching on food, browsing through
the wares of booksellers, and watching bands and musicians perform
on a stage located near one end of the festival. At several points during
the day the What Cheer? Brigade, a local marching band, would materialize replete with propulsive drumming and piercing horns, re-
splendent in motley attire that one would be hard pressed to call
uniforms. Their appearance changed the nature of the situation because as they would enter the space people would begin to dance and
frolic around with them as they moved through the space, rather than
staying fixed upon the stage as a focal point, one that clearly marked
the difference between those who were performing and observing.
This increase in the generalized level of conviviality affected not only
those directly involved in the dancing, but seemed to move beyond
itself as those around it somehow found new reasons to converse and
interact with people they hadn't spoken with before.

The marching band may most commonly be experienced as an ap-
pendage to the state form, as a space defined by tightly scripted and
controlled lines and the military insignia. They are encountered at the
military or civic parade, or perhaps as a motivational soundtrack to a
sports competition.[6]   And it is perhaps this association that makes
their playful détournement and reappropriation to serve other ends
all the more delicious. March music might usually typically have resonance with the workings of the war machine, but as Deleuze and
Guattari would remind us, this war machine can never totally be integrated into the workings of governance: there is always something
that escapes. It is a process that exceeds that subject and existing communicative structures yet paradoxically one that creates a space where
the possibility of transversal commonality exists. And the war machine, understood as a space of exteriority to the state, can also be understood as a transformation machine, as the nomadic flows and

machinations that constitutes spaces of possibility.

Stencil art and graffiti as well as street performances play an important in breaking down the forms of relations created by artistic activity as separated or removed from daily life because they can be inscribed within the flows of people's everyday lives, in the streets, and in subways. But this does not inherently mean that such activities contain the possibility for reorienting people's expectations or will result in certain responses. And indeed, it is possible that what was once an innovative creative activity can become standardized and expected in such ways that the affectivity it initially generated is longer as intensive or effective in its workings. And if Banksy, or someone as marketable as him, should come to your town, it can drive up the real estate values as well. Even the most apparently subversive imagery can be reincorporated and recuperated back into the workings of the spectacle.

This constituent and affective space for creating new relations is not one that can be created and continue to exist without interference or difficulty. Temporary autonomous zones are temporary for a reason, namely the realization that attempts to create such spaces will inevitably face repression and recuperation. Thus, it is often not tactically sensible to create a space and maintain it (investing time, energies, and cost) against all odds. These moments and spaces are described quite well by the Leeds May Day Group as "moments of excess" (2004). One can see how with phenomena as diverse as the rise of punk and social centers to culture jamming and Critical Mass, through different mixes of cooptation and legal action, a space that once vibrant and full of possibilities comes to be a bit lackluster. But the compositional capacities of these ruptures are not unlimited, for they too through repetition become ritualized and fall back into solidified patterns of circulation. The question becomes one of keeping open the affective capacities of the created space: to finds ways to avoid the traps of spectacular recuperation and the solidification of constituent moments and possibilities into fixed and constituted forms that have lost their vitality.

It's in this way that the concept of the art strike, as originally proposed by Gustav Metzgar, and then further developed by Stewart Home and the Praxis Group in 1990 – 1993, becomes useful for the composition of struggles. At a juncture where capitalism is increasingly reliant on the production of new images, relations, and affects for its continued existence, struggles to find ways to intervene in these somewhat more ephemeral realms. This is why Home argues that the importance of the art strike lies less in its feasibility or its concrete success, but rather in the possibility it opens up for extending and intensifying class war: "By extending and redefining traditional conceptions of the strike, the organization of the art strike intends to both increase its value both as a weapon of struggle and a means of disseminating proletarian propaganda" (1995: 27). The withdrawal of artistic labor needs to be collective in a significant way to have any effect, for to only have one artist striking against the institutional machinery (as with Metzgar's first strike), or a handful (as with the Praxis Group), while quite conceptually interesting, has little in the way of effects.[7] The withdrawal of artistic labor can only be aided by disruption of artistic production and communication by inducing of confusion and distortion of communication guerillas in the mystifications of the post-Fordist world. As the autonome a.f.r.i.k.a. gruppe argues: "When information becomes a commodity and Cultural Capital a most important asset, the distortion and devaluation of both is a direct attack against the capitalist system. To say it in a swanky way: This is Class War" (2003: 89). This is much the tactic explored in the discussion of the IWW Starbucks campaign: in so far as the production and ambiences is central to Starbucks, monkey wrenching their image production process can be understood as industrial action. Or, as Patrick Reinsborough describes it, "direct action at the point of assumption" (2003: 40).

This would mean to work with a sense of aesthetic politics and interventions that are not necessarily or totally based upon the elements contained within the work itself, but on understanding the possibilities created for affective relations, spaces, and interactions and their intensification and deepening by the process of artistic creation. And to continually modify the composition of these situations, subtracting them from circulation and visibility, and turning towards disruption, confusion and illegibility, in the face of recuperation. This is to understand artistic creation as what George Hubler describes as the shaping of time: art as a succession of works and productions distributed through time that embody the development of forms of collective time and relations. That is, a process that is not necessarily predicated upon the creation of meaning, but as an intervention or opening into a system of relations, connecting innovations that are passed along and mutated through the modulation of the relations in which they exist, on a terrain and topology of time "where relationships rather than magnitudes are the subject of study" (1962: 83). It is in these chains of relations that radical innovations in work, form, idea and practice are passed along, mutated, and linked in a succession of works embodying forms of collective time and relations. Hubler proposes that

Every act is an invention. Yet the entire organization of thought and language denies the simple affirmation of non-identity. We can grasp the universe only by simplifying it with ideas of identity by classes, types, and categories by rearranging the infinite continuation of non-identical events into a finite system of similitudes. It is in the nature of being that no event ever repeats, but it is in the nature of thought that we understand events only be the identities we imagine among them (1962: 67)

Similarly, affective composition, as a form of aesthetic politics and composition, is also ultimately an act of non-identity, or at least of any identity that is ever finally set in a fixed, sovereign form. The creation of affective spaces and possibilities, the common spaces and moments that underlie and make possible intensive forms of politics, is not a task that happens once and is finished, or ever could be, but is an ongoing task of the self-institution of the radical imagination. Self-management, as organizational form and practice for the continual reworking and renewal of affective composition, will be explored in the next chapter. As an ever-renewing process, moving and intensifying from the public sphere to constituent spirals of possibility, focusing of the affective composition of these moments means to focus on the possibilities for collective self-creation drawing from the relations created by shared creation.

Notes

1. One of the most interesting aspects about Raunig's work is his excellent exploration of the ways that a dialectical sublimation of art into revolution maintains a hierarchical relation between them. The argument for a total fusion of art and life have tended to come to ends far less desirable than initially imagined: "In cultural political endeavors that have ended up being too large and too abstract, the ideals of the inseparability of art and life, instead of questioning rigid boundaries between aesthetic and political practice, absolutized these boundaries or made them reoccur somewhere else" (2007: 203). This does not mean it is necessary to abandon the impulse that led to the desire for the fusion of art and life, as there are questions still raised about the way to connect and overlap art and revolutionary machines. This, however, is a more limited and modest question. This chapter and the text overall can be thought of as teasing out some tentative answers to this ongoing question.
2. For materials on the avant-garde and politics, see Poggioli (1965), Buchloh (2001), Negt and Kluge (1993), Weiss (1994), Kiaer (2005), and Cleveland (2008).
3. This example is taken from the *Martian Encyclopedia of Terrestrial Life, Volume VIII: Art* (2008). One of the interesting things about this text is despite the introduction of othering effects into the narrative to disorient approaches to already formed conceptions of contemporary artistic production (which can be quite alienating in themselves), the same examples are continually referred

to, with repeated references to Duchamp and Joseph Beuys. This is interesting in that these attempts to disarticulate the borders of artistic production then become so inscribed as the constant reference to keep inscribing those borders even the othering effect of the alien visit narrative still keeps reproducing them, almost despite itself.

4. For another critical commentary on relational aesthetics, see Bishop (2004).
5. This is quite similar to the shift that Donald Kuspit (1993) describes in the shift to the post-war neo-avant-garde, one that he characterizes as a shift from the former therapeutic role of the avant-garde to one based around increasing narcissism and the production of novelty and ironic effect rather than political intervention and social vision. While it is questionable whether the avant-garde really had anything that can be taken as a therapeutic role, nonetheless certain aspects of this description quite accurately describe the shift towards entrepreneurial artistic collectivism.
6. The author admits to briefly playing trumpet in a high school marching band.
7. For an exploration of the relation between aesthetic labor and emotional labor, specifically the kinds of embodiment found in their conjunction, see Witz et al. (2003).

:: VII :: The Labor of Imagination ::

Let us imagine, for a change, an association of free men working with the means of production held in common, and ex-
pending their many different forms of labor-power in full
self-awareness as one single social labor force... The total
product of our imagined association is a social product...
This, however, requires that society possess a material foundation, or a series of material conditions of existence, which
in their turn are the natural and spontaneous product of a long
and tormented historical development. – Karl Marx (1973:
171/173)

How can one establish, in the intervals of servitude, the new
time of liberation: not the insurrection of slaves, but the advent
of a new sociability between individuals who already have,
each on his own, thrown off the servile passions that are in-
definitely reproduced by the rhythm of work hours? The absence of the master from the time and space of productive
work turns this exploited work into something more: not just
a bargain promising the master a better return in exchange
for the freedom of the workers' movement but the formation
of a type of worker's movement belonging to a different history than that of mastery. So there is no paradox in the fact
that the path of emancipation is first the path where one is liberated from the hatred of the master experienced by the rebel
slave. – Jacques Ranciere (1989: 67/83)

Sisyphus is a paradoxical figure. He is said both to have been the
wisest of mortals and to have practiced the trade of a highway robber.
Sisyphus stole the secrets of the gods, cheated death, and for this was
condemned to an eternal life of pointless labor: the pushing of a boulder up a hill only to never be able to reach the summit with it. For
each time he neared the top the boulder slipped away, and he was
forced to see it roll down again, and cursed to return down the hill to

begin the task again. It may seem odd to begin a discussion of self-management with the image of Sisyphus. Or maybe not. As Albert Camus informs us, Sisyphus was indeed the proletarian of the gods, one both powerless and rebellious. Sisyphus is the absurd hero, one who is condemned to his position by his scorn of the gods, hatred of death, and passion for life: condemned to an eternal labor of no accomplishment or end. And just as the dreadful nature of Sisyphus' punishment is a condition of eternal, futile, hopeless labor, so is the position of the working class: trapped in dynamics of seemingly eternal repetition of the same tasks, one that "is tragic only at the rare moments when it becomes conscious" (1983: 121).

And it is this way that the figure of Sisyphus opens up an interesting avenue for thinking about worker self-management.[1] Self-management, as a demand, practice, and concept long circulating with the various milieus of radical politics and labor organizing struggles, all too often finds that the gains made by various campaigns and struggles slip beyond grasp before ever reaching that glorious plateau of the end of capitalism. The form of intervention (unions, the party, networks) escapes the conscious intents forged, often threatening to flatten the forms of protagonism themselves. Thus they roll back down the hill yet again, through moments of counterrevolution and recuperation. Despite this, if it is still held to be a desirable goal to move through and beyond capitalism, to create a new world of self-determining communities and socialites, the problems posed by the question of self-management are still all the more pressing: namely, the creation of new selves in this world that further enable moving through this world and on to the creation of another.

So, why raise the question of self-management again, now? In many ways this might be absurd (perhaps almost absurd as Sisyphus) – and because of that necessary. After all, if we live in such a period of intense globalization, is there any sense of thinking through an ethics of the liberation of labor on the level of a single organization? In other words, if the intense amount of competition and pressures created by global economic flows (through processes such as outsourcing, downsizing, the creation of regional trade blocs, the power of corporate conglomerates, etc.) mean that it is largely futile for governments to act as bulwarks against economic pressures, how can one really think through trying to remove oneself from these conditions on a comparatively much smaller scale? Would not even the best thought campaigns and forms of self-organization, subjected to such pressures, become fodder for another renewal and regeneration of capitalism? One can see this dynamic in the ways that demands for flexibility at work were realized as the imposition of precarious labor, so too the demands for self-management and self-determination at work raised during the 1960s and 1970s came be implemented, in a perverse form, through the rise of new management strategies, in the formation of quality teams, as 'responsible autonomy,' total quality management, and other implementations that can hardly be described as liberation. In the workings of the heavily symbolic post-Fordist economy there are many tasks that have come to be taken on as self-managed, but more often than not constitute the self-organization by the workforce of the means of its own alienation. Again, hardly liberating (even if arguably potentially containing some of the necessary tools for liberation). These pose weighty questions and concerns for the seemingly Sisyphean task of the liberation of labor and creativity, in the composition of non-alienated life within the confines of the present to create ways stretching through and beyond it.

What I want to do in this chapter is to try and see if it is possible to distill something of a radical kernel, or part of the notion and practices of worker self-management, which can be salvaged from the many qualms, difficulties, and complications that confront it, particularly in regards to its potentiality within fields of cultural production. That is, to see how self-management can contribute to what Ranciere describes as a movement not of slaves filled with *ressentiment*, but those living and embodying a new time of sociability and cooperation, creating resources and skills that can spread out from this, rather than being caught and contained by the conditions of it own creation. Drawing from my own experiences working in Ever Reviled Records, a worker owned and run record label, I want to ferret out, conducting something akin to an organizational autoethnography,[2] hints as to whether or not self-management could be useful for radical social struggles today (and if so how).

The most immediate concern that arises in considering the subversive potentialities of forms of self-management is essentially a definitional one: just what is meant by self-management? If the modifier worker is added, how (and around who) are the boundaries of what is considered work drawn? There is a wide variety of phenomena that have at times been described as a form of worker self-management (WSM), varying from workers occupying factories – seizing the means of production and running it themselves – to schemes of codetermination where workers are given slightly more voice in the operations of their workplace, within boundaries and parameters still beyond their control, for a slightly better deal in the divvying up of the wage pie. WSM can be used to describe broader revolutionary conditions where the economy is collectivized as a part of a general radical reorganization of social life (for instance as in Spain in 1936), or the takeover of production by workers during an economic down-turn where businesses have been abandoned by their owners (such as the classic example of Lip factory and some factories in Argentina more recently).[3] WSM can be oriented toward and eventual goal of getting rid of the capitalist market altogether, or it can be a partial so-cialization and amelioration of some of the more odious aspects of it, paradoxically possibly strengthening the rule of the market over social life.

One could carry on, indeed for some time, continuing to list the widely varying and discordant forms of social organization that have been described at one point or another as WSM. The varying mani-festations of WSM can be differentiated (although this would not be the only way to do so) by how particular forms of social organization configure the interactions between socialized labor and state power. This sort of a conceptual distinction helps to explain the difference between WSM as a form of market/social democracy (McNally 1993), versus the formation of cooperatives, or compared to nation-alization of production in a top down fashion as directed by a military regime. However, I'm not particularly interested in trying to create an airtight definition of WSM, but rather the ways such varying phe-nomena can contribute to furthering an overall and much larger ant-icapitalist and anti-statist project intended to reduce, deconstruct, and abolish the many and varying forms of social domination that exist.

Ever Reviled & the Building of Imaginal Machines

Ever reviled, accursed, ne'er understood, thou art the grisly terror of our age. – John Henry McKay (1999: 1)[4]

Ever Reviled Records was started in 1998 by Darren "Deicide" Kramer, first as a venue to release 7"s and albums by a band he was in at the time. It was named after a line in a poem by late 19th century anarchist John Henry McKay. Shortly after starting the project Dar-ren decided that it would be a better idea (and more consistent with the political ideas behind it) to run the project as a workers' collective, and that such a project could provide a useful model for self-organi-zation in the various overlapping communities centered around punk and radical politics. For the first several years of Ever Reviled Records existence I was not directly involved in the running of the project, although I had met Darren and several of the people involved in it at various shows and events. We also distributed each other's re-leases and helped promote shows and other events (at the time I was involved in running my own attempted record label, Patriotic Dissent, whose main activities was putting together various compilation CDs and shows that brought together multiple genres of music in unexpected ways and combined art events such as poetry readings and exhibitions with musical events).

I became involved in ERR in December 2002, around the time that the collective was starting to shift from being a label that only released music by punk bands (such as the Hopeless Dregs of Humanity, Rational Solution, and Give Us Barabbas) to one that was considering releasing a broader spectrum of music united by a focus on radical politics rather than any specific musical genre. Or, as it was often phrased in meetings and discussions, to go about taking part in building a radical democratic counterculture. As this idea was taken further subsequently ERR would come to release political folk music, hip hop, and blues. The particular path by which I ended up becoming involved in the project was by coordinating a radio show and interview for David Rovics (a well known political folk singer that the collective was interested in working with) and Graciela Monteagudo from the Argentina Autonomista Project to discuss the one year anniversary of the Argentinean economic collapse and the various social movements in Argentina that had sprung up over the past few years. ERR was at the same time planning a show to take place in New York City that David Rovics and other artists would be performing at. So I ended up taking part in planning and running that show, and thus became more interested in the direction the record label was taking, and discussed joining the project.

During the years I was involved in Ever Reviled (2002-2006) I was coordinated many of the tasks of running the collective. Indeed, one of the main principles characterizing ERR was that anyone could and should be involved in any of the aspects necessary to its continuing operations. In other words, to try and consciously avoid the emergence of a fixed division of labor and the forms of implicit hierarchies that can be contained in such divisions. Having said that, the majority of activities I was involved with for ERR consisted of design related tasks (such as designing CD inserts, flyers, updating the website and promotional materials, etc.) and writing the ERR newsletter, as well as planning promotions and distributions, deciding which artists to sign, as well as the more mundane tasks such as moving around boxes, posting flyers, and filling orders and taking them to the post office.

Despite the attempt to avoid the emergence of a division of labor, which is common among many such projects (and usually attempted by means such as rotating tasks and other measures), there was a tendency in ERR that solidified into certain roles based upon the experiences and skills of the various members of the collective. For instance, the work of filing taxes and other legal forms most often fell upon Uehara, not because he particularly enjoyed such tasks, but because he was the only member of the collective who understood the tasks well enough to get them done. Similarly I ended up doing much of the design work not necessarily because I wanted to do the majority of it myself, but because I was the member of the collective that had the most experience with these sorts of tasks. It seemed that greatest fluidity of tasks and who took part in them was in the jobs that were relatively unskilled, or the 'grunt work,' as it was often referred to, such as moving packages around and stuffing envelops. But these tasks, too, were subject to a division of tasks based on who had access to the physical resources (several members of the collective lived in Colorado, and in 2004 I moved to the UK).

Cultural Subversion & Laboratories of Cooperation

The goal of ERR can be understood as a attempted form of cultural subversion in multiple senses. It is both to create a vehicle, a platform, for the dissemination and circulation of political ideas through the cultural field (by releasing music and planning events that express radical political ideas), but also through the propagation of itself as an incipient model of post-capitalist production and relations. In other words, to conceive of Ever Reviled's internally democratic structure and propagating it as a form of propaganda through spreading a model of pre-figurative politics. This is what is meant by the idea of creating a radical, directly democratic counterculture: to embody and practice the possibilities of cooperative social relations in and through the means of subversion, to not separate the end goals of radical politics from the means created to work towards them. These efforts are constrained by the conditions under which they occur (the existence of the market, dealing with the state, constraints on time, etc) – but the idea is to take methods of moving through and beyond these conditions from within them. To use the practices of DIY found within various punk communities and find ways to extend them to other areas of life in the present (Holtzman et al 2004).

At its best such a project becomes a laboratory for the creation of forms of social cooperation and subjectivities that arguably would form the basis of a post-capitalist world, and to cultivate them in the here and now. I found that this argument resonated greatly with my personal experiences of working, which by large are not designed to extend and deepen forms of autonomous cooperation and workers' self-activity. Indeed, I can remember clearly the reason why I started to wonder about alternative forms of work organization, which was spurred on by working in a gas station and mini-mart for several years. It seemed obvious that the organization of the workplace was utterly absurd and there must be more sensible ways to organize people's lives and labor. From the alienation I felt going about what seemed like absurd tasks, arranged and coordinated in bizarre ways dictated by company policy, to the disenchantment I could palpably sense from almost every person who wandered into the store on their way to work at 6am.

Being aware of the very real disenchantment felt by almost everyone I knew about their jobs, the workers, to borrow Erik Petersen's words, whose "song weighs a thousand pounds," there was much focus in ERR on building links and forms of solidarity between various projects and networks that shared goals to similar to ours. The idea being not just to develop sociability within forms of autonomous self-organization, but also to build solidarity in between and amongst them. And to connect organizing and struggles around what might be more clearly recognized and economic, workplace, and labor issues with broader concerns about sexuality, race, state oppression, and other concerns. And perhaps even more importantly, to create links between projects working on creating forms of self-organization and directly democratic relations to be separated from more directly contestational forms of political action.

Thus ERR at various times worked on events and campaigns with groups such as Food Not Bombs, New Jersey Anti-Racist Action, Palestine Solidarity, the New Jersey Indymedia Center, and various unemployed workers unions and community groups in Argentina. An important part of creating this web and networks of solidarity and co-operation was organizing and planning workshops, events, conference, and encuentros where people could meet, exchange information and experiences, and find common grounds from which various struggles could cross-pollinate. Among these events was the Festival del Pueblo, multiple years of National Conference on Organized Resistance, the Life After Capitalism gathering, and Enero Autonomo in Argentina.

Forms of autonomous self-organization and self-management in the workplace operate as critiques of existing forms of work organization as they stipulate that there exist other possibilities for how workplaces might operate. They function as what could be described, even if this is not usually done, as forms of "propaganda of the deed" and as direct action (Flynn, et al. 1997). This is not to say that they are in any way violent or confrontational at all as is often assumed about such practices, but rather that they embody a form that follows this spirit and inspiration, namely that of taking political action without recourse to the state as a locus of making demands. For example, the idea behind acts of "propaganda of the deed" is that they will inspire others to take part in forms of political action and organizing that they would not otherwise. Worker self-management then can be understood as overturning the violence of dispossession and command instilled in wage slavery from the founding acts of originary accumulation to the myriad methods of discipline, control and surveillance often deployed on the job directly. Similarly, direct action does not necessarily indicate any form of violence at all, but rather acting outside the mediation and forms designated by the state or other bodies. So, while this can take the forms of a blockade outside the meeting of a questionable financial meeting or military base, intervening in the situation based on the notion the authority of the state is illegitimate, is it can equally be understood as the creation of spaces and method for autonomous self-organization and community without appealing to the authority or assistance of those beyond who are involved in the process of co-creation.

Problems of Self-Exploitation

In the days of Marx, the main problem was the liberation of the working man from the capitalist. The contribution of Yugoslavia to socialism is in the liberation of the working-man from the state. But socialist labor-management cannot assume the position of leading the world system, which belongs to it, until it liberates the working man from himself as a collective capitalist. – Jaroslav Vanek (1977: 48)

Worker self-management, at its best, takes part in creating times and relations that are, at least partially, outside of the existing reality of capitalist work. But, perhaps not surprisingly, not all is sunny and sweet in the land of creating forms of self-management. Indeed, this is perhaps not all that surprising, because as much as they aim to create the incipient forms of organization and sociality that forms the basis of a more liberatory society, they also exist within the confines of the present, and thus have to work against the ways in which current conditions constrict these possibilities. And this conflict leads to many tensions, ambivalent dynamics, and other problems that cannot just be wished away. This wishing away occurs not necessarily through obvious and visible means, but rather through the assumption that self-directed creative labor is inherently other to alienating and exploited labor. This is a widespread assumption that is often found in many places that are otherwise very critical in analyzing the workings of capitalism. In an issue of *Capital & Class* on the cultural economy, Gerard Strange and Jim Shorthouse draw a sharp distinction between artistic work (which they see as an expression of creative capacity through self-determined labor) and managed creativity (which they see as reduced and alienated work within orthodox capitalist re- lations of production), from which they argue that "artistic labor is inherently linked to autonomy and self-determination, if it is to be a real and genuine expression of creative labor power" (2004: 47).[5]

The problem with such an argument isn't that artistic labor and creativity cannot be part of creating conditions of autonomy and self- determination, but that they are not as nearly discrete or separated as this kind of distinction would have it. The assumption that artistic labor is inherently tied to autonomy and self-determination, reduced to managed creativity within capitalism, overlooks the ways in which self-directed forms of artistic labor are always tied up within various fields of power which complicate things even within self-managed forms of cultural production and economic arrangements. This is a point well explored by Jacques Godbout, who notes that based on this perceived connection the tendency for artists to want to constitute some form of lost community composed only of producers, and there- fore that would be able to assert this autonomy. The irony is that this is formed around the myth of the artist, which is a "kind of mythic negation of the fact that the real production system destroys the pro- ducer" (1998: 87). This finds its expression in the idea that the strug- gling artist, through this image of creativity and authenticity, rather that this position and its mythic foundation is continually functional and useful to capital through willing self-exploitation. Andrew Ross (2003), in his excellent study of no collar workers, refers to this dy- namic within circuits of artistic labor as sacrificial labor, one that is essential to the continued workings of the cultural economy.[6] When I first heard the idea of self-exploitation being discussed in workshop on self-management at the Festival del Pueblo in Boston in 2002 it struck me as being absurd. After all, if one's labor is not alienated by being commanded by a boss, if it is self-directed and organized, then surely it could not be alienated labor, at least not the in the usual Marxist sense. And, if one is organizing and directing one's own tasks during work, then the answer to self-exploitation would seem quite easy as one could just reduce, alter, or transform the way in which one was working. Maybe simply just work less. But silly or not, self- exploitation is indeed a real problem and concern precisely of how easily the pleasures of self-directed (especially creative labor) and forms of self-exploitation can mingle and overlap.

The quandary of worker self-management is then when a project or enterprise is self-directed it is quite easy to put much greater amounts of energy, effort, passion, commitment, time, and work, all the while often expecting far less from it, or excusing it if it does not happen otherwise. This is to integrate much more of one's creative capacities and abilities than one normally would if it were being directed by someone else (and this is similar to the way that many small businesses manage to succeed, because those initiating them are willing to put an immense amount of work, beyond the usual, into starting precisely because the endeavor is self-directed). To put it in autonomist terms, the formation of the social factory involves the dual movement of capitalist work relations outside of the workplace and greater energies of social creativity into the workplace. For instance, while working with ERR I often would work many more hours, at not terribly convenient times, and for amounts of money so low that if it were any other job I would most likely be throwing a fit. Why did I do this? Why does anyone? There are many reasons, most of them involving a desire to see the project succeed, an agreement with the political aims and objectives of the project, and the very real forms of pleasure and enjoyment that often characterize self-directed projects. Another was the notion, of which we often reminded ourselves, that as the conditions improved in the project (in terms of generating revenue) we would have built the conditions for ourselves to be involved in a form of work that was enjoyable, politically satisfying, and so forth. In other words, that it was building towards something worthwhile. It should be readily obvious that it's extremely unlikely that any of us involved in the project would have accepted the less satisfying aspects (low pay for the hours, etc.) were it not for these other aspects.

At its worst WSM can become little more than the self-organization and management of one's own misery and exploitation, gladly taken on and exalted as a positive thing. This is not to say that all projects of self-management go in this direction, as indeed many do not approach anything as such a stark characterization – but that does mean that the potential (and usually the tendency) towards such a direction is not at play. After all, ultimately it is impossible to create conditions of self-management in an unrestricted sense under capitalism because one is still subordinated by the demands of market forces, of having to generate profits, etc. As p.m. argues in his classic text *bolo'bolo'*, as long as the planetary work machine continues to exist, self-management and autonomy "can only serve as a kind of recreational area for the repair of exhausted workers" (1995: 50). Creating a haven of internal economic democracy does not necessarily by itself do anything to change the large macroeconomic conditions, contribute to ecological sustainability, or even guarantee that what is produced by the particular project is desirable.

Forms of self-management tend as they persist under capitalism to increasingly take on characteristics of more typical capitalist forms.

This is perhaps not so surprising, for dealing with certain forms of market pressures over time (for instance the basic imperative of keeping costs low enough so the project remains viable, etc.) can easily, over time, especially as the initial impulses and political drives which often led to the foundation the project, get forgotten or laid by the wayside (or perhaps there are new people involved in a project who do not necessarily subscribe to the core notions that brought it together). This can be seen in the way that many cooperatives after enjoying a period of success are sold out by their original members and come to take on the structure of a much more traditional capitalist firm.

It has been noted, by Harold Barclay for instance, that forms of worker self-management and cooperatives are much more likely historically to appear during periods of economic crisis and generally instability and for these same projects to tend toward more typical forms of capitalist organization once this period of crisis is completed. Economic cycles, projects of WSM, cooperatives, and labor managed firms being formed during economic down turns, and then reverting to more traditional forms of organization during better periods. As Hajime Miyazaki (1984) has argued, how this process occurs is largely dependent by the particulars of the interactions between different projects and the political, economic, and social environment they exist in. In this way one can distinguish between forms of self-management emerging out of moments of crisis or rupture, for instance through factory occupations or after business have been abandoned by their owners, versus those that are created and inaugurated as cooperative enterprises from their inception. This is supported by the work of Ann Arnett Ferguson (1991), who makes the argument, drawing from an ethnography of a cooperative bakery in the Bay Area of California, that when considering the longevity of collective projects one cannot separate the particular project from the social context in which it exists. This is particularly important for understanding the long term success of cooperatives in places like the Bay Area, which can easily form vibrant networks to support each other, exist in a community where there is a great deal of support for this kind of work, and have a steady supply of highly motivated politically sympathetic employees.[7]

Perhaps one of the sharpest critiques of self-management, even if a bit overstated, was produced by the Negation Collective (1975) in response to the worker takeover and management of the Lip watch factory in the early 1970s. The takeover of the factory, which occurred after it was abandoned by its former owners, was argued not to represent a positive stage in the socialization of the productive apparatus, but rather the socialization of the Lip workers themselves into the role of collective capitalists.[8] Based on this, it was argued that Lip (and similar forms of self-management), are potentially counterrevolutionary, in that the crisis limited to one industry (or one firm for that matter), and thus did not represent any real break with the logic of capitalist command. Thus the actions of Lip workers could inadvertently end up functioning as a means of shoring a temporarily flagging sector of the economy, securing rather than rupturing capital's valorization as a total process. There is some truth to this, embedded in the ambivalent character of self-management, although perhaps the better question is building upon the social energies unleashed through such struggles so that they are not trapped and confined into a self-limiting position and into the roles of collective capitalists.

Another potentially unsettling dynamic that can emerge is found in patterns of self-surveillance. To take an example that is perhaps fairly well known, there is one scene in the documentary *The Take* (2004), about self-managed factories in Argentina, where during a discussion with some of the workers from a plant, it is mentioned that while the factory was under the control of the previous owner it was acceptable for the workers to try and find ways to take extra breaks, to slack off here and there, and to find ways to make a little space for themselves in the work day. But now that the factory is owned and run by the workers, to do that would be bourgeois, and so now everyone was to watch everyone else to make sure that no one's slacking off or neglecting their tasks. I experienced a similar dynamic in Ever Reviled as we came up with better-developed accounting and labor tracking methods. Although the situation was much different it yielded a similar dynamic, naming a willingly embraced form of self-surveillance and discipline. This, of course, is not to dispute that there were not valid and useful reasons for why these kind of dynamics occur (for instance in order to know how to effectively plan and for everyone to do one's fair share of work), that doesn't change the fact that even the best intentioned and thought out plans and projects can develop dynamics that can indeed run counter to the intent of the project.[9] The higher level of time and concern that often goes into a self-directed project, part of the amorphous webs of what Tiziana Terranova (2004) describes as "free labor," eventually exhausts itself. And perhaps this process has created greater possibilities for the self-reproduction and expansion of social movement, but oftentimes it simply does not in a significant way.

The ultimate and most important criteria for considering the relevance and usefulness of projects of self-management for radical politics is really quite simple: what kind of selves does the particular arrangement of self-management tend to produce? In other words, as a process of socialization does it tend to create forms of subjectivity and interactions that provide building blocks for a larger revolutionary social process? This is an important and often difficult question to ask for self-management projects precisely because of the historical trends for such to appeal more to particular compositions and stratas of workers: namely those with higher levels of skill and technocratic knowledge who often already possessed greater degrees of job autonomy to begin with. Or, as Sidney Verba and Goldie Shabad put it, there arises conflicts between "egalitarian and technocratic values, between democratic and meritocratic criteria for participation, and between tendencies towards 'workers' solidarity' and tendencies towards functional and status differentiation based on expertise" (1978: 82). Vladmimir Arzensek argues that in situations where there are not unions autonomous from the structures of self-management this tends to reinforce the bias of workers' councils toward highly skilled and professional workers (1972). Similarly Rudy Fenwick and Jon Olson claim that those with *perceived* higher levels of job autonomy tend to be more supportive of worker participation and forms of self-management (1986). While Robert Grady (1990) argues that forms of possessive individualism can be used to further self-management and industrial democracy, the question is how that would not lead to a further reinforcing of the dynamics where those who already possess more empowering and rewarding forms of work tend to argue for greater forms of participation and those who do not, don't, recreating the same patterns of power. This poses a problem because, if, following the Comrades of Kronstadt, it is held that "the concept of worker's autonomy bases itself on a qualitative change in human relations, not simply changes in the ownership of the means of production" (1990: 6) the existing of tendencies towards favoring participation of particular strata of workers creates the tendency of implicitly reinforcing certain questionable forms of power dynamics and hierarchies within the workplace *despite* increasing degrees of democratization.

Movement of the Imaginary Away from Self-Management?

Capital affords us to project ahead, work it from within, knowing all too well that it will be quick to instrumentalize any creative move, turning it into binary opposition, however radical they claim to be, proven recipes that failed repeatedly *because they have become inadequate to think the complexity of the contemporary* reality. – Sylvere Lotringer (Virno 2004: 17-18)

While worker self-management played an important role in the imaginary and formulation of demands during the late 1960s in the new left (Katsiaficas 1987), since then there has been a general shift away from a focus on self-management as a locus of revolutionary energies. While it has been argued that the division between an artistic and social critique and their differential trajectories of recuperation, to use Boltanski and Chiapello's suspect distinction (2005), this is highly questionable because of how fused together these elements of radical thought were in the radical imagination of the time. WSM and council communist ideas were stressed heavily by the Situationists (who more or less borrowed a large chunk of these ideas from *Socialisme ou Barbarie* when Debord was a member), who despite that are used as the emblem of an artistic critique that has forsaken class dynamics. Although the reasons for such a shift in the composition of the radical imagination are multiple and complex (including the reality that the increased importance of various struggles such as feminism, student movements, struggles against racism and homophobia, and so forth broke down the hegemonic imaginary of the industrial worker as the central and most importance locus on struggles – a focus which tends to legitimize a focus on self-management as a key point of contestation), one of the perhaps most interesting for such a shift is the reality that many aspects of aspirations for self-management were realized during the 1970s – just in a form nearly inverse from the desires of those struggling for them, and in directions that cannot be described as particularly liberatory.[10] As an example, proposals to use state subsidies to fund workers taking over their workplaces, a proposal which is sometimes touted as a radical project (for instance currently by some movements in Argentina), was advocated for by parts of the World Bank and the Wharton Business School during the late 1970s and early 1980s as one way to regenerate the economy. It was even argued that this represented a new form of industrial policy, for even if it might be marked by some overtones of class struggle, this was not of much danger.

Similar to the way that demands for flexibility at work and the widespread refusal of work came to realized as imposed forms of precarity, energies of social insurgency channeled through demands for self-management came to be realized in inverse form through managerial schemes and methods of integrating and co-opting these dissatisfactions. Responsible autonomy, co-determination schemes, work quality studies, co-determination, total quality management, employee participation, and a whole host of other terms and practices developed during the 1970s to address the very real dissatisfactions and complaints which were causing massive industrial unrest.[11] This is not to say that these responses to the 'blue collar blues' and the discontent

with people's working lives did not address some real concerns in oc-
casionally positive ways (because almost despite themselves such
measures sometimes did), but rather to point out that these efforts addressed such concerns in ways that by partially but not totally addressing these sources of discontent themselves provided necessary
forms of social stabilization at work while at the same time harnessing
increased forms of social wealth and creativity brought into the workplace by these participatory schemes.

It also has been argued that this period and its transformations
ushered in an era where the social forces congealed around the potentiality of living labor were no longer sufficient to provide social insurgencies and the radical imagination with the fuel for inspiring
continued resistance and revolt. Habermas, for instance, describes the
situation where we find ourselves as "the New Obscurity," a condition
while seemingly characterized by the retreat of utopian energies from
historical thought, reveals rather the end of a particular configuration
of utopia based on the potential of a society based upon labor; these
social energies no longer have the same social resonance "not only
simply because the forces of production have lost their innocence or
because the abolition of private ownership of the means of production
has clearly not led in and of itself to workers' self-management. Rather
it is above all because that utopia has lost its point of reference in reality: the power of abstract labor to create and give form to society"
(1989: 53). While it is true that the twentieth century is littered with
remnants of revolutions proving definitively that simply eliminating
private ownership of the means of production does not necessarily
guarantee a revolution that goes all the way down to address the multiple forms of social domination – and likewise that the operation of
various labor markets have been transformed such that continuing to
rely on the same narrowly formed embodiment of a resistance imaginary would have been ridiculous – this nowhere close to means that
all potentiality for revolt through the labor of the imaginary, the imagination of labor, has disappeared.

What occurred following the revolts of the 1960s and 1970s, leading up the present situation, was not a total transformation or withdrawal of the subversive potential of labor's imagination, but a series
of transformations and permutations in how these imaginaries, movements, and practices were conceived: a displacement of a hegemonic
imaginary by a diffuse, multiple, and often contradictory and conflict-
ing array of imaginaries. In other words, it's not that there were class
movements and labor organizing (existing as unified, hegemonic
wholes) that were replaced by a series of fractured and diffuse movements (i.e., the so-called movement toward identity politics:

environmental issues, feminism, questions of cultural and ethnic difference, etc.). Rather, beneath the image of the unified and coherent
class movement already existed a series of multiplicitous subjectivities,
that while they indeed embody varying forms of class politics are not
simply reducible to them. Rather than there being 'new' concerns
which were different than those found within 'old social movements,'
ones that because they might at first seem quite different and distinct
from previous politics might even be looked upon with suspicion, it's
a question of seeing how those demands and desires were already
there, but were lumped together and erased by the false image of a
necessary unity that could not accommodate difference within it. This
embrace of difference within a radical labor imaginary was not something new, as the history of the IWW and the movements of migrant
labor and the multitude of workers who have always been precarious
shows, but it was these very movements that had been erased by the
enforced imaginary of the institutional left, the very imaginary that at
this point was shattered. Thus, this was not a new phenomenon by
any means, as one can see in Gerald Raunig (2007: 67-96) and Gordon Clark's (1984) exploration of the varied forms of neighborhood
self-organization and constituent practice, rather than workplace dynamics underlying the Paris Commune. This isn't to deny that there
has been transformation in its internal composition of the radical
imaginary, but rather that this is a constant and on-going process.
Rather than a sharp or sudden break, it was the recognition of a transformation in the imaginary, which was new.

Perhaps self-management is a fish that is only well suited to swim
in the struggles of Fordist waters. In other words, it's suited for struggles occurring in a productive context based on the necessity of certain forms of dead capital (machinery, equipment, factories and so
forth) that are worth winning. To the degree that post-Fordist labor
is founded on forms of social creativity, on forms of imagination and
labor that are already and immediately collective (because as much
as management may wish it was possible to colonize and harness all
cognitive labor, this is simply not possible), struggling to possess them
in common makes little sense because they already are in common.
That is not to deny that there are still great proliferations of mechanisms, laws, and procedures to ensure capitalist valorization from this
productive common (whether intellectual property laws or forms of
legal enforcement and government funding of new forms and institutions for these forms of production), because there clearly are. Rather
it is to indicate that the imaginary that used to fuel drives to self-management (we can take over the factory and use the tools in a liberatory
way now that they have been collectivized) makes less and less sense

because the tools are already owned in common and founded in co-operation. The struggle then becomes one of subtracting oneself from the forms of capitalist valorization, the parasitic rent on the productive commons (Vercellone 2008), without recreating the collective self as yet another form of collective capitalist. This is the problem that Jaroslav Vanek identified in his analysis of self-management, and in many ways it remains the problem of worker self-management today.

The question then is not trying to restate a notion of WSM or labor radicalism as a hegemonic imaginary that could exist within present conditions (if such would be either desirable or possible), but rather to consider what degree the ideas and practices of self-management can take part in constructing forms of social resistance that, much like the potentiality of labor itself, is always predicated upon an ability to go beyond itself, to be super-adequate to itself (Spivak 1985), to not let its constituted form inhibit the continued expansion of its constituent potentiality. This would be to reconsider self-management not as creating a set and stable economic arrangement to be defended against the pressures of the capitalist market, but rather creating such spaces with the intent of creating resources and possibilities to expand and deepen other struggles as well. This is not a restatement of the usual "spillover" argument, or a claim that forms of industrial democracy and worker participation would tend to lead to other forms of democratic renewal in other spheres of life. That does not mean that cannot happen; that liberatory transformation in one area of social life is closely connected to other areas makes a good deal of sense, but that does not mean that this necessarily occurs in any easily predictable or mechanical manner. In other words, projects of WSM divorced from a broader-based social reorganization tend to reinforce market-based behavior rather than subverting it, which is almost the direct opposite of what a 'spillover' model would expect (Greenberg, et al. 1966). This would be a self-management of constant self-institution, of the collective shaping of the imaginary (both collectively and individually) in ways that create resources for expanding radical forms of social movement: squatting, the autoreduction of prices, and other forms of labor struggles spreading from the recognized work places all over the social field. It is these labor struggles outside the recognized factory spaces that congealed during the 1970s into the autonomist's notion of the struggle of the socialized worker and Raoul Vaneigem's call (n.d.) to move from wildcat strike to generalized self-management. In other words, to retain the subversive core of labor struggles and movements towards to self-management, but stripped of their narrowly workerist focus.

Between Sisyphus & Self-Management

And so where does this leave the conceptual territory and practices of self-management? Best consigned to the dustbin of history?
Tempting, perhaps, although to do so would be a bit hasty, and likely
an instance of throwing out the baby with the bathwater of our discontent. WSM can play a vital role in social resistance, but one that
is more limited than I thought several years ago when I started thinking about this in a more concerted fashion. WSM can play an important role in creating networks of knowledge and cooperation
laboratories for experimentation and the development of resources
and skills for 'building the new world within the shell of the old,' to
use the old Wobbly phrase. But is important to never forget that this
new world is being built within the shell of the old, within the iron
cage of capitalist rationality, which is far more likely to impinge upon
its growth than to be torn asunder by other forms of social life developing within it. Practices of WSM exist in a cramped position, as a
form of minor politics and composition, and their radicality is in this
position and its capability to create resources and time, and in consciously avoiding becoming a major or representative form (Thoburn
2003). In other words, WSM can help to create space and time that
foster the cultivation of other possibilities, other possible worlds
emerging, but that not does mean that we can just 'buy back the
world' from the capitalists, or that it can serve as a means to overcome
without difficulties the vast arrays if questionable forms of power that
exist. WSM is not an unambivalent outside to the realities of capitalism, but it can create time that partially is one.

It is also fundamentally important that self-management, as an affirmation of the creative potentiality of non-alienated labor, does not
unwittingly find itself sliding back into an affirmation of the dignity
of work that has haunted various forms of labor organizing and radicalism from times immemorial (and has been the target of radicals
more prone to celebrate the refusal of work and argue for its reduction, from Lafargue to the Italian autonomists, Bob Black to the Situationists). The idea would be rather to extend and deepened the
relation between the refusal of work and its self-management, as when
Raoul Vaneigem called for the unity of workers' councils and the refusal of work (1994: 277). This is not nearly as paradoxical (or silly)
as it might seem at first. Rather it is an argument based on the realization that socialized labor's potentiality is revealed most clearly by
its absence (which is the basic concept underlying strikes after all),
therefore the way to affirm such potentiality is not under conditions
which limit it absurdly within the present but by the constant imma-
nent shaping of a collective imagination and creativity that will not

allow itself to ever be totally bound within a fixed form.

This is to understand and learn from WSM such that it acts, to borrow the argument of Maurice Brinton, as a means to liberation rather than liberation itself (2004: 33). One could extend this argument further, as the Comrades of Kronstadt do, to argue that "the only valid self-management activity for the workers is therefore that of self-management of struggle, that is direct action" (1990: 33). But not just any old direct action, but direct action as an open ended activity that consciously avoids closure and fixity within any given form. Perhaps this is quite close to what John Asimakopoulos, meant when he called for a "new militant working class strategy of direct economic civil disobedience," one linking radical actions with real outcomes (2006).

And this is why Sisyphus is paradoxically a quite appropriate image to discuss the nature of worker self-management. The tragedy of Sisyphus is that he is fully aware of the impossible nature of his condition. Sisyphus is cursed by the awareness of the futility of his position, much in the same way the proletarian condition is cursed by an awareness of ultimate futility of trying to create forms of non-alienated life and self-determining community that can continue to exist under the current conditions of capitalism. The boulder is pushed up the hill, only to roll down again it yet another round of enclosure, counterrevolution, recuperation, or whatever your preferred name for the process might be. This of course does not mean that there is no value in the pushing, as absurd as it might often seem. The resilience of Sisyphus' insurgent spirit, his overcoming of his position, is found within his capacity to find joy and possibility in walking back down the hill: through this he overcomes his cursed position and defies his fate, for "at each of these moments when he leaves the heights and gradually sinks towards the lair of the gods, he is superior to his fate" (Camus 1983: 121). Indeed, there is no fate that cannot be overcome by scorn.

The labor of the imagination, or the imagination of labor, is based on the realization that self-determination within existing conditions is ultimately absurd. But that does not mean that practices of self-determination and the building of autonomous communities are useless, rather that the conditions preventing the emergence of such are absurd and deserve to meet their destruction. Perhaps it is useful to understand it in the way that Boltanski and Chiapello describe the absorption of critique by capital, which they also describe using the image of Sisyphus: "But the effects of critique are real. The boulder does indeed go up the full length of the slope, even if it is always rolling back down by another path whose direction most often depends on the direction it was rolled up" (2005: 41). Between the changing directions of the boulder's role and the grimaced face of Sisyphus pushed against it is the space of an absurd freedom. But this is an absurd freedom that is hard to endure, for it is difficult and draining, especially if these conditions are individuated rather than confronted collectively through the creation of affective relations and communities (a topic to be discussed in the next chapter). And so if it is the machinations of the gods pressing down upon us, then it very well be time for another storming of the heavens.[12]

Notes

1. For some general writings on worker self-management see Balfour (1997), Berman (1984), Chaplin and Coyne (1977), Cole (1972), Greenberg (1986), Gunn (1986), Jansson and Hellmark (1986), Mason (1982), Thornley (1981), Vanek (1975), Wiener with Oakeshott (1987), Wright (1979), and Blumberg (1968).
2. For a recent argument for the importance of such an approach, see the special issue of *Culture and Organization* on organizational autoethnography edited by Maree Boyle and Ken Parry (2007).
3. See for instance Dolgoff (1974), Sitirin (2006), Negation (1975), Vanek (1970), and Lavaca (2007).
4. For a recent assessment of McKay from a GLBT perspective, see Highleyman (2007).
5. For an excellent consideration of artistic labor see the work of William Morris, whose work is particularly strong in elaborating the potentiality of craft and labor without falling into fetishizing any reductive version of working class culture or a static notion of authentic working class labor (1993).
6. Ross argues that this dynamic can be thought of as fundamental to the continued existence of cultural production. Artists (and also those involved in forms of labor that come to take on aesthetic qualities in the labor process), "are predisposed to accept nonmonetary rewards – the gratification of producing art – as partial compensation for their work, thereby discounting the cash price of their labor. Indeed, it is fair to say that the largest subsidy to the arts has always come from art workers themselves, underselling themselves in anticipation of future career rewards" (2003: 142).
7. The Bay Area provides an excellent example of how networks of cooperatives can support and benefit each other. For more on how this dynamic see the work of Network of Bay Area Cooperatives, No BAWC (pronounced "no boss"): www.nobawc.org.
8. For more on this dynamic in the eastern European context, see the Barricade Collective (2008).
9. For more on the dynamics of self-surveillance in self-management, see Martin (1994).
10. See for instance Keith Bradley and Alan Gelb's two books (both from 1983) on the Mondragon collectives and worker-managed capitalism as a tool of industrial renewal and regeneration. See also Boltanski and Chiapello (2005). Another interesting and bizarre example of this style of thought has been the argument for both creating increased forms of employee participation and self-management along with a general neoliberal restructuring of the state.

For this unique piece of ideological mish mash, see Biagi, (2002).

11. For more on this see Bass and V.J. Shackleton (1979), Vallas (2003), and Fenwick and Olson (1986). One could also connect this to other currents and concepts with management and organization studies, such as Andrew Friedman's notion of responsible autonomy and the work of the Tavistock Institute.

12. This image is first used by Marx in 1871 in a letter to Dr. Kugelmann about the Paris Commune. It has since been picked up and used within varying contexts, such as the Italian autonomist milieu of the 1970s (and was then used as the title for Steve Wright's book on the history of Workerism), and is alluded to in Ellio Petri's 1971 film *Classe Operai va in Paradiso* (*The Working Class Goes to Heaven*).

:: VIII :: Questions for Aeffective Resistance ::

Each wound accumulated over the years, each hope frustrated feels a part of your pain and disappointment. Often I wonder, what the heck keeps us going on, despite such hurt affected in a walk that is supposed to be beautiful, trustful, liberating, juvenating? I do not know any more, or forgot what I once knew. Perhaps those glimpses we have had, here and there, planned or spontaneous, with friends or with strangers, glimpses of "the best" in each one of us, in love, risk, togetherness, joy, labor, and, yes, in pain and disappointment. It seems to me that there is no obvious "reason" we must hang in there, except the reasons we can provide for and with each other in the midst of this insanity that passes for reality, left and right. What can I say, but that if we fail to be that reason, let us, at least, fail better. – Ayca Cubukcu[1]

I'm tired. It's 3 am. The desk is stacked tall with too many things to be done, too many projects that have fallen behind schedule, and ideas that would come to fruition beautifully if only there was time for them to be born. If only there was time. But there never seems to be. The endless march of everyday pressures and gripes mounts endlessly – the moment it seems that they have been beaten back, that there are conditions of respite to move from with thought out intentions – the flood just sweeps in again. And my whole body aches. It never seems possible to catch up with this mounting pile of tasks. Sometimes I wonder whether this constant sense of growing tiredness might just be something that's *my* fault, something *I* caused by taking on too many projects and not managing time effectively. Perhaps. Surely there are few foolish enough to make this kind of mistake, voluntarily taking just enough so that they don't totally collapse, but always teetering close to doing so.

But it's not just me. No, far from it. If it were only me it would be much easier to dismiss this as just a personal issue – *something* that I need to deal with. But that's not so. It seems that nearly all my friends and comrades are constantly faced with similar dilemmas. At times it seems one could compose a calendar of varying and interlocking seasons of burnout cycles: intense periods of hyperinvolvement, manically attempting to balance fifteen different projects at once, trying to hold them all together, and to a large degree succeeding. But that can never last. Eventually exhaustion kicks in and forces one to withdraw, to cut back a little, and to find some time to gather one's energies again. Periods of isolation and withdrawing from communities of resistance more often than finding support in them, followed by another cycle of the same crests and crashes. And so it goes on, our own little angel of history looking back on the mounting pile of personal wreckage and emotional catastrophe.

And so we feel guilty for not having done enough. For needing time for ourselves. Everyday insurgencies are sublimated, almost as if there was a voice constantly reminding, commanding that we have failed in our task, that we need to do more to prove our chosen status and assure our ascension to heaven... I mean revolution. And so the grounded reality of resistance is dematerialized, transformed into an imaginary – promised but never to be achieved – realm, always beckoning, almost mocking us.[2] Perhaps this is what Suzanne Cesaire had in mind when she observed that "if we see a suffering and sensitive – at times mocking – being, which can be recognized as our collective self, appearing in our legends and stories, we would seek in vain the expression of this self...We sense that this disturbing age will see a ripened fruit burst forth, irresistibly invoked by solar ardor to scatter its creative energy to the winds" (1996: 96). Or maybe instead we are caught in a process and dynamic marked by a strong consumerist undertone: we must do something now! It doesn't matter what as long as we do it now! Satisfaction that we have done something, whatever that something may be and regardless of whether it is effective or not, whether it is connected in any way to a long term sustainable strategy of building capacities to sustain joyous lives of resistance rather than brief moments, is largely irrelevant. It is sacrificed to the imperative to do something now. Satisfaction guaranteed, no warranties implied.

But surely the struggle to create a better, joyous, freer, more loving world is not one that is premised upon a constant struggle that leaves one tired and run down. The question is one of creating communities of resistance that provide support and strength, a density of relations and affections, through all aspects of our lives, so that we can carry on and support each other in our work rather than having to withdraw from that which we love to do in order to sustain the capacity to do those very things. To create a sustainable culture of resistance, a flowering of aeffective resistance – that is, a sustainable basis for ongoing and continuing political organizing, a plateau of vibrating intensities, premised upon refusing to separate questions of the *effectiveness* of any tactic, idea, or campaign, from its *affectiveness*. Affect here in the sense used in a line of thought beginning with the work of Benedict de Spinoza, who defined it as "the modification of the body by which the power of the body itself is increased, diminished, helped, or hindered, together with the idea of these modifications" (1949). In contrast to Descartes, whose idea of the mind/body split in many ways forms the basis of inherited philosophical thought for some time, Spinoza saw the mind and body not as two substances but as differently articulated versions of the same substance. His ideas have been taken up by those working in a counter-history or submerged lineage to that of Descartes (as well as Hegel), and thus was taken up by figures such as Gilles Deleuze, Louis Althusser, Antonio Negri, and various feminist strains of thought focusing on the body.[3] These varied notions of affect, considered as a creative power of immense potentiality, particularly in creating new forms of relations, finds it way into the text, even if not explicitly cited.

The simple gestures, even sometimes ones that seem insignificant, are often the ones that mean the most in creating affective community. Not that they are glorious tasks by any means – asking how someone is doing, taking an extra five minutes to work out what's bothering someone or why they're pre-occupied – but because of this it is easy to overlook how important they really are.[4] They form the basis underlying our on-going interactions, lodged within the workings of our affective memory (Titchner 1895). Immersed within the constant and ever-renewing nourishment contained within the gift economies of language, motions, and affections, all too often we fail to appreciate the on-going work of social reproduction and maintaining community that these acts entail (Vaughan 2002).

Creating a vibrant political culture, one that exists "beyond duty and joy," to borrow the phrasing of the Curious George Brigade, is not an easy task (2003). Here the Curious George Brigade uses joy when arguably what they are contrasting is overly serious, dogmatic "duty" activism with that based on pursuing and engaging in things for the pure, ephemeral thrill of them (read: irresponsible politics), which they use the word joy for. This more than any is perhaps indicative of the lack of a conceptual vocabulary to describe forms of commonly felt joy, a condition that Spinoza commented on. Indeed, as our very joys, subjectivities, experiences, and desires are brought further and further into the heart of the production process, creating autonomous spaces based upon their realization becomes all the more tricky. Fortunately some people have begun to explore and find ways to cope with and overcome the traumatic stress and tensions that can build as a part of organizing (Activist Trauma Support 2005).[5] But what about the less spectacular or obvious forms, the damage of the everyday? What happens as all the constantly mounting and renewing demands on our very being, our capacity to exist and continuing to participate in radical politics, build up? We find ourselves in ever more cramped positions, unsure of how to work from the conditions we find ourselves in. Do we carry on as we can, slowly burning out, and finally withdrawing from ongoing struggles, perhaps consigning them as some part of our former youth that had to be left behind to deal with other things?[6] Might there not be other options and paths to take?

To take part in what has been described as the "affective turn," to use the title of a recent collection put together by Patricia Clough (2007), that is, to foreground questions of our individual and collective capacities to affect and be affected by the world around us, means that questions and concerns about sustainability, personal relations, and caring for each other are not insignificant concerns that can be brushed aside to tackle whatever the pressing demand of the day. As famously observed by Gustav Landauer, "the State is a condition, a certain relationship between human beings, a mode of human behavior; we destroy it by contracting other relationships, by behaving differently" (1973: 226). Politics is not external to the relationships and interactions we have – it grows out of, is intensified by, and ties them together. Affect, developed through interaction and care, exists as expansive and creative powers: "it is a power of freedom, ontological opening, and omnilateral diffusion... [that] constructs value from below" and transforms according to the rhythm of what is common (Negri 1999: 86).

Aeffective resistance, as one might gather from the name, starts from realization that one can ultimately never separate questions of the effectiveness of political organizing from concerns about its affectiveness. They are inherently and inevitably intertwined. The social relations we create every day prefigure the world to come, not just in a metaphorical sense, but also quite literally: they truly are the emergence of that other world embodied in the constant motion and interaction of bodies. The becoming-tomorrow of the already here and now. And thus the collective practices of relating, of composing communities and collectives, exists at the intersection of "the interplay of the care of the self and the help of others blends into preexisting relations, giving them a new coloration and greater warmth. The care of the self – or the attention that one devotes to the care that others should take of themselves – appears then as an intensification of social relations" (Foucault 1984: 53). And so it is from considering the varying affective compositions, dynamics, and relations that these questions aeffective resistance begins. It is the unfolding map that locates what Precarias a la Deriva have described as the condition of affective virtuosity, where "what escapes the code situates us in that which is not yet said, opens the terrain of the thinkable and livable, it is that which creates relationships. We have to necessarily take into account this affective component in order to unravel the politically radical character of care, because we know – this time without a doubt – that the affective is the effective" (2006: 40).

Autonomous Feminism & Aeffective Revolt

Strike or unemployment, a woman's work is never done. – Mariarosa Dalla Costa and Selma James (1973: 30)

To find inspiration and some kernels of wisdom for teasing out a basis to expand the concept of aeffective resistance, perhaps one could turn to the experiences and knowledges in the history of autonomous feminism,[7] from the writings of figures such as Mariarosa Dalla Costa and Silvia Federici to campaigns like Wages for Housework and the more recent organizing of groups like Precarias a la Deriva. Because their efforts come from experiences where the very basis of their being, the capacity of their bodies to care and relate are directly involved in necessary functions for the reproduction and continued existence of capitalism, but in ways that for a long time went unacknowledged by large segments of the so-called progressive and revolutionary political milieu, one can learn from their insights into organizing from such tricky positions to find routes and passages toward more aeffective forms of resistance. Despite the importance that autonomist feminism has played in the development of autonomous politics and struggles it is commonly relegated to little more than a glorious footnote of figures emerging out of *operaisti* thought.[8] George Katsiaficas, for instance, argues that in many of the most significant dimensions of these movements, the meaning of autonomy, feminist currents are the most important source (2001).

Strangely enough, because housework, caring labor, and many other forms of social labor were not directly waged, it was often assumed that they simply took place outside of the workings of capitalism, as if they existed in some sort of pre-capitalist status that had mysteriously managed to persist into the present. Organizing around gender, affective labor, and issues of reproduction posed numerous important questions to forms of class struggle that focused exclusively on the figure of the waged industrial worker (Hardt 1999). The revolts of housewives, students, the unwaged, and farm workers led to a rethinking of notions of labor, the boundaries of workplace, and effective strategies for class struggles: they enacted a critical transformation in the social imaginary of labor organizing and struggle. Because the labor of social reproduction and unwaged work was not considered work, was not considered to produce surplus value or to be a relevance for capitalism, it was often ignored and looked over as an arena of social struggle. Relegated to an adjunct status compared to what was held as the real focus of power, economic power and class struggle, it was assumed that these sorts of concerns would be worked out after capitalism had been overthrown. But, as argued by Alisa Del Re, there is a great importance in learning from and taking seriously the concerns put forth by autonomous feminism, precisely because attempting to refuse and reduce forms of imposed labor and exploitation without addressing the realms of social reproduction and housework amounts to building a notion of utopia upon the continued exploitation of female labor (1996).

Autonomous feminism, by exhorting that this simply was not going to stand anymore – that it was ridiculous to be expected to constantly care for and attend to the tasks of social reproduction, from childcare to caring for parents to housework all the while being told that what one was engaged in was *not work at all*, shattered the ossified and rigid structures of the narrowly and dogmatically class-oriented radical imagination. One should also note that the recognition of forms of gendered labor as work doesn't necessarily mean that struggles around them start from a better position. As Angela Davis notes (1981), black women were paid wages for housework for many years in the US before the advent of the Wages for Housework campaign, but that didn't mean they were in a better position in their struggles around such work. This should make clear that the potentiality political recomposition found within a strategy such as Wages for Housework is always dependent on the particular social situations it is deployed within.

As observed by Elisabetta Rasy, feminism is not external to politics nor is it necessarily part of class struggle in an already determined manner, rather it is a movement within these various groupings, a movement creating conditions for the emergence of other subjects and experience to finally be acknowledged and learned from: "feminism opens up a magnetic crack in the categoric universe of the male-Marxist vision of the world, painfully exhibiting a history of ghosts behind the slippery façade of facts and certainties. The absolute materiality of the ghosts who embody need and desire stand in contrast and opposition to the phobic philologies of the existent and the existed" (1991: 78). Issues such as legalizing and access to abortion, divorce, contraception, sexuality, and violence against women, while not reducible or contained within the framework of class struggle, organizing around them embodies a challenge to forms of class-based social domination as it exists through the ability to control and restrict possibilities for social reproduction.

This shattering of the previously hermetically sealed dead end of the radical imagination opened up a long needed avenue for contesting and confronting forms of domination in all aspects of capitalist society: in the family, the street, the factory, the school, the hospital, and so on. As argued by Leopoldina Fortunati, while it may have appeared that the processes of production and reproduction operated as separate spheres governed by different laws and principles, almost as if there relation was "mirror image, a back-to-front photograph of production," their difference was not a question about whether value was produced, but rather one of how the production of value in social reproduction "*is* the creation of value but *appears otherwise*" (1995: 8). This is directly contrary to claims that housework and forms of domestic labor produced use values and thus were not involved in the production of value for capitalism. Mariarosa Dalla Costa and Selma James emphasized the point this way: "We have to make clear that, within the wage, domestic work produces not merely use values, but is essential to the production of surplus value." (1973: 33) It was on this point, the domestic labor produced value, surplus value in the Marxist sense, that provoked a great deal of controversy, particularly from those who held to their sense of Marxist categories regarding the dividing lines between productive and unproductive labor. It was often argued that women produced use values, not surplus value for capitalist production, and therefore were in a position more akin to feudalism or pre-capitalist relations. Alternately it was argued by people like Carla Consemi, not that women were not producing surplus value or that they definitely were, but that the relations of mediation and all the layering forms of social relations involved in such makes it difficult to see quite how that works: "[Housework] does not produce 'goods,' it will not be transferred into money – unless it is in a very indirect, incalculable way (which is still to be examined)" (1991: 268).

In some ways the question of whether domestic labor does or not *really* produce surplus value might seem a bit silly from the outside of it. But to appreciate the significant of this it is important to remember that in debate carried on in the terrain of Marxist thought, to argue that such forms of labor did not produce value was an important part of marginalizing and arguing against their importance. Thus one can see how making the argument that domestic labor does produce surplus value expands the spaces where labor struggle occurs precisely because it is organizing around the production of value necessary for the functioning of capitalism. As argued by James and Dalla Costa, "The possibility of social struggle arises out of the *socially productive character* of women's work in the home" (1973: 37). It might be possible to argue that domestic labor either does not produce value, or does so in a way that is indirect, subtle, and ephemeral, while still affirming the importance of feminist struggles around domestic labor. This was not an argument commonly made, and would be somewhat strange and difficult to continue to make within a Marxist framework centered on issues of exploitation in value production. In other words, by only focusing on certain forms of social labor and the exploitation involved in them (which was considered the basis for an antagonist political subjectivity capable of overthrowing capitalism), this analysis overlooked myriad forms of social power and exploitation that operated within fields of social production and reproduction that because of their unwaged status did not appear as such. And perhaps even more importantly, this blindness, a situation created by the obfuscation of the theoretical baggage, also blinded radicals to the possibilities for political action emanating from these positions. But, as long as housewives, or the unwaged, or the peasants, or other populations were excluded from the narrowly defined Marxist framework of analysis and politics, "the class struggle at every moment and any point is impeded, frustrated, and unable to find full scope for its action" (Dalla Costa and James 1973: 35).

Wages for/against Housework

We want to call work what is work so that eventually we might rediscover what is love and create what will be our sexuality which we have never known. – Silvia Federici (1980: 258)

Slavery to an assembly line is not a liberation from slavery to a kitchen sink. – Mariarosa Dalla Costa and Selma James (1973: 35)

There has long existed a relation between the nature of social reproduction and women's forms of political self-organization.[9] But this relation is not specifically between women and the form of political organization as much as the influence of the resources and possibilities available for supporting social reproduction. Rather, it is more often women because of their location within specific articulations of social roles and relations that are affected with greater intensity by various forms of political domination and power that attack the basis of social reproduction. Just as the destruction of the commons was accompanied by the enclosure of the female body (Federici 2004), and largely came to replace the role formerly played by the commons through countless hours of unacknowledged labor, neoliberal assaults from the 1970s until the present have coupled together attacks on forms of collective ownership with a politics bent upon the destruction of the meager gains congealed in the form of welfare state programs and conservative backlashes against what small gains feminism had managed to thus far win.

Given the often-harsher effects that capitalism and the whole array of forms of social domination have on women, it really should not be of any great surprise that they would play important roles in struggling against these forms of domination precisely because of how intensely it affects their ability to exist and live. From the mothers' demand for "bread and herring" that started the Russian revolution,[10] to the role of women in struggling against the IMF and World Bank imposed structural adjustment programs and austerity measures that accompany the disciplinary devices of international loan slavery, the importance and roles played by females all too often get ignored or passed over because they do not fit into the form of what is generally recognized as political action (Dalla Costa and Dalla Costa 1995; Federici and Caffentzis 2001). This makes the reluctance by much of the left, from Marxist theoreticians to union organizers, to see the relevance of feminist organizing as a class issue all the more exasperating. It's one thing to be exploited constantly and seemingly throughout all moments of the day and spaces of one's life, but then it's another, even worse condition to find that one's allies and comrades don't consider your struggle against these conditions to be part of a common endeavor. In other words women found themselves in conditions trapped not only with a "double shift" of work – both in a formal waged sense and in various tasks of social reproduction – but also that in which their work during the "third shift," or efforts expended on behalf of unionizing and political organizing campaigns, many of which were replete with people who did not value these multiple layers and difficulties and treated organizing around them as "reactionary" and "divisive" (Huws 2003). Or, as quipped by Silvia Federici, "We are seen as nagging bitches, not workers in struggle" (1980: 255). Given that, feminist separatism is clearly a totally sensible response to "comrades" that are often times little more than condescending and patronizing allies.

Autonomous feminism is thus not just important in itself, which it clearly is, but also in that it works as an important re-opening and cracking apart of the sedimented imaginary of struggle that could not see outside of the blinders it had created for itself. By demanding that housework and caring work be recognized as work, that labor takes place not just in the physically bounded workplace, but also exists all throughout the tasks of social reproduction and community life, autonomous feminism opened a space for a reconsideration of many of the concepts and tactical baggage that had been held on to: "Once we see the community as a productive center and thus a center of subversion, *the whole perspective for generalized struggle and revolutionary organization is* re-opened" (Dalla Costa and James 1973: 17). In other words, the personal is political, but it is also economic, as well as social and cultural. Struggles around issues of care and housework, of the tasks of the everyday, are not just individual concerns unrelated to broader political and economic questions – they are the quotidian manifestations of these larger processes. Recognition of their connections, as well as the connections against questionable power dynamics in the home, school, office, hospital, and all spaces of social life, is an important step in socializing and connecting minor moments of rupture and rebellion into connected networks of struggle. As James and Dalla Costa argue, there is great importance in understanding the relation of domestic labor and its exploitation to struggles diffused throughout society precisely because, "Every place of struggle outside the home, precisely because *every sphere of capitalist organization presupposes the home*, offers a chance for attack by women" (Dalla Costa and James 1973: 38). Organizing around domestic labor acted as a key point in the developing of autonomous struggles because of its locations within intersecting dynamics of gender, race, and class;[11] thus learning from these struggles is all the more important precisely because of the multiple constraints and difficulties they faced, and ways that they found to contest multiple forms social power and domination.

One of the ways these demands would become embodied was in the various "Wages for Housework" campaigns inspired by these ideas. Originating initially in Italy and the UK, these campaigns, based on demanding the recognition of the countless hours of unpaid work involved in typically female labor, quickly spread to many locations across the globe. Originating from struggles of both women of the classical working class (such as demands around equal pay in the workplace), student groups and the new left, and various feminist organizations, the campaign used many of the concepts and framing of Marxist categories while at the same time attempting to move past the limitations and assumptions about the "true" revolutionary subject that often accompanied them. Admittedly the campaign and demand for remuneration for housework was controversial and received much criticism both from the right and the left.[12] In particular it was argued that the campaign could have the effect of further consigning and limiting women to be confined within a domestic sphere, this time in a way that had been argued for through a feminist lens.[13] Alternately it was argued that the demand for wages represented a further commodification of yet another aspect of life and was harmful in that way. But what is perhaps most inspiring in such a campaign and contains key insights for aeffective resistance is the ways which such was formulated from working within and based the position that women found themselves, formulating demands and antagonisms based upon that position. In other words to find ways to socialize and connect struggles around the ways their capacities and very existence were being exploited. This could be understood as its function as a pole of class recomposition and route for the increasing of collective political capacity of struggle. In the words of Mariarosa Dalla Costa:

> The question is, therefore, to develop forms of struggle which do not leave the housewife peacefully at home, at most ready to take part in occasional demonstrations through the streets... *The starting point is not how to do housework more efficiently, but how to find* a place as protagonist in the struggle: that is, not a higher productivity of domestic labor but a higher subversiveness in the struggle (1973: 36).

The various Wages for Housework campaigns attempted to do just that: to find positions of higher subversiveness in struggle from where it was possible to organize against the isolation and misery that accompanied the miserable conditions of capitalist patriarchy.

In that sense the ultimate goal of such campaigns could be seen not as the demand of wage themselves, but rather using the demand for wages to ferment and spread antagonisms against the structural systems of patriarchy and capitalist control that has instituted and relied upon the unwaged and unacknowledged burden of women's labor to begin with. This was the source of much of the antipathy towards the campaigns, based on confusing the demand of wages for housework as object (from which it could be seen to keep women in the home, the commodification of caring labor, etc.) rather than as a perspective and catalyst of struggle. This confusion, argues Silvia Federici, separates a moment and temporary goal of the struggle from the dynamics of composition and the formation of collective capacities, and thus overlooks "its significance in demystifying and subverting the role to which women have been confined in capitalist society" (1980: 253). The demand for wages for housework is not then an embracing of and struggle for waged status, but is a moment in finding effective methods to struggle against the imposition of work and the dynamics of class power that exist under capitalism. That is, Wages for Housework is precisely the construction of a composition of social forces that make possible to struggle against the forms of housework, social roles, and dynamics of exploitation that underpin them: "To say that we want money for housework is the first step towards refusing to do it, because the demands for a wage makes work visible, which is the most indispensable condition to begin to struggle against it" (1980: 258). In other words, Wages for Housework is a moment in the struggles of wages against housework, a dynamic of composing class power from the position that women found themselves in thus that they could attempt to find ways to escape from that position. In the words of Roberta Hunter-Hendersen, "The essential task was to re-appropriate our own energy, intellectual, social and emotional, and it meant working together with patience as we unfolded our constricted limbs, began to stretch our oppressed kinds, and learnt again to interact with each other" (1973: 41).[14]

We've drifted a Long Way (or have you?)

The oppression of women, after all, did not begin with capitalism. What began with capitalism was the more intense exploitation of women as women and the possibility at last of their liberation. – Mariarosa Dalla Costa and Selma James (1973: 23)

Despite the amazing feminist upsurge that entered public visibility and consciousness during the 1960s and 1970s, many of the issues that inspired it continue to exist, even if there have been vast improvements in addressing some of them. Disparities in wages, gender discrimination and differences in power, and violence against women continue to be major issues for almost the entire world to some degree or another. The neoliberal onslaught of the 1980s and dismantling of the welfare state in much of the industrialized west have also created difficult questions for many women. And perhaps most depressing in some ways, large sections of the left, and even the "radical left" continue to largely ignore issues around gendered labor and forms of organizing around them.

It is from this regrettable condition that Precarias a la Deriva, a feminist research and organizing collective (who are one of the most interesting inheritors of this strand of feminist politics existing today), emerged. Precarias a la Deriva began in 2002 starting out of a feminist social center, La Eskalera Karakola, initially as a response to a call for a general strike. It was realized that the call for the strike did not address the forms of labor that many of the women were involved in, namely forms of caring labor, informal work, invisibilized jobs, intermittent and precarious work. These are forms of work that if this involved in them attempted to participated in the strike it would be very unlikely to have any effect on their circumstances and could very easily end with them losing their jobs altogether. In fact, a majority of people who were increasingly involved in such forms of work, which have come to be discussed under the concept of precarity (which will be discussed more in depth in the next chapter), were not even that affected by the proposed changes in labor legislation that inspired the call for strike because their social position is already so unstable.

The members of Precarias a la Deriva (PAD) thus set out to find methods to investigate and understand the changing nature of work and social relations and to develop methods of generating conflict that would suit this changing terrain. The method they initially chose to work with was that of the dérive, which is drawn from the ideas of the Situationists, who employed forms of wandering through the city while allowing themselves to be attracted to and repulsed by the features of the city, and thus hopefully to open up new spaces and experiences that would otherwise and usually be ignored or looked over.[15] Precarias a la Deriva modified the concept of the dérive, which they argue in many ways was particularly marked by the social position of the bourgeois male subject who had nothing better to do. Instead they sought to update the dérive to drift through the circuits and spaces of feminized labor that constituted their everyday lives. Arguably there could be seen to be some tension in this kind of updating. Notably, if the purpose of the dérive was to open up unforeseen possibilities and connections through the drift's openness, stipulating an already understood framework and space for drifting then could foreclose possibilities for connection that might exist outside of that framework. Alternately one could argue that the Situationist notion of the dérive already had an understood framework and space of its operation (provided by the subjective positioning of those involved and the understood spaces of the city) that was not quite as open as they would have liked to believe. PAD's transformation of the practice thus has not limited its possibilities per se, but make more explicit their framework and positioning compared to that which was left implicit in the Situationist version. The drift was thus converted into a mobile interview, a wandering picket that sought out women who were involved in the many forms of precarious and caring labor, to find out how the conditions affected them, and how they might work from them. They decided to investigate five overall sectors and interconnected spaces: 1. domestic 2. telemarketing 3. manipulators of codes (translators, language teachers) 4. food service (bars, restaurants) 5. health care. This method of mobile interview / picket was used

> to take the quotidian as a dimension of the political and as a source of resistances, privileging experience as an epistemological category. Experience, in this sense, is not a pre-analytic category but a central notion in understanding the warp of daily events, and, what is more, the ways in which we give meaning to our localized and incarnated quotidian (2003).

PAD used this practice of drifting as means to explore the "intimate and paradoxical nature of feminized work," wander through the different connections between the spaces of feminized labor, and to find ways to turn mobility and uncertainty into strategic points of intervention: to "appropriate the communicative channels in order to talk about other things (and not just anything), modify semiotic production in strategic moments, make care and the invisible networks of mutual support into a lever for subverting dependence, practice 'the job well done' as something illicit and contrary to productivity, insist upon the practice of inhabiting, of being, a growing right" (2003). They aim to use these forms of intervention to construct what they describe as points of aggregation, which borrowing from the Buenos Aires militant research group Colectivo Situaciones (who they have corresponded with a great deal), will be constructed based not a notion of aggregation capacity (the construction of mass forms of organization) but rather on consistency capacity, or the ability to form intense and dense networks of relations.[16]

The practice of the dérive, the drift, as wandering interview and as a form of militant research, was thus an important starting point (and continues to be an importance practice) for PAD because it operates, in their words as a form of "contagion and reflection," whose potentiality is not easily exhausted; it is "An infinite method, given the intrinsic singularity of each route and its capacity to open and defamiliarize places" (2003). The shifting and transformation of everyday social relations and realities does not cease after the first phase of engaged research and intervention into a social space. Thus the need to continue to ask questions about how that space is formed and those living within it carries on as a pressing question, all the more so in that as methods for visible political intervention change the composition of a particular space the relations within it also change. While often times militant research is employed for a brief period of time to get a sense of the territory in which forms of intervention will take place (the most famous example being how such methods were employed in Italy in the 1960s), often after the initial inquiry the projects cease, and organizers continue to rely on their knowledge of the composition of social relations and realities that had previously existed, not taking into account how they have changed and been transformed. PAD, by emphasizing the openness and fluidity of the drift, of its capacity to defamiliarize environments of habit, thus emphasized the need to keep the questions and inquiry open, and to keep circulating and exchanging knowledges (which they often do through the forms of workshops, gatherings, encuentros, and publications) which are then fed back into other projects.

For PAD in many ways find themselves, though they have drifted quite far to discover new methods of intervention, having to confront many of the same questions that faced feminist organizers in the 1970s, particularly those involved in campaigns such as Wages for Housework. While PAD argues, "care is not a domestic question but rather a public matter and generator of conflict," they are also quite aware of the difficulty in this task, for as they observe, "the question of how to generate conflict in environments which are invisible, fragile, private" (2003). This division between the political and the personal, the public and the private, has long been one of the dividing lines that feminists have confronted as a barrier to the raising of *their* concerns and demands without having them merely consigned as their concerns and demands. One can see this dynamic, for instance, in the ways which concerns about retreat from public life(the specter of bowling alone), overlooks the invisible networks of civic engagement embodied through forms of care which are typically overlooked as possible forms of political involvement (Herd and Harrington 2002). In other words, the process by which discussions around gender become understood as "women's issues," rather than the way that construction of gender roles and social roles more broadly (which involves, although this is not discussed nearly as much, the construction of masculinity and norms of heterosexuality). Or the ways in which domestic labor and care, even in their discussion within radical political circles, can become assigned and narrated as a feminist issue alone, rather than seeing the ways in which these forms of labor, interaction, of the tasks that are perhaps the most primary in keeping together a society (as they are critically involved in primary socialization) relate to and are enmeshed within larger frameworks of power that are being contested.

PAD's answer to this encompasses multiple parts of their overall project and centers to a large degree around questions of affect. Rather than treating issues of domestic labor, the role of empathy and the creation of relations, interaction, sexuality, and forms of care as separate issues and concerns, they rather see them as existing along a continuum, which they logically describe as the communicative continuum sex-attention-care. This continuum connects the diverse sectors and areas of their investigations, along which they point out that sex, care, and attention are not pre-existing objects but socially narrated and constructed ones. They are not means naturally formed into a specified arrangement (although they are often *naturalized* as if this were the case), but rather are "historically determined social stratifications of affect, traditionally assigned to women" (2006: 34). It is along this continuum that they see the role of affect as being key, existing at the center of the chain that "connects places, circuits, families, populations, etc. These chains are producing phenomena and strategies as diverse as virtually arranged marriages, sex tourism, marriage as a means of passing along rights, the ethnification of sex and of care, the formation of multiple and transnational households" (2003).

This perspective at looking at the interconnections between forms of activity that have often been constructed as feminine is extremely important, especially in a period where the forms of activity described as such have become mush more enmeshed and widespread across the functioning of the economy, from the "service with a smile" or "phone smile" of the McDonald's employee and telephone operator to the hypervisibility of the body (particularly the female body) in media and advertising as a way to excite libidinal desires for the glories of consumption. And it has been argued that those involved in caring labor, which constitutes an estimated 20% of the work force, tend to be more highly class conscious regardless of the gender of those involved (although notably there are higher percentages of women employed in such positions) (Jones 2001). Thus the question of aeffective resistance, attention to the dynamic of affective labor, becomes all the more pressing because those involved in such work contain a potentiality for rebuilding an inclusive revolutionary class politics at a moment where it seems that such in many ways retreated from the realm of existing possibilities.

Arguably the increasing rise of forms of human resource management, particularly those stressing the appreciation of diversity and cultural difference, as well as attention to issues of gender, are also part of the growing presence and importance of skills of communication and interaction extended through the social fabric as directly productive activities and abilities. But this "becoming woman of labor,"[17] which as an ambivalent process has highlighted the potentiality found within forms of affective labor and relations, has also continued to be marked by forms of social division and domination in which gender relations are historically embedded: "a tremendously irregular topography, reinforcing, reproducing and modifying the social hierarchies already existent within the patriarchy and the racial order inherited from colonialism… [upon which] the global restructuring of cities and the performances and rhetorics of gender are imprinted" (2003).

Precarias a la Deriva thus proposes a typology for considering forms of feminized and precarious labor, not based upon overall transformations in social and economic structure (although such is clearly related), but rather on the nature of the work and the possibilities it opens up or forecloses for insurgencies against it. Typologies based on specific forms of economic transformations in labor markets (for instance distinguishing between chainworkers and brainworkers) lacks coherence, they argue, and tends to overlook the many ways in which similar dynamics overlap and affect multiple positions (as well as tends to homogenize various positions and particularities). Developing this typology based on unrest and rebellion there are three general types of labor:

> 1. jobs with a repetitive content (telemarketing, cleaning, textile production) which have little subjective value or investment for those involved – tendency for conflicts based upon refusal of the work, absenteeism, sabotage
> 2. vocational / professional work (anything from nursing to informatics, social work, research, etc) where there is a higher subjective component and investment – conflict tends to be expressed as critique of the organization of labor, how it is articulated, and the forms it takes
> 3. jobs where the content is directly invisibilized and/or stigmatized (cleaning work, domestic labor, forms of sex work) – conflict tends to manifest as a demand for dignity and recognition of the social value of the work (2005)

The question for PAD, as already observed, is finding points for commonality and alliances, lines of aggregation where intense forms of relations and communities can emerge and are strengthened. PAD have also been involved the creation of various social centers and feminist spaces where such can occur and have been involved in the EuroMayDay Networks and parades which have acted as key points of visibility for those contesting existing conditions: In their words:

> The Mayday Parade constitutes a means of visibilization of
> the new forms of rebellion, a moment of encounter for the
> movements, and practices of forms of self-organized politi-
> cization (social centers, rank-and-file unions, immigrant col-
> lectives, feminists, ecologists, hackers), a space of expression
> of its forms of communication (the parade as an expression of
> pride inherited from the movements of sexual liberation, but
> also all the media-activist artillery developed around the global
> movement against the summits of the powerful of the world)
> and a collective cry for rights lost (housing, health, education)
> or new ones (free money, universal citizenship), which day to
> day and from each situated form we try to begin and to con-
> struct from below" (2005)

Thus the central problem, and one that has become much more
pressing in recent years, centers around the issue of security. The military and neoliberal logic of security,[18] involving anything from increased border controls and migration regulation to the proliferation
of private security firms and NGOs, has risen during the past 20-30
years during the same period that the decline of the welfare state and
apparatuses of social security and welfare measures have been taken
apart. It is a condition where an overall shift in the macropolitical situation is articulated in what PAD describe as a "micropolitics of fear"
that is directly related to the regulation of the labor market (and the
configuration of state-labor-business) and increasing forms of instability and precarization of life that extends over the whole of society
as regimes of discipline. The increasing importance, or perhaps overwhelming nature, of the logic of security is such that PAD have argued that it is "the principal form of taking charge of bodies and
organizing them around fear, contention, control, and management
of unease" (2005). As particular regimes of security, visibility, and exploitation comes together in a particular kind of state-form that at the
same time it dismantles the meager bits of itself that served the purpose of maintaining some sort of social safety net, PAD see it as a moment where it is necessary to put forth a logic of care as the
counterpoint to the logic of security which has become the hegemonic
dispositif of politics in many locations, because, as they argue, "Care,
with its ecological logic, opposes the securitary logic reigning in the
precaritzed world" (2006: 39).[19]

This involves four key elements: affective virtuosity, interdepend-
ence, transversality, and everydayness (2006: 40-41). These four elements are used to address questions of the sustainability of life, of the

ability to continue in the everyday tasks of life, labor, and communication in which we are constantly immersed; in doing that, in particular in attempting to find ways to contest the arrangements that they have been articulated in at the present, organized by a logic of security that is based on the generation of fear and negative affects (Sharp 2005), it becomes possible to create cracks in these forms of articulation, and by doing so, focus on the role that forms of care, affects, and relations have in the continual process of social reproduction, to develop "a critique of the current organization of sex, attention, and care and a practice that, starting from those as elements inside a continuum, recombines them in order to produce new more liberatory and cooperative forms of affect" (2006: 41).

PAD have pursued this through two related proposals, arguing for what they have described as "biosyndicalism" and the proposal of a "caring strike." Biosyndicalism, which as the name itself implies, is a drawing together of life and syndicalist traditions of labor struggle while stripping them of their more economistic elements. This is not to propose that life has "become productive" or that it has "been put to work," as starting from a feminist analysis of affects, caring labor, and social reproduction makes it quite clear that affects have always been productive, productive of life itself, even forms of life existed for many years that were not enmeshed in capitalist relations because they did not exist yet. Rather than arguing that it has become productive, it is rather that there are changing compositions of capitalism, modulated as eruptions of social resistance and flight which have been reintegrated into the workings of capitalism, that have altered these arrangements in such ways that forms of affective labor and social (re)production occupy a more directly exploited, more central position, in these arrangements. Similarly, it is not that conditions of instability and a precarious existence are a new phenomena (as they have been perhaps more the rule rather than the exception for the vast majority of the history of capitalism), rather that this process of precarization comes to currently encompass a much broader swath of the population than it has in recent times. Biosyndicalism for PAD does not mean that labor struggles are no longer important, far from it, rather it indicates that as processes affecting the composition of labor and social life are in no ways restricted to any clearly definable sphere of "work" that conflicts over them likewise cannot be easily marked in one area or sphere. Rather, it becomes all the more important to learn from these struggles and their successes (as well as their failures) in order to "invent forms of alliance, of organization, and everyday struggle in the passage between labor and non-labor, which is the passage that we inhabit" (2005).

Thus they propose what they call a "caring strike," a strike carried out at the same time by all those involved in forms of work all along the sex-care-attention continuum, from those involved in domestic labor to sex work, from telecommunications workers to teachers, and so forth. While this in many ways is close to the idea of the general strike so cherished (and fetishized) within the syndicalist tradition, the difference is here a combined strike by those involved in related forms of labor involving the dynamics of care. It is these dynamics, that are increasingly productive and important to the workings of the economy, are those that are the most often invisibilized, stigmatized, looked over, and underappreciated. While campaigns like Wages for Housework were built upon bringing visibility to forms of struggle and care within the home, PAD are for expanding this notion to not only include domestic labor, but the same dynamics and processes involved in such that are spread across the economy, and bring visibility to them, to organized around them, and to consciously withdraw their productivity, that which holds together the whole arrangement. In their words

> because the strike is always interruption and visibilization and care is the continuous and invisible line whose interruption would be devastating… the caring strike would be nothing other than the interruption of the order that is ineluctably produced in the moment in which we place the truth of care in the center and politicize it (2006: 42)

This is not that PAD have magically solved all the most pressing questions of revolutionary politics for today. Indeed, there are difficulties contained in what they propose; what about forms of caring labor that are difficult (and perhaps sometimes even impossible) to refuse? For instance, for those involved in critically intense forms of healthcare, of caring for relatives and children, and so forth? The rhetorical weight and power of such a proposition might very well lie in the reality that it is nearly impossible for those engaged in these forms of "affectively necessary labor" (and perhaps more varying forms of socialized labor) to go on strike at all (Spivak 1985: 40). PAD's proposal of the caring strike and their concept of biosyndicalism do not solve these difficulties per se, but do rather productively reopen these questions in much the same way that campaigns like Wages for Housework opened the question of feminist organizing and class. In this way PAD bring focus back to aspects of gendered labor and feminist organizing in ways that should not be forgotten, and with the proposal of the caring strike take part in an on-going process of bringing visibility to underappreciated aspects of social reproduction (including for this discussion the social reproduction involved in maintaining the lives of communities of resistance) and by doing so raise the question of what it would mean to withdraw them. While there is great potential for social rupture and upheaval to be dérived from the sometimes manic movement of the radical imagination, it is likewise important to never forget the conditions and processes that underlie the possibility of its emergence and continuation.

A Thousand Aeffective Plateaus: Anticapitalism & Schizophrenia

I think Utopia is possible, I see Utopia in humanity. We can reconsider our existence as completely utopian. Bringing a baby to life or simply the act of walking or dancing are examples of utopist action. Utopia should be in our streets. – Anita Liberti (quoted in Kendra and Lauren: 23)

The problem that confronts us today, and which the nearest future is to solve, is how to be one's self and yet in oneness with others, to deeply feel with all human beings and still retain one's characteristic qualities. – Emma Goldman (1998: 158)

It's 3am again… and several months after when I initially began writing this. And I must admit that in some ways things don't seem a whole lot clearer than when I began. There are still too many things to do (the pile in a different order than several months ago, is about the same height) and I'm still tired. Have things ended up right back where they started, with the circle unbroken, by and by, but with no pie in the sky when I die? Joe Hill already told me that was a lie. And perhaps that is the point after all: that any sort of politics which promises all the glories of heaven / revolution to come some day after one spent all one's time and effort in devotion / organizing is deeply troubled. And perhaps most trouble in the sense of without the attention to the on-going forms of care, interaction, and relations that constitute a community, and perhaps even more so communities in resistance, it is very unlikely that such community will be able to hold together for very long.

It is in this space that a focus on care, on affective relations, reveals just how important it really is: when it is framed as the question of aeffective resistance. For as PAD argue, "Care as passage to the other and to the many, as a point between the personal and the collective" (2005). Aeffective resistance, the creation of new forms of community and collectivity, involves the creation of subjectivities that are produced in the formation of these emerging communities. So it is never possible to clearly differentiate between the formation of subjective positions from the formation of collective relations, as they emerge at the same time and through the same process. But by focusing on this process of co-articulation and emergence, not as a means to stated political goals, but as political goals in themselves which are related to a whole host of other emerging communities, concerns, and articulations, the care of self in relation to the community in resistance is clearly understood as a necessary and important.

This is, perhaps not very surprisingly, quite close to arguments that are made and have been made within strains of radical political thought for some time, from arguments about the importance of prefigurative politics (the refusal to separate the means of organizing from their ends leading to creating forms or organization which prefigure the kind of social arrangements to which struggles are organized) and the more recent emphasis on creating open spaces, networks, and forums (Nunes 2005). The difference here is that one cannot overlook the very real forms of labor, effort, and intensity that are required for the on-going self-constitution of communities of resistance. To do so all too often is the ways in which patterns of behavior that communities in resistance are working to oppose and undermine (sexism, racism, homophobia, heteronormativity, classism, etc) reappear, as people falling back on structures of thought and assumptions that have become normalized through their daily lives in other ways that often get looked over precisely because it assumed that they been dealt with.

Aeffective resistance does not proceed by making a giant leap through which all existing dynamics that one could wish to do away with are magically dispersed forever more. Indeed, if it were possible to radically change all the structures of thought, mental schemas and short cuts, and forms of socialization construct our lifeworlds at once, it would be very difficult to do without approaching that closely approximated insanity. Schizophrenia even. Rather it is, to borrow a phrase from Italian feminist theorist Luisa Muraro, about creating "relations of entrustment," an attention to the composition of relations as a necessary basis for revolutionary politics (Muraro 1991). It is to understand the composition of relations and affections as an important pole for a process of political recomposition, one that underlies and is necessary for such a compositional process. To prevent the radical imagination from ever settling into a notion that politics occurs "over there" or at certain moments, rather than as something that grows out of the very relations and ethical interactions that constitute the fabric of everyday social life.

There are cracks in the structure of the everyday, uprisings, moments of excess, where it is possible to create new forms of relations and sociabilities: moments of excess. But it also very difficult to maintain them for any length of time. The grounds of radical politics are precarious, constantly shifting and transforming, and offer no firm foundation but one that must be continually recomposed, as we will explore in the next chapter. Rather than assuming a given ground for politics, perhaps it might make more sense to wander towards creating a thousand plateaus of aeffective intensities, vibrating locations where forms of energy, community, and intensity can be sustained and build links between other plateaus as they emerge. Thus aeffective resistance is not something that needs to be built from scratch, nor something that only concerns relations within movements themselves. Rather it is a focus on intensifying and deepening both the relations and connections that exist within movements as well as finding ways to politicize connections and relations throughout everyday life. Gestures of kindness and care, random acts of beautiful anticapitalism, exist and support life in many more places than just where black flags are flown and revolutionary statements issues. Aeffective resistance is about working from these intensities of care and connection, of constantly rebuilding the imaginal machines from them, rather then considering interpersonal and ethical concerns as an adjunct and supplement of radical politics.

Notes

1. E-mail June 4, 2006.
2. This argument is borrowed from, or perhaps inspired by, similar arguments made in the introduction to the 2004 *Slingshot Organizer*. For more information see http://slingshot.tao.ca.
3. Related currents of thought about affect are also found, oddly enough, in post-Kantian German idealism. For more on strain of thought see Redding (1999)
4. Even within activist communities these things frequently end up by default as the tasks taken on by females, although such is rarely stated or acknowledged (or done anything about).
5. See www.activist-trauma.net
6. For an exploration of the management of feeling, particularly the repression of negative emotions to maintain social peace, and the gendered dynamics of this, see Erickson and Ritter (2001) Wharton (1999).
7 The category I'm employing here, autonomous feminism, is admittedly a bit clunky. While in this particular piece I'm drawing mainly from currents of thought coming out of the autonomous Marxism of operaismo (unorthodox Italian radical politics coming out of the 1960s and 1970s), this category is not meant to be a delimiting one. It is definitely not intended to be a historically or geographically closed category. Autonomous feminism can thus be

understood as any feminist current focusing on the autonomous capacities of people to create self-determining forms of community without forms of hierarchy of political mediation and direction.

8. The worst offenders in this regard are Antonio Negri and Paolo Virno, who often tend to overlook and not mention any of the work on these issues, except for an occasional passing footnote. There is some irony, which the author is thoroughly enjoying, in noting this in a footnote.

9. See Brenner and Laslett (1991), Balser (1987), Ong (1987), and Raunig (2007: 67-96). Of particular importance is Ong's argument (1991) that the widening gap between current analytical constructs and workers' actual experiences is from a limited theoretical grasp of both capitalist operations and workers' response to them.

10. According to Pitirim Sorokin, "The Russian Revolution was begun by hungry women and children demanding bread and herrings. They started wrecking tramcars and looting a few small shops. Only did they, together with workmen and politicians, become ambitious enough to wreck that mighty edifice of the Russian autocracy" (1950: 3).

11. Particular articulations of power relations through gender and class are obviously enmeshed within dynamics of slavery, colonialism, and imperial conquest, and how their effects continue to live on and shape social relations. In the US, for example, organizing around domestic labor was very important for African American women still living within a social context shaped by the lingering effects of slavery, particularly in their struggle to clearly define their roles as independent employees (rather than servants of household masters). For more about this relation of race and the organizing of domestic labor, see Rio (2005), Kousha (1994), Palmer (1984), and Van Raaphorst (1988).

12. For information on some of these controversies, as well as useful background information and history see Malos (1980). It is also worth noting that there is some divergence and disagreement about whether the analysis put forth by Mariarosa Dalla Costa, which would be the inspiration for the use of demand for wages for housework, supports this strategy. The main text of *The Power of Women and the Subversion of Community* seems to imply that this demand would not be a suitable basis for organizing, while the footnotes appended afterwards in subsequent editions printed by the Wages for Housework Campaign, not surprisingly, claim that it is. There also seem to be some questions about which parts were jointly written. For more information on this apparent lack of sisterhood in struggle, see Sullivan (2005). For a more recent overview and reinterpretation of these issues from multiple theoretical perspectives, see Caffentzis (1999).

13. Anna Ciaperoni makes this argument: "It is insidious to try to re-establish – even through filters from feminist experience – a theoretical value for the age-long confinement of women to domestic activities, though unconstrained, because how many women actually choose housework? In this way one risks erasing ten years of feminist struggle and practice, for the destruction of the ideological basis of female subordination." (1991: 270).

14. There is a quite large collection of interesting resources, papers, and materials coming out of socialist feminist discussion and debates housed at the archives of the London School of Economic library, which hopefully will be made accessible in some form to those not close enough to London to access them in person.

15. For more on the dérive see Debord (1958). Also, see Plant (1992).

16. For more about Precarias a la Deriva's dialogue with Colectivo Situaciones, see Colectivo Situaciones (2005).
17. For a discussion of this concept see Negri (2004), Corsani (2007), and Osterweil (2007).
18. Precarias a la Deriva's translators have often used the phrase "securitary logic" to indicate the difference between more onerous forms of security (military, border, etc) and security as a more positive value (sense of personal safety, freedom from assault). While such seems a useful distinction to make, I find "securitary logic" to be quite awkward and thus have avoided using it. This should not be taken to be a dismissal of attempts to found a politics based upon other notions of security, such as the True Security action during the protests against the Republican National Convention in 2004 (which tried to put forward a notion of security appropriate to the building of self-determining communities as opposed to a military logic of security). See also Brown (1995).
19. For more on the relation of security, surveillance, and the regulation of bodies, see Ball (2005).

::: IX :: Precarious Politics ::

The condition today described as that of the precarious worker is perhaps the fundamental reality of the proletariat. And the modes of existence of workers in 1830 are quite close to those of our temporary workers. – Jacques Ranciere (1989: xxxiii)

During the past decade in Italy and Spain, but now having spread more broadly, there has emerged a discussion about precarity and precarious labor.[1] Describing conditions of unstable, short term, flexible, and highly exploited labor, these discussions and the organizing based around them have sought to find new ways, or revive and renew existing methods, to contest forms of social domination and exploitation found within neoliberal capitalism. This is a timely and needed intervention, as ever-increasing populations are involved in part-time, contract, and temp jobs: from 16.8% in the US to 46.1% in the Netherlands, as reported in the *Greenpepper Magazine* issue on the subject (2004). Thus elaborating methods of contestation fitting to the current political and social situation, to explore directions for recomposition corresponding to these dynamics, becomes an increasingly important task. What I want to do in this chapter is not to reopen the question of precarity in its entirety, for to do so would be to reopen the entire history of capitalism in so far that precarity is a foundational dynamic within it, constrained and contained during certain periods by forms of social resistance and the incorporation of these energies into the apparatus of governance, the current composition of capital-labor-state relations. Rather than reopening the question of precarious labor in total, the angle will be to explore precarity as a moment and trope for movement building, to explore the ways in which it has functioned as a point of political recomposition, and the formation of imaginal machines within this compositional space.

Precarious Understandings

We know that precariousness is not limited to the world of work. We prefer to define it as a juncture of material and symbolic conditions which determine an uncertainty with respect to the sustained access to the resources essential to the full development of one's life. This definition permits us to overcome the dichotomies of public/private and production/reproduction and to recognize the interconnections between the social and the economic. – Precarias a la Deriva (2005)

The discussions about precarity are inspired by the legacy of workerist and autonomous politics in Italy originating from the 1960s and 1970s. But in some ways the stark contrast between the nature of the precarity discussed, separated by several decades, makes them appear to be almost totally disconnected conversations. One might say that there seems almost to be two (if not more) kinds of precarity, or that the precarity discussed in the 1970s is something completely different from the kind discussed today. This is not because that actually is the case (at least in the concept itself), but rather the two conversations occur in different compositional moments, where the precarity discussed today is almost the inverse form of that discussed in the 1970s. In the 1970s it was common to employ the phrase *precario bello*, or that precarity was beautiful. And when one thinks about it in context, this is an eminently sensible thing to say when you think about what the kind of 'security' and 'stability' is created by working in a petrochemical factory or on an automobile assembly line for forty years. The Fordist-Keynesian deal, made possible (or perhaps more accurately made necessary) by long term waves of labor struggle and radical politics, had created conditions for certain kinds of material stability and security within sections of the industrialized west, although this came at a cost in other aspects. Assuaging working class populations through increased material consumption had long been a feature of this arrangement (think for instance of Ford's higher wages for assembly line work), but this had limits to which it could be effective.

These growing disenchantments expressed themselves in massive waves of strikes (many of them wildcat strikes) and bouts of work refusal. This was perhaps even more the case in Italy, which unlike sections of the US or Germany that had been operating with a factory system for several decades, Italy's economic and development 'miracle' of the 1950s and 1960s meant that industrial production had been established there for less time.[2] The wave of internal northern migration in Italy also resulted in large amounts of workers who did not feel themselves particularly welcome within the ranks of the Italian Communist Parties or larger unions, thus feeding waves of discontent leading to the proliferation of industrial action not coordinated by the unions or the party. These revolts against work, against the factory and the production line, coalesced into the figure of "Gasparazzo" as a mythical embodiment of industrial action and resistance. There is a rough correspondence to the figure of the slacker or dropout within US (and broader) counterculture and politics, although this comparison perhaps obscures as much as it clarifies. Obscures in the sense that the refusals and forms of exodus occurring within the factories and metropolitan spaces in Italy were by and large of a collective character, while not surprisingly in the US the direction of drop out and withdrawal tended to take (or at least was ascribed) a much more individualistic character. It is for this reason that one of the most interesting and important aspects of workerist politics, working class refusal and the drive to collective exodus, is misunderstood precisely because it is assumed that the politics of withdrawal and exodus are necessarily a middle class politics precisely because it does not seem possible for it to be otherwise.

This hatred of the factory and the assembly line, congealed in the figure of Gasparazzo, over time found itself differently expressed, as the resistance of the mass worker spread throughout the social fabric. This was theorized as the movement of the resistance of the socialized worker, which occurred within the diffused factory. This also found expression in the rise of precarious patterns of work embraced as a positive feature, for instance working for several months to raise funds for a trip, or project, or a period of finding some escape from wage labor. This came together in the German context as the jobber movement, finding ways to work when necessary to raise funds, but then to use those resources (as well as squatting and other forms of collective appropriation) to create spaces and times outside of the constant discipline and requirements of wage labor. There was also a concomitant rise of forms of self-organized, small scale, flexible production and work organization that provided forms of material sustenance. All of these together created a sense that precarity was something that indeed could be thought of as beautiful, as a means out of the confines and standardization of factory labor, particularly as experiments in collective living and securing material resources provided the support for the emergence of vibrant forms of community and living.

It is this sense of a beautiful precarity, of a greater sense of flexibility and life arrangements, and ability to collectively subtract (at least partially) from capitalism, that necessitated and determined capital's response, thus leading to the inversion and transformation of precarity into the sense now used. Flexible and dispersed forms of production and organization were adapted and developed within capitalist firms (these forms, such as autonomous work teams and groups, as well as flexible production methods, come to increasing prominence and attention within management literature in the 1970s), and the forms of flexibility and contingent working embraced as beautiful precarity come to imposed as used as means of discipline and control. Capital's response to these diffuse and creative forms of resistance, emerging forms of sociality, was something like saying "You want flexibility, fine, we'll give you flexibility!" – flexibility in an imposed, rather than embraced sense. It could take the form of a part time job that always remains at a level of hours low enough to not qualify for benefits or health insurance, or to be able to survive on just one job. But forced and imposed flexibility was not just something that comes about through changes in bounded workplace environments, it was also embodied in an overall change of regime of accumulation and mode of governance, namely that of the transition to a neoliberal economic order that occurred starting in the late 1970s and 1980s. It is one thing to be able to embrace precarity as beautiful when there is a strong welfare state and means of social support existing (not to mention the existence of support through movement networks and communities), it is another to attempt to do so when both the social support programs have been attacked and scaled back and the movements and communities have been crushed, dispersed, or fallen apart.

Precarity then is not just the absence of the state, or its withdrawal, or rolling back social programs, although in some ways it is all these things. It is not the passive non-presence of the state in spheres in which it was once active, but rather the active withdrawal of government activity from certain areas of life, such as those regulating work relationships or providing welfare programs. As Olmedo and Murray show (2002), drawing from the Argentinean experience, precarious labor arises through the active withdrawal of the state from these areas in a way that formalizes and establishes their non-regulation, or more accurately their regulation through non-intervention. Thus precarity is not only characteristic of the informal and quasi-legal labor markets, but rather an implemented destructuring of regulations that is the capitalist response to social struggles. Or, more accurately, that was taken on as the capitalist response to struggle entering the neoliberal phase (as opposed to the Fordist-Keynesian adaptation of resistant energies with a framework based around that form of state and approach to policy). Although more often it is not presented this way, but rather is explained as a means of attaining a higher degree of global competitiveness, as an inevitable effect of the dynamics of globalization, as an outcome of a structural adjustment program, or any number of variations on similar themes.

Although the term precarity had been used previously (although the 'beautiful precarity' of the 1970s is often ignored or forgotten within more recent discussions),[3] its contemporary usage derives from the efforts of the labor organizing and media activism collective Chainworkers, a Milan-based group which formed in 1999-2000. Their aim was to find ways to merge together the methods of IWW-inspired anarcho-syndicalist labor organizing and subvertising to find ways to contest forms of labor found within post-industrial capitalism (Foti 2004). The IWW has long been a key point of reference in autonomist politics, serving as a model of radical labor politics outside party structures that found ways to organize forms of labor often ignored by other unions, and also employing varied forms of cultural politics within its organizing. In conditions where work to a large extent no longer occurs primarily within centralized locations of productions (such as factories), but is distributed across much larger geographic scales, in the diffuse workings of the social factory.[4] The task was drawing from this history of subversion and reformulating it within present conditions, or finding ways to articulate the politics of a communicative Wobbly, weaving affective-linguistic territories through organizing across the social field. Or as Ben Trott phrased it in his discussion of precarity as a machine for moving back to everyday resistance,

> Perhaps, then, we require something along the lines of a Post-Industrial Workers of the World in order to provide an open, horizontal structure within which a multitude of resistances can coordinate themselves; an organizational form which, as was the case with the original IWW, allows for all of those involved in acts of social production to 'plug in' to the network as and when they need, to draw upon resources, experience and the solidarity of others, whilst constructing basis-democratic forms of organization on both a local and a global level (2005: 230)

Given the drastic changes occurring within forms of work, it was necessary to update and reformulate labor organizing tactics to address them. While there have long existed many forms of contingent and precarious labor, they have become increasingly central since the neoliberal reaction to the social insurgencies of the 1960s and 1970s which gave rise to capitalist counterattacks in the 1980s. The Chainworkers thus moved their area of focus increasingly to the cultural and media spheres, trying to find bases of antagonism not primarily or even necessarily within the usually recognized locations of work, but through all the social fabric and areas into which capitalist dynamics have seeped. As the formerly existing space of the workplace was fractured by changes in the nature of work, organizing through cultural politics attempted to create a shared basis for a politics which was not based upon being located in the same physical workplace, but rather through the creation of shared positions and commonality in various cultural fields. In other words, being located with the same workplace gave workers a common experience and space from which it was possible to organize, a space which no longer exists in the distributed forms of production and swing shifts that are more common in today's economy. Thus the strategy shifts to using forms of cultural politics and symbolism to form a common space to organize from.

This is based on an understanding that cultural production is not an adjunct or addition to the "real work" of capitalist production but increasingly (particularly within highly industrialized areas) *is* the work that is a key component of it. That is not to say that workplace culture and culture more generally were not important to the working of capitalism before; the existence and importance of workplace and working class culture is quite extensive. The workplace has always been a cultural field, the change is the degree of importance that cultural production has within the process of production, not whether the production process is cultural. This is to say that the cultural sphere has come to play a more integral role within the current composition of forces, actors, and positions enmeshed in the workings of capitalism. The changed compositional role of cultural production within the workings of capitalism means that the potentiality for struggles contained within it is transformed, not necessarily because it is the most advanced sector of capitalist development, but because as cultural production plays an important role within capitalism it offers more possibilities for disrupting capitalist dynamics, for connecting multiple struggles. The struggle over culture within production is not new, not at all, but is rather a question that is reopened within a changed compositional context. As Andrew Ross explores with great skill (2003), despite all the hoopla about the allegedly non-hierarchical and non-exploitative new media workplace that circulated during the 1990s and through the dot.com frenzy, the new boss was just as horrible as the old one, and even more so for those who didn't occupy the few relatively privileged positions in such workplaces that had become emblematic of this transformation.

In some ways a number of the difficulties discussed in relation to Ever Reviled Records – a self-organized form, as discussed in a previous chapter, and the tensions in self-managed forms – have come to more broadly affect sections of media and cultural labor. This does affect those involved in these workplaces in the same ways in that most projects are not founded on the political goals of abolishing capitalism and the state, although there is perhaps much in that rhetorical line that they would borrow from in terms of liberating human potential and creativity, humanizing the workplace and so forth. And in this way many new media workplaces and cultural labor generally is caught in many of the same binds, even if not for the same reasons. This is not so surprising, because as already argued, precarity in many ways is the inversion of the forms of struggle and exodus that emerged during the 1970s. Capital found ways to take people's desires for less work and for forms of flexible labor and arrangements and turn them into increasingly uncertain conditions as social welfare provisions and neoliberal deregulation were brought into the effect. Precarity emerges as a discourse and focus of organizing in conditions where it is those very conditions that are being strategized through and against.

Back to the Everyday

If we accept that capitalism is a social relation, and one which has escaped the confines of the factory wall and permeated every aspect of society at that, there is no particular reason as to why the cities, streets and golf greens surrounding international summits should not themselves become sites of struggle. The problem, of course, is not really that mobilizations take place around international summits, but that these mobilizations become reified and fetishized as the *de facto* form of anti-capitalist resistance today. – Ben Trott (2005: 227)

At its best, precarity as a conceptual terrain and area of focus is quite useful in creating an opening for the politicization of everyday life and labor relations. This served an especially important role in a period where the social energies unleashed by the anti-globalization movement and protest summits had reached their limit and encountered with increasing intensity the problems of their own predictability, the increased ability of police to control them (as well as their recuperation by media starlets and the Bonos of the world), and the flagging of their creative vitality. The anti-globalization movement functioned in finding ways to contest and make visible networks of power and governance in the neoliberal order, forms which because of their diffuse and somewhat abstract character were difficult to frame in a way that directly connected with people's everyday lives (although admittedly this was more of a difficulty in the Global North, in much of the world struggling under the brunt of structural adjustment programs and privatization this was much less of a concern). This explains the large focus on consumer politics, sweatshop production, and related concerns that provided a large degree of focus for movements during the 1990s, as they were points of focus where one could clearly articulate how one's everyday actions and decisions connected to a global system of capitalist exploitation, connecting shopping malls in Minnesota to the factories of South Asia. Summit protests proved a logical compositional step from this focus, as a congealing of forces articulating how these varied forms of economic power, ecological destruction, and antidemocratic forms of power were linked through transnational institutions in which much of the world's population has little or no say over the decisions made that directly and quite significantly affect them. The problem is that the everydayness of anticorporate politics were somewhat lost within the spectacular form and manifestation of the summit events. In other words, attention was shifted somewhat towards the particular spaces oriented around the summits. This led to some quite sharp debates on how to bring these social energies back into community organizing and politics.

A focus on precarity opened up a space for deploying a cultural politics based around a realization that the unstable and uncertain forms of social life that now existed were closely connected by a series of new enclosures to the forms of debt and financial bondage being created: each imposition of structural adjustment programs by the International Monetary Fund in the Third World is connected to the dismantling of social services in the First, the enclosures of common lands is related to the increasing enclosure of people's time, energies, and creativity, and so forth. And most importantly did so in a way that shifted attention to people's everyday lives and relations by focusing not just on a transnational form of governance, an institution over there, or a sweatshop half way across the world, but the forms of domination and exploitation connecting low wage and unstable jobs, migration controls, restrictions on health care and social support, and so forth. And also quite importantly began to address these areas by drawing from the resources, creativity, and imaginal arsenal developed within the anti-globalization movement, bringing a new sense of vitality to organizing.

This was accomplished through the development of an array of cultural symbols and actions, such as the figure of San Precario, which detourns and uses the common image of the Catholic saint to represent the figure of the precarious worker and her desire for communication, transportation, housing, resources, and affection. Originally developed as a means to "celebrate" the newly generalizing conditions of working on Sundays (which had until recently been quite rare in Italy), San Precario quickly caught on as a meme. As Marcello Tarì and Ilaria Vanni observe, his image functions "as a rhetorical device to move into the public arena a critical awareness of the changes in conditions and forms of work, of the shift from permanent positions to casual" (2005). San Precario has since appeared at numerous rallies, actions, parades, and events, where followers have had "miracles" performed for them such as the autonomous reduction of prices. There is even a sanctuary devoted to San Precario (the gazebo of the beach occupied during the Venice Film Festival) and a Saint's Day, February 29th, itself a precariously occurring day. This practice of autoreduction, or negotiating by mob, originated in Italy during the 1970s to combat rapid inflation in costs of food, clothing, electricity, and other necessities (accompanied by squatting and a massive refusal of payment). This practice was renewed at a guaranteed income demo on November 6, 2004 at a supermarket owned by the former Italian prime minister Silvio Berlusconi when 700 people entered the store demanding a 70% discount on everything, chanting that "everything costs too much." While negotiations occurred many people simply left with food and provisions, many of whom had not been involved in the demo at all.

Another innovative tactic was the holding of fashion show by the designer Serpica Naro to highlight conditions of precarious workers.[5] In February 2005 during the Milano Fashion Week anti-precarity activists disrupted a high profile Prada catwalk, and then threatened to disrupt a fashion show for the controversial designer Serpica Naro, planned to be held at a car park in Milan only accessible by one bridge. Police contacted the show's agent to warn him about the possible disruption. But as the event began, the police became confused when the crowd (which was supposed to "disrupt" the show), starting laughing at them, instead of being angry and frustrated since the police were preventing them from moving. Even stranger was that they were accompanied by the models and organizers themselves, who then proceed to produce the permits showing that it was they who had organized the show to begin with! There was no Serpica Naro – it was all a hoax based on a clever rearranging of "San Precario." When the media began to arrive, still largely unaware of this, they were treated to a fashion show highlighting the precarious conditions of those involved in the fashion industry and related sectors (such as garment manufacture). This event turned the tables in a highly media saturated political climate like Italy (where much of Berlusconi's power was through his use and control of the media) and managed to break down expectations of what constitutes activism and political action.

The most visible expression of the concept, which starting in 2000 had started to become adopted by various sections of the anti-globalization movement, are the EuroMayDay Parades,[6] which started in Italy in 2001. Employing carnival like forms of protest and tactical absurdity these events sought to revive the Wobbly tradition of humor and satire in politics as well as breaking with more traditional trade unions and social democratic parties, which had taken part in the institutional decision making that ushered in the increasingly intense and unstable social conditions. Precarity was used a rallying cry to find points of commonality between forms of labor and generalized social situations of insecurity, for instance between the positions of lowly paid workers in chainstores, computer programmers and data manipulators, and the highly exploited and blackmailed labor of undocumented migrants. The goal was to tease out these common points and positions, build alliances across the social sphere, and find ways to bring together antagonisms against these common but differing forms of exploitation. The first May Day parade in Milano brought out 5,000 people and created a flying picket that succeeded in shutting down all the major chainstores in the city center. By 2003 the event has grown to 50,000 people and inspired similar events across Europe. A European network was created in 2004 during the "Beyond the ESF" forum in Middlesex that took place at the same time as the European Social Forum and led to events taking place in 20 cities across Europe in 2005. Although it seems that the success (at least in terms of attendance) of the EuroMayDay marches has waned since then, and as Chris Carlsson has explored, perhaps more fundamentally, has been waning from several hundred thousand over the past several decades (2006). Although this involves a transformation of what was traditionally a large event coordinated by the Communist Party to one being put together by a much more diffuse network of organizers and media activists rather than a formal party structure.

And in many ways this seemed a very fitting approach, for the concept of precarity described quite aptly many of the situations of various emerging movements, such as the Intermittents du Spectacle, a group of seasonal arts and cultural workers who attracted attention by organizing against their uncertain situations by disrupting live TV news broadcasts and the Cannes Film Festival. The concept also seemed to capture well the organizing of casualized Parisian McDonalds workers who occupied their workplaces; migrant organizing against detention and deportation (such as the often celebrated *san papiers* movement of undocumented migrants); and many other of the

struggles that have emerged recently. It could arguably be used to describe organizing such as the actions against recent changes in immigration law in the US and around the conditions of domestic and sex
workers, the recent (and first) demonstrations by workers against
Wal-Mart that occurred in Florida, as well as campaigns such as the
IWW Starbucks Workers Campaign, the New Zealand based "Super
Size My Pay" campaign, and the Taco Bell boycott campaign put together by the Coalition of Immokalee Workers (and the Student-
Farmworker Alliance that grew out of it). These are claimed as signs
of the emergence of a new social subject, the precariat, which is the
condition of autonomous proletarian self-activity in the increasingly
exploitative conditions of neoliberal capitalism.[7]

The problem, compositionally (or one of the problems) is that
while the networks and connection of the anti-globalization movement
and its form of political composition was quite important as a starting
point for the building of these networks, they also tended to keep organizing around precarity confined within that space. There was a
shift in focus and rhetoric within the organizing, but one that also fal-
tered around the limits of the composition of the anti-globalization
movement rather than going beyond them. So while a focus on precarity was useful as a means for thinking about the kinds of power
and exploitation in everyday life and organizing around that rather
than summit convergences necessarily, this form was recreated within
the organizing anyways. In other words, rather than focusing on the
ordained symbolic events of disrupting transnational institutions, the
focus switched to organizing around the EuroMayDay parades.

There is nothing inherently flawed in organizing around a May
Day event, but the problem is when that becomes the main focus,
to such a degree that it is hard to see in what ways struggle around
precarity is actualized in forms other than the EuroMayDay parades. This again is to reduce a diffuse and creative politics of the
everyday into a fetishization of particular moments, albeit an array
of movements that at least are arranged according to the timeframe
of those organizing them rather than the dates and places chosen
by any number of transnational institutions aimed to be disrupted
(and thus has less of a reactive character). This dynamic and limi-
tation is perhaps not all that surprising. As one of the members of
the publication *Wildcat* pointed out to me, organizing around precarity had in some ways merely transferred the activism of the anti-
globalization movement into a changed rhetorical framework
without really working through the tensions and contradictions and
tensions faced there. There is a degree of truth in this, although it
still seems sensible to appreciate the creativity and usefulness of

this move even and despite the unresolved tensions it still carried within it.

Networks, Structure, Logic

The proletarian experience is 'naturally' one of being organized (interpolated) but this organization also imposes the necessity of an ambivalence in that structuration – in other words, the organization of workers by capitalism is already/always by capital, for capital and against capital. – Frere Dupont (2007)

A kind of waiting madness, like a state of undeclared war, haunted the office buildings of the business park. – J.G. Ballard (2000: 3)

There are perhaps more fundamental questions and tensions facing those organizing around precarity, although it must be said that these are in some ways the same tensions that would be likely to confront the project of recomposing radical politics today, to some degree, regardless of the particular focus. One of these is the difficulty of moving beyond the existing forms of networks, connections and compositions found within a movement, to find ways to be self-expanding and create waves and cycles of struggle, rather than falling into a self-marginalizing or limiting patterns of social interaction. To take an angle that might seem strange at first, and likely a bit provocative later, it would be useful to draw from Barbara Ehrenreich's (2005) ethnography and exploration of the forms of insecurity and instability (and might we say precarity) that have slowly crept over the years into the lives of a group of people who generally are convinced that they would not have to deal with such, namely middle and upper middle class professionals, aspiring executives, and the denizens of the corporate world. Yes, even the lives of the suit wearing, management guru listening set, have come to be afflicted by degrees of uncertainty and job insecurity that would have been unthinkable only several decades ago. She describes the shadowy world of internet job searches, job coaching and image management, and networking and social events designed to assist the middle class executive "in transition" (read, not unemployed, that's something for the rabble) to a new form of employment, at a cost, of course. Aside from getting a glimpse into this dynamic and the surrealness of the corporate world, Ehrenreich makes some quite interesting observations about the logic of networking, which is constantly proclaimed by all the job coaches and advisors as being the most important, practically a job in itself for the precarious individual.

What Ehrenreich draws out of this is the blunt instrumentality of networking logic, one that undercuts the possibility of collective identity, commonality, and struggle based on these. In short, if through networking one is induced only to see others as possible contacts, leads, and sources of information, it is that dynamic that effectively prevents the emergence of any sort of real discussion of the common position of these people, of the reality that they are caught within such a bizarre world of pop psychology and quaisi-magical aspirational thinking precisely because of the systemic instabilities of capitalism. Now, true, she is describing those who have been kicked to the curb of the corporate world, which is a somewhat different sort of habitus from the social existence of the people who have been involved in organizing around precarity. But putting aside the particularities of the individualizing logic of middle class executives and the specifically corporate world, it might be there is a similar dynamic occurring here, even it is a strange parallel. In corporate culture and management literature there is a constant injunction to see oneself as a creative, dynamic individual that is alone responsible for your success or failure. This sort of combination of quasi-mystical belief in the self as creative and the source of success, combined with a networking logic; how different is this from still-lingering romantic notions of artistic production and the logic of networking that is all too prevalent among cultural and media workers as well as those involved in artistic fields? Once one has stripped away the outward appearance of difference (they wear suits, the cultural workers look more boho, they both go for drinks in Shoreditch), this tendency to narrate collective problems within an individualizing narrative has the same dynamic of undercutting the possibility of collective identity or struggle. For just as we have yet to see the insurgent organization of displaced executives, the radicality and struggles of cultural and media workers in general (often despite the beliefs and politics people will lay claim to if asked) often leaves one a bit underwhelmed.

This is not to say that such couldn't happen, but rather that there are dynamics and tendencies found within the class composition of media, cultural, artistic labor that tend to work against the sort of alliances and connections that could most productively be made based around a focus on precarity. The point is not to dwell on these as a sigh of despair of organizing in such sectors, but rather to realize that doing so requires working against certain patterns of ingrained assumptions that tend to exist within these areas. There are useful tools for this found within the writing of Bifo, who has argued a number of different positions, that much like his politics in general, alternates between an infectious and joyous optimism, to a quite pessimistic and near mournful analysis inflected by all sorts of sad passions. For instance, in response to struggles of precarious workers and students in France, in 2006 he argued that this could provide the beginning of a new cultural and political cycle in Europe. That is not to say that the protests of the French students against changes in employment law could in itself defeat precarity. This is in absurd suggestion, for he argues that such a victory would actually be just the defeat of the legal *formalization* of precarity, which would then be posed within other contexts. But this in itself is a significant victory in that it could open a "phase of struggle and social invention which, beyond neoliberal slavery, will make it possible to formulate new rules, new criteria of regulation of the labor-capital relation" (2006). But this seems to contradict other arguments he had made about the possibility for organizing around precarity.

The year before he had argued that precarity was not a new condition, but rather was the black heart of capitalist relations, the transformative element in the whole cycle of production, and a dynamic that had only been regulated against with some degree of success for a limited period of the twentieth century under the political pressure of unions and workers, the presence of a relatively well functioning welfare state, and more or less full employment. It is only with these conditions that the violence and instability endemic of capitalism could be given some limits, conditions that as we have seen are no longer present. Furthermore, for Bifo the essential is not just the becoming, or one should say re-becoming of labor's precarity, but rather what he describes as "the dissolution of the person as active productive agent, as labor power" taking place as labor is fractalized through dispersed technological and communicative networks (2005). Bifo argues that this process of fractalization and deeper enmeshing of labor within technological networks, in flexibilized forms, creates a problem that prevents the struggles of precarious workers from launching a cycle of struggles:

> Fractalized work can also punctually rebel, but this does not set into motion any wave of struggle. The reason is easy to understand. In order for struggles to form a cycle there must be a spatial proximity of the bodies of labor and an existential temporal continuity. Without this proximity and this continuity, we lack the conditions for the cellularized bodies to become community. No wave can be created, because the workers do not share their existence in time, and behaviors can only become a wave when there is a continuous proximity in time that info-labor no longer allows (2009: 34).

The thrust of Bifo's argument is that those engaged in precarious cognitive labor are capable of acts of rebellion, minor strikes, and so forth, but that they lack the conditions for those acts to coalesce into a wave or cycle of struggles. While the lack of physical proximity in some senses is understandable as a hindrance to organizing (after all, how much of labor organizing begins when someone turns to the person next to them in the line and says something to the effect of "this is a bit messed up"), this does not seem to be a fully adequate explanation. Historically there have been many instances of organizing lacking spatial proximity and overcoming that through creative means, from glyphs and marks left on walls to digital communications. Perhaps the problem of creating waves and struggles has more to it than just physical proximity and has more to do with what Bifo refers to as an existential temporal condition, a condition of not sharing existence in a common time or framework that prevents individuated understandings and subjectivities finding their commonality. This seems to overlap a good bit with the tensions and difficulties Ehrenreich identified within a overriding logic of networking preventing commonality and solidarity from emerging precisely in such a logic it is only possible to regard others in a time frame working towards one's end, rather than ever occupying a common time or position.

While these are important questions to be raised, they are somewhat odd in that it is precisely these very concerns that organizing focusing on precarity hopefully would have addressed: to find ways to create common positions, understandings, and forms of collective time in a social and political context marked by the fractalization of labor and common time within the bounded workplace. To find ways to foster and develop these understandings and commonalities within a broader and more diffuse cultural politics precisely because of the difficulties faced on using the assumed experience of a common space, time, or framework. The question then becomes why such a project has stalled (or has appeared to have reached the limits of its creativity, as one might tend to think given the waning of EuroMayDay and the lack of renewed ideas and movements), and how the factors leading to the slowing or halting of a compositional process can be understood precisely to work through, within, and beyond them. This, after all, is perhaps *the* lingering question, one that most definitely lingers because it is never fully solved, at least not for good. To get at that, there are some questions to be raised around time, epochal divisions, and precarity. In many ways, haven't we been precarious for quite some time? As Jacques Ranciere observes in the quote that begins this chapter, a precarious existence is perhaps the defining condition of the proletariat: indeed, the bloody terror and dispossession of primitive accumulation is precisely the process through which a state of precarity, the inability to effectively live outside of capitalist relations, is created.

And what does it mean to speak about precarity, if used as a unifying concept or framework, in situations that have a far different political, economic, and social context? Nate Holdren comments on this in an essay on the question of why there is no discourse around precarity in the US, or why one has not emerged in a similar manner (2007). For Holdren one might say that this is the wrong question, for framing it like that tends to overlook the ways that such a discussion exists, both in the sense of occurring under the banner of other terms but addressing the same questions (for instance in terms of casualization or marginalization) as well as occurring within sections of the milieu of cultural politics and organizing (for instance in forms like the *TempSlave* zine and the long running publication of *Processed World*). One can also see much the same questions being addressed in organizing around migrant labor and the work of the IWW as well as during the 1990s in the Love & Rage Anarchist Federation (which had a committee basically on precarity, or what they referred to as "anti-austerity work"). The difference between a US and European context is not a lack of addressing precarity per se, but rather that this has not come to fruition in any sense of mass mobilization per se (although one could see the massive organizing against the new immigration laws in 2006 precisely as organizing against precarity in many ways). From this Holdren concludes that the question about the lack of a discourse around precarity in the US is really a lament for stronger movement cultures and traditions, such as those that continue to exist in more pronounced ways in places like France, Italy, and Spain.

For instance in the US, where to a large extent there have never existed the forms of job contracts and increased forms of labor protection that are now under attack in places like France and Spain, it is silly to talk about the process of social relations becoming precarious, because they have been for a very long time. And in countries where such protections existed, they only operated for a relatively brief period of time, namely the era of the Fordist-Keynesian welfare/warfare state that existed from the end of WWII until the 1980s. In a sense this is exactly the question that a focus on precarity reopens, that questions of the welfare state and its legacy, or the lingering presence of social support programs that still exist. But this is a question that is different within varying national contexts, for despite the tendency of enclosures in one place to be connected to and necessitate enclosures in other locations, the destructuring of the welfare state under neoliberal assaults is uneven in the same way that process leading to its formation was also uneven. The varying trajectories of the formation of the welfare state largely reflect how the insurgent energies of labor movements and social movements were territorialized and incorporated into a governing apparatus. So while the social and political context of the times could lead Richard Nixon to declaring in the early 1970s that 'we are all Keynesians' now, being a Keynesian in the US has a different inflection, with its unique history of responding to the radical left (by and large repression as opposed to varying forms of accommodation more common with an European context).

Turning to precarity as a focus brings into consideration not just the ways that labor regulations and social welfare measures were taken apart as a part of a neoliberal trajectory, but also the history of their formation, the process leading to the congealing of insurgent energies into forms of state. The question of precarity involves making sense out of this legacy, and what it means to a recompositional process today, how it enables and or disables movement, how it is possible or not to build from these trajectories. There is no great surprise in saying that in some ways arguments around precarious labor emerge out of, and are based upon, certain latent assumptions and conditions concerning the role of the welfare state and social democracy. They rely implicitly upon people recalling what might, in general, be described as the greater success that various European attempts at social regulation of the economy and creating forms of security for their populations, admittedly measures taken because of the larger and more militant social movements that have existed there. This is perfectly sensible, as access to health care, a sense of security of life, material resources, and continued access to means of social reproduction are not just 'immediate demands' to be transcended into some purer form, but rather the very questions that underlie and make possible supporting livelihoods and communities. That their gratification and stability would hover as a constant theme in the imaginary of radical politics is nothing new, and has been a key feature of the radical imaginary from time immemorial. It is a question of finding ways to both defend the legacy of the welfare state and social support programs (that which continue to exist) but to also go beyond them, to continually remember that while they are important and worth defending they are not enough. The important difference is whether this is an unstated assumption, and if it is, what sort of less seemly dynamics are inadvertently brought along with these assumptions. In other words, whether it is a process of re-opening the question of welfare state and social solidarity, how to find ways to construct new social rights and institutional forms for their continued provision today, or falling back into an older model of the welfare state without considering the tensions and contradictions contained within it. This could take a form, for instance, where the provision of welfare is attached to an exclusionary or nationalist project, thus taking on a reactionary role in the policing of that border even while taking on a benevolent role to those marked to be within bounds.

This can be seen in the usage of ideas posed as a response to precarious conditions, such as basic/guaranteed income and flexicurity. Basic income is an idea popularized in the milieu of 1970s autonomist politics (although it has a much longer history),[8] particularly in Italy, to argue that people held the rights to a basic form of subsistence and ability to survive regardless of what forms of recognized labor in which they were involved. This was important both in acknowledging the importance of the many activities of social reproduction (housework, caring for children and the elderly, etc.) that are usually unwaged, and in trying to separate income from labor time spent in forms of capitalist work. Flexicurity as a concept has emerged more recently, most noticeably as a policy of the Danish government, which has taken the somewhat paradoxical approach of both deregulating labor markets and forms of employment while also strengthening the provision of social welfare services (as opposed to the usual tact of dismantling the apparatus of the welfare state at the same time). Social movements have thus used notions of flexicurity across Europe, usually inflected with a more radical tinge, to argue for measures to support people's ability to exist under conditions of instability and uncertainty. In other words, the argument is made that it is not the uncertainty of flexible conditions and employment itself that is necessarily undesirable, but rather that there are not measures existing to ensure that people can be secure in these conditions: thus the idea of flexicurity, or flexible security.

It should be readily obvious how such arguments are inflected to various degrees by social democratic assumptions. After all, who's going to provide this basic income / flexicurity? If not the nation-state, then where are the measures enacted from, say, the EU? Some other political space that has not clearly emerged yet? As Brian Holmes argues, forms of violence and racism have already injected themselves into the notion of flexicurity and thus overdetermine it in a context marked by exclusion (2006). In other words, a concept that emerged in a context of racism and forms of social domination, in this case a reliance on the hyperexploited labor of migrants and in domestic spaces, cannot easily be separated from this context without being shaped by it. This is not to say that such is necessarily the case, but rather that there needs to be serious discussion about how those kinds of dynamics can be avoided, particularly if a concept such as precarity is to be used in places like the US, which has a long standing and particularly intense history of intersecting dynamics of race, class, gender, and social power. This is also an important consideration for using the concept anywhere outside of the social and cultural context from which it emerged. One should also note that Holmes, somewhat like the discussion of Bifo previously, has expressed both great hope and sensed possibility in organizing around precarity as well as reservations. For instance in an essay he wrote previous to the one just mentioned he noted the possibility that flexworkers can reinvent the welfare state (2007: 28). This is not to point out a contradiction, but rather perhaps that there was a common trajectory of responses to organizing precarity, one that started very hopeful and perhaps naively optimistic in some ways, but has since become more cautious about the possibility of large scale cultural and institutional change and the ways and forms that could occur through and in. As Holmes emphasized in his later article, what's important is keeping open the question of the welfare state rather than assuming it settled, either by being outmoded by neoliberal transformation or a simple reinvention of mechanisms for creating conditions for flexicurity, or flexible security.

Also, and perhaps more fundamentally, there is a risk of identifying common positions and grounds for struggle by drawing out the implications of changes in the forms of labor that do not necessarily resonate with those experiencing them, or do not necessarily produce unproblematic alliances. Or to put it another way, while a common technical composition of labor is often useful in building alliances along that shared condition, a shared technical composition does not necessarily create conditions of shared political composition. To take technical composition for political composition neglects the labor of composition, the labor of self-organization that necessarily sustains and supports the emergence of collective antagonism. As the Madrid-based feminist collective Precarias a la Deriva observed, while those involved in designing a webpage and providing a hand-job for a client can both be understood to engaged in a form of immaterial labor (forms of work more based on cultural or symbolic rather than physical production), one which is connected through overall transformations on structures of labor and social power,[9] these are two forms of work hugely inflected by the social value and worth assigned to them. And thus any politics that is based on the changing nature of work has to consider how differences in access to social power and the ability to have a voice about one's conditions affect organizing from those conditions, and the possibility, as well as difficulties, of creating alliances between them. To continue using the same example, how do we form a politics based upon those conditions without those involved in a form of labor with greater social prestige (for instance web design or computer-based work) speaking for those who do not have the same access to forms of social power and ability to voice their concerns (in this instance, sex workers). There is a huge potential to recreate a form of paternalistic liberal politics, only this time based upon an understanding of a connected position in an overall form of economic transformation.

Or to use another example, one could argue that both the people involved in the riots that started in the Paris suburb *Clichy-sous-Bois*[10] and spread across France last year, and those involved in the massive student and labor protests and occupations against the introduction of new flexible labor contracts for young workers, are involved in organizing against the same dynamics of uncertainty and exclusion. That, however, does not mean that there is easily or necessarily a common basis for political alliance between those positions based upon that shared condition. Or at the very least there is not a basis for alliance between those two situations until political organizing occurs which draws upon those conditions to create common grounds for alliance rather than assuming one exists based on large scale transformations in social and political power. This is the mistake that theorists such as Negri tend to fall into, which lends credence to the argument that the concept of the multitude effaces differences within itself in ways that are not particularly helpful for movement building.[11] To borrow another argument from Precarias a la Deriva (2005), perhaps rather than using a notion of precarity and its forms based on the changing compositions of labor (such as those embodied in an understanding of the difference between a chainworker and a brainworker), it would be more useful to consider how differences in social position and conditions creates possibilities for differing forms of insurgency and rebellion, and how to work between these various possibilities. This would be to push precarity even more explicitly in the direction of a specifically recompositional machine rather than an analytic framework or structural analysis. That is not to say that analysis and structure are not important and functional to recomposition, rather that they are components within the imaginal machine rather than setting the framework for its construction.

Creative workers may indeed be held by many to be the exemplary figure of post-fordist labor, enmeshed in circuits of immaterial, precarious production, but as Angela Mitropolous points out, "this requires a moment in which the precarious conditions of others are

declared to be a result of their 'invisibility' or 'exclusion'" (2005: 91).
This argument about exclusion and invisibility is more problematic
than it might seem at first. As Mitropolous continues, the framing of
migrant and precarious labor as invisible and excluded is most often
then used, even if only implicit, as an argument for reconstructing a
plane of visibility based on thematics of inclusion and recognition by
mechanisms of governance. In this way she argues a strategy of exodus and refusal, one acknowledging and working from within a respect for autonomy and self-organization,[12] instead is transformed
into a form of politics of juridical recognition and mediation through
visibility. From that she poses the following:

> Transformed into organizational questions: how feasible is it
> to use precarity as a means for alliances or coalition building
> without effacing the differences between Mimi and the
> Philosopher, or indeed reproducing the hierarchy between
> them? Is it in the best interests for the maquiladora worker to
> ally herself with the fashion designer? Such questions cannot
> be answered abstractly. But there are two, perhaps difficult
> and irresolvable questions that might be still be posed (2005:
> 91).

What Mitropolous gestures to here is the way the precarity as a
focus has a danger of translating the core themes of workerist into
categories of mediation, thus reintroducing the problematics of state
thought and governance into the discourse. It is to that problem we
will now turn.

Governance, Stepping Aside, and State Thought

The proletarian subject lacks nothing, certainly not more organization. It is always adequate to its situation... Organization of the proletariat by capital against capital is immediate
because it is also latent, it is of the class, by the class, for the
class – this is the nature of assigned subjectivity. Any further
organizational structure introduces less not more ambivalence,
more and not less ideological mystification. In the real world,
there can be no conscious proposal for an organizational structure that is not also a proposal for either a non-class based
leadership and/or a mystification of the proletariat's true ca-
pacities/position in the social relation. – Frere Dupont (2007)

The problem is that by and large this has not been worked
through well enough within discussion around precarity. Rather the
discussion is usually framed by, whether explicitly or implicitly, a

narrative of precarity as a structural condition (and one that is generally understood to have emerged relatively recently) that can be
countered by developing new means of social support, flexicurity, or
a basic income. The latter is often spoken of in tones taking on an almost reverential or messianistic character, as though the coming of
basic income will save us all from the ravages and demons of capitalism. Praise be! That is not to ignore more nuanced versions of an argument for a basic income, particularly ones based on an
understanding of it as a recompositional pole, and also taking into account the varying national trajectories and political milieus where
such demands are compositionally different within them. But given
that related measures were contemplated by noted radicals as Richard
Nixon and Daniel Patrick Moynihan (1973), it is curious that they
keep resurfacing within a political context still laying claim to some
form of radicalism. Now we are all Nixonians?

More fundamentally, and more problematically, is the role this
discourse plays in creating a conceptual space of stepping aside, a moment or space that appears to rise above the process of direct and concrete struggles. This operates through arguments of a common
situation of precarity that is countered by measures to remediate that
state. The forms of remediation do not seem to necessarily have to
connect to the particularities of the situations and struggles which
have been effaced in the transcendent structural condition. Thus they
no longer flow from the real movement that struggles to abolish the
state of things, to use a worn but still lovely phrase, but rather from
an almost state-like function of thought that has preserved itself
within the radical imaginary, cleverly hiding its nature. In this moment
of stepping aside an uncritical focus on precarity carries within itself
a state function, a mechanism of governance that operates by eluci-
dating from populations their grievances, conditions, and concerns in
ways that they may be more effectively governed through this enunciation. The problem is not necessarily that there is a form of governance or a strain of thought that has some state-like characteristics
(unless one is being a purist about such matters). Rather, the problem
is that because the potential governance function of a discourse on
precarity operates as one but appears to do otherwise, it operates on
a level where the power effects it animates cannot be apprehended by
those who are involved in it. The dispersal of the state is only possible
through an understanding of the forms of labor and the functions contained within them, the imaginaries, collectivities, and sociability embedded within the state even if not reducible to it (Harney 2002).
Otherwise, the dispersal of the state could very well just mean the rise
of governance as state function, less visible but all the more effective.

In terms of political recomposition, this would mean that there very well could be a pattern where the appearance of increasing movement mobilization and building of cycles of struggle could paradoxically be accompanied by an internal decomposition of this movement itself through functioning of unrecognized state thought and mechanisms of governance within it.

And this is the question that ultimately determines whether a focus such as precarity is useful: can it be used to contribute to constituting a common ground of the political that does not recreate conditions where certain groups assumptions are hoisted upon others or where the implicit social democratic assumptions work their ways unseen into radical politics? The idea is not to import a discussion around precarious labor and radical politics from Italy, France, or Spain, in the hopes that such ideas and practices could just be translated and reused unproblematically. It is not just a question of literal translation of the words, but a translation that finds resonance with a particular cultural, social, and political context. Rather, the task is to learn from the way that discussions around precarity have been developed to ferment political antagonisms and everyday insurgency in a particular context, and to see how a process like that can occur elsewhere, drawing from particularities of the location. As Brett Neilson and Ned Rossiter point out, "the opposite of precarity is not regular work, stable housing, and so on. Rather, such material security is another version of precarity, consuming time, energy, and affective relations as well as producing the anxiety that results from the financialization of daily life" (2005). Rather than reclaiming life for work it a question of reclaiming a freedom of life from work, by being determined only by one's capacity as a form of labor, and the re-invention of value as the importance of sociality and interaction one is already engaged in that is not reducible to an economic calculus (Graeber 2001).

It is on these grounds that self-reproducing movements – or movements which take into account the conditions of their social reproduction, to use Silvia Federici's phrasing – are fostered (2008). It was this approach to movement building and composition, an aeffective one, that requires continual fostering and development. Indeed, the grounds of politics themselves are precarious, composed of an uncertain and constantly shifting terrain. Also, it is vitally important to not forget that precarity was once a beautiful concept, one that indicated a space of freedom and time for life. The translation and contextual reworking needed not only involves, as Klaus Neundlinger wisely points out (2004), not only countering the effects of neoliberal deregulation, but also turning around the concept of precarity itself, to find

ways to reclaim and learn from the compositional potential is possessed. Their precarity as a condition of uncertainty is not just a hindrance (although it is some ways), but also a potentiality, an openness
based on the fact that it is not fixed. Whether a concept such as precarity is useful for recomposing the grounds and basis for a radical
politics is not something determined by the concept itself, but rather
how those who use it employ it. It is this recompositional politics,
turning what has been recuperated from insurgencies and movements
back into useful tools, practices, and energies for social movement
and autonomous politics, that we turn to in the next chapter.

Notes

1. For more on precarity and organizing around it in general see the special issues on it: *Mute* (www.metamute.org/en/Precarious-Reader), Republicart.net
   (www.republicart.net/disc/precariat/index.htm), *Fibreculture* (journal.fibrecul-
   ture.org/issue5/index.html). See also the blog Precarious Understanding
   (precariousunderstanding.blogsome.com) and that of Angela Mitropoulos
   (archive.blogsome.com).
2. For a good history of Italy that deals not just with this period but also the
   "Years of Lead," see Ginsborg (2003).
3. Some examples of previous use of precarity can be found in the work of
   Leonce Crenier, Dorothy Day (2006 [1952]), Sergio Bologna (1980), Federici and Fortunati (1981), and Bourdieu (2003), who referred to the current
   generation as a "precarious generation."
4. One could find similar inspiration in the organizing of the Independent Union
   of All Workers, an IWW inspired militant union that existed from 1933-1937,
   and focused on organizing all people in a town rather than specific workplaces. The aim was to achieve 100% unionization, a goal that according to
   Peter Rachleff (1996; 2008) was reached or almost reached in some locations.
   The little that is known about the history of the IUAW still leaves some lingering questions, such as how conflicts between different workplaces and
   their varying interests would be reconciled. Also, given the claims of the density and intensity of their organizing, their quick dissolution after some
   branches affiliated within the CIO seems rather unusual. One can find more
   contemporary organizing along similar lines in the work of the Vermont
   Workers Center who also organize on a town-wide rather than craft or union
   basis (www.workerscenter.org).
5. For more on this see www.serpicanaro.com.
6. For more on EuroMayDay: www.euromarches.org
7. Some of these examples are discussed in the chapter on minor composition.
   For more information see Goldner (2006), Caffentzis (2006), as well as
   www.ciw-online.org and www.supersizemypay.com.
8. Among the more noteworthy supporters and advocates of a basic income are
   Martin Luther King, James Tobin, John Kenneth Gailbrath, and Andre
   Gorz. One can also trace connections to the idea of the social wage and similar
   practices within guild socialism, anarcho-syndicalism, and cooperativist
   movements. For more on basic income, see Raventós (2007) and www.ba-

sicincome.org.

9. And, as Guillaume Paoli points out, just as the transformation of gold coins into electronic funds did not completely transform the nature of money, the dematerialization of labor does not mean the end of its compulsive and coercive character nor the bodily exertion involved in it (2004). For more on the relation between gender, precarity, politics, and the debates around their conjunction, see the *Feminist Review* special on contemporary Italian feminisms, in particular Fantone (2007).

10. For an interesting analysis of the 2005 riots see Emillio Quadrelli's essay "Grassroots Political Militant: Banlieusards and Politics," which explores the ways that the riots were not racial or religious in character but primarily directed against capital, the state, and institutions of domination. This is a useful counter to the typical argument that such riots are meaningless and purposeless nihilism, or alternately the cry of those who are seeking some form of representation within the space of liberal politics. Quadrelli explores the riots as being organized through an infrastructure of collective intelligence that while perhaps not readily visible exists. The riots for Quadrelli can be understood as form of endocolonial conflict and guerilla warfare. Quadrelli's essay and a critical response to it were published by Mute Magazine in the collection Scum of the Republic (2007). For an insurrectionist analysis of the same events, see Argenti (2007).

11. Hydrarchist comments on this tendency within movements in Italy: "Social movements in Italy function best when external factors oblige cooperation and marginalize intra-movement rivalry, yet an inability to coldly appraise the efficiency of discarded strategies threatens to nullify the benefits of experience. The Gordian knots of representation, relations with the institutions, and internal and network democracy are not going away. With a centre-left government on the horizon, and the fertile ground for reactionary demagogy that promises, the challenge will be to maintain abrasive contestation, autonomous from the party system, without being relegated to the margins, where the only dividend is unceasing police attention" (2005: 38).

12. For Mitropolous' analysis of these issues, exploring the relation between the autonomy of migration and workerist thought, see her essay "Autonomy, Recognition, Movement" (2007). This thematic informs her work on technology, borders and migration more generally and raises a number of important considerations that could use to be taken to heart and considered by autonomist movements. For a take on invisibility and labor that does not fall into this sort of trap, one finds a number of interesting ideas explored in Sergio Bologna's writing on self-employment and the forms of organization it takes (2007).

:: X :: Dance, Dance Recomposition ::

What we need to think about – and discuss widely through the libertarian left – is the *political content* of an activity that *consciously* seeks both to avoid recuperation and to be relevant to the conditions of today. An ongoing reassessment of the degree to which one's former goals have been recuperated is the most effective antidote to the malaise on the left, and the only possible prescription for remaining a revolutionary. – Maurice Brinton, November 1974 (2004: 168)

As much energy needs to be put into combating recuperation as into avoiding repression – Anonymous, September 2005 (2005: 180)

Recuperation as a concept and/or process is deployed with great frequency within various communities centered around radical politics, arts, and the diffuse world of 'social resistance.' Strangely, and despite that (or perhaps because of it), there is usually little to no discussion of what this word actually means. It is constantly employed as if its meaning were already clearly known and understood by all involved in whatever the discussion may be; in other words, the standard mode of operation is to fall back on an implicitly understood meaning developed within the general circuits and collective intelligence of the forces of social resistance. Much the same could be said for related and overlapping conceptual terrains such as 'co-optation' and other ways to describe the process through which a formerly radical form of social interaction becomes integrated into 'the system's' logic, turned against its former vitality, and so on and so forth.

This is not to discount the value of the knowledges and concepts developed, even in sometimes fuzzy ways, through diffuse and disparate discussions and debates where more often than not there is no neatly packaged product that comes out of the other end of the theoretical sausage factory. Perhaps one of the greatest developments in that diffuse area known as 'autonomist' thought, particularly that of Italian *operaismo*, was precisely to cast the whole of capitalism as necessarily existing and gaining its continued solely from its ability to exist as a system of recuperation drawing from the vitality of working class resistance (and to emphasize this resistance as the determining factor of capitalist development). Or, as Jacques Camatte phrases it, "capital is a form that always inflates itself on an alien content (recuperation)" (1995: 154). Or further yet, the way in which Silvia Federici (2004) shows that the rise of capitalism itself is a response to the power of movements organizing to overthrow feudalism. Social movements perhaps gain a greater degree of flexibility in their actions and responses precisely because of the ability to deploy, break down, and reform conceptual and political frameworks with greater ease than if such had been painstakingly built upon over time in the hopes of creating *the* framework that would establish definitely the workings of whatever apparatus of power was being contested and the sure means to dispatch it.

As one can see from the two quotes that appear at the top of the chapter, united in their concern for putting a greater focus on processes of recuperation while divided by over thirty years in when they were written, recuperation is often recognized as a pressing threat for radical movements. The concept of recuperation has likewise haunted this text, always lurking in the background as something that needs to be dealt with, looming like a specter over the moors of the radical imagination. For instance, during the period of organizing that the second quote describes (the anti-G8 mobilizations taking place in Scotland in 2005), organizers were confronted not only with the obvious threat of the deployment of a small army of riot cops, but also the mediated offensive of Bono and Live Aid telling people to welcome the G8 so that they can 'solve' the problem of poverty. While the riot cops posed the most direct threat to be dealt with, in terms of movement building perhaps it is the second which is more menacing precisely because it created situations where people concerned about the ravages of neoliberalism found their concerns for dealing with such being supposedly addressed (although not really much at all) by the same people who had inflicted these harms! Meanwhile, organizers from *Dissent!* and other anticapitalist networks found themselves marginalized by this 'reasonable' expression of concern. It was the advent of what George Caffentzis refers to as neoliberalism's "Plan B," or how people such as Jeffrey Sachs (also personally responsible for engineering a great deal of poverty) hedged their bets on saving capitalism in the long term by the use of non-commoditized social relations (health care and social service provisions, the same things they had argued needed to be rolled back in the first place) in the short term (2005). The Plan 9 of originary accumulation and the zombification of struggle slides effortlessly into the Plan B of recuperation, just as formal and real subsumption crisscross and striate each other over the social field in shifting patterns.

The problem with the concept of recuperation is that because it is used in such undefined, flexible, and varying ways, this almost comes to serve as excuse or explanation for many forms of difficulties within movements that are not necessarily a problem of recuperation as well as providing little in the way of developing theoretical or political tools for responding to such a process. To speak of recuperation then becomes a lament, a coda to sing when the magic of the insurgent moment has faded, a dirge to sing that gives the illusion of explaining the frustration of a movement that could not realize its goal... but used in this way it becomes an end of discussion, a final explanation, rather than a reopening. Recuperation becomes a confirmation of what Brinton describes as the "malaise of the left" rather than a scream against it, a pole of political recomposition that is most needed in the moments of decomposition that comprise processes of recuperation. So what I would like to at this juncture is to connect a number of the concerns discussed through the book thus far, is to explore in a more thorough way processes of recuperation and related concepts (co-optation, integration, etc), to bring it together with other ideas that could possibly add subtlety and nuance to it,[1] and then suggest some possible ways to think through responses to recuperation through the framework of invisibility.

Counterrevolutions of Everyday Life

People who talk about revolution and class struggle without referring explicitly to everyday life, without understanding what is subversive about love and what is positive in the refusal of constraints, such people have a corpse in their mouth.
– Raoul Vaneigem (1994: 68)

The basic notion of recuperation is, perhaps not so surprisingly, simple enough. The concept entered English in its current form through the work of the Situationist International, which used it to describe the way that radical and oppositional thought is made ineffectual, converted into a functioning part of the spectacle, and through such a process deprived of any radical vitality that it formerly possessed. Or in their phrasing, it is "the activity of society as it attempts to obtain possession of that which negates it" (1969). Recuperation was thus used as a tool to understand why so often movements, falling short of the goals they professed to be struggling towards, found themselves in a condition where the very substance of their demands was redeployed against them. As the Situationists themselves emphasized, the moment of recuperation and political decomposition are tied together, tied together to such a point that it becomes hard to distinguish the difference between them except through an analytic gaze (1966). The Situationists developed the notion of recuperation to try to understand why revolutionary movements rather than destroying the machinery of governance kept ending up perfecting it. Or, as continually intoned by Vaneigem and Debord, recalling the words of Saint Just, those who half-make revolutions dig their own graves.

Despite being most closely associated with the Situationists, perhaps the clearest and most useful definition of recuperation appears in Ariel Dorfman and Arman Mattelart's seminal text *How to Read Donald Duck: Imperialist Ideology in the Disney Comic*, which defines recuperation as "the utilization of a potentially dangerous phenomenon of the social body in such a way that serves to justify the continued need of the social system and its values, and very often justify the violence and repression which are part of that system" (2003: 56). This they argue is part of a process by which people are induced into the self-colonization of their own imaginations, or when recuperation as external phenomena becomes a process of self-regulating and internalized alienation, and thus the negation of revolutionary potentiality. In other words, not only do radical politics become turned against themselves, but people are induced into the initiation of this process themselves. It has been suggested that perhaps Dorfman and Mattelart might have been reading their Donald Duck comics a little bit too closely (somewhat like the people who manage to find Satanic messages when you play the Mr. Ed show backwards), but, nonetheless, this is a helpful starting point and definition of recuperation.

The Situationists were of course not the first group in the course of history to be stymied by this phenomenon. There are, however, particular reasons why this question and focus became much more pressing for them. These reasons, which were mirrored by similar conditions in Italy and elsewhere in Europe, was that of fairly massive and well organized left communist and socialist movements that found themselves unable to move forward with their agendas. And worse than that they often found themselves confronted by governments where right wing forces implemented many of their stated objectives (nationalization, increased access to healthcare and social resources and provisions) while at the same time the very forces that one would easily expect to be allies in the question for revolutionary transformation (the larger socialist and communist parties) were acting to prevent these very things from happening at best, to acting as the agents of introducing austerity measures and increased forms of discipline on the working class. The context that the Situationists found themselves in thus was not one where recuperation was a marginal and incidental phenomena, but rather an ongoing process that largely structured this context; therefore it is not surprising that their analysis would take this reality as a focus for their critique and strategizing.[2] Recuperation was also of great concern for the SI because of the tradition of radical politics they were working from, namely drawing from avant-garde currents such as Dada and Surrealism, which stressed the necessity of the negation of art due to the role such had played in the creation of nationalist and colonialist imaginaries and other objectionable fields of power.

And this, to a large degree, explains why the SI placed such a large emphasis on the everyday as the focus and locus and organizing (as opposed to grand moments of visibility and convergence). The SI's response to their concern with recuperation was that their ideas were slowly finding their ways into everyone's heads, but through the submerged infrapolitics and everyday resistance and networks of communication. It is this fluid and shifting space that Vaneigem describes as where there exists "an infra-language which the economy tries to recuperate," in line with its need to conquer those areas of life it still does not control, "for it is exactly around the black holes of language where declarations of power dance wildly" (n.d. 24). In other words, the Situationists developed a model of resistance based on submerged networks of invisible connections that would elude the constantly becoming-image of capitalist development and its ability to integrate forms of resistance to its image array.

Before proceeding, it is interesting to note that Ken Knabb, who has been one of the main (and earliest) translators of the writings of the Situationists, no longer thinks that the French word (*recuperation*) which he formerly translated as "recuperation" should be translated as such because it normally has a different sense in English (indicating a period of physical or mental recovery). Instead he suggests that it would more accurately and clearly rendered as "cooption."[3] The SI themselves commented that the two words only seem to be mean the same thing, but in fact do not (1969). While the case for finding precision, clarity, and accuracy in translation is often a quite good one way to make, in this case perhaps it is not (especially as the circulation and usage of the word, accurate or not, has taken on within itself meaning that has social validity regardless of the accuracy or not of the translation). The concept of recuperation, as it describes such an ambivalent of murky process, might actually be enhanced by how the multiple and contradictory connotations of the word mesh against each other. For instance, does not the recuperation of revolutionary ideas by capitalism and the state represent a period of recovery from the illness (the foreign bodies of insurgents and rebels) that have invaded it, threatened its existence, and attempted to repurpose its social wealth for other ends? Similarly, when workers took over their factories during the economic collapse in 2001, what exactly was recuperated? Who was recuperated? In one sense it is arguable that by providing means for the workers to sustain their livelihoods they had taken back by the machinery of production from the capitalist class; but at the same time by doing so, by taking on the role of collective capitalist, this enabled the recovery of the economy precisely because the increased investiture of social energies into the production process enabled their survival when otherwise it would have not been possible. This explains why the government reacted to such factory takeovers in a somewhat schizophrenic manner: they both acted as an attack of the relations of private property and acted as an engine of economic recovery. So who recuperated whom? Most likely a truthful answer would be that it went both ways.

There is always a risk of reducing the concept of recuperation to simple cog in the machinic formation of a knee-jerk mass society analysis. In other words, turning recuperation into an individualized notion of resisting forces of social integration. The concept is more subtle, broader, and more useful than that. Indeed, individualist desires and allegedly anti-conformist notion are perhaps the greatest force of marketing flows and forces that exist within the post-industrial, low run customized commodity west. This is the argument that Hal Niedzviecki makes: that individuality has become the 'new conformity,' and forms of rebellion, rather than working towards anything operating against the system rather function as means to gain access to it (2006). But to reduce the notion of recuperation to the individualistic politics of consumer behavior and preferences is to precisely miss the point, for it is a notion rooted in collective class politics. This is the very reason why the SI comments that recuperation might seem to be the same thing for how the word 'cooption' is used in the left, but precisely the reason why they do not think so. The SI is not interested in individualist strategies of resistance any more than they are interested in forms of politics that they associate with such. To render recuperation as co-option is to make in a meaningless concept that easily fits into a defeatist narrative, because any particular individual cannot by him or herself resist co-optation any more than to raise the subversiveness of struggle on an individual level. This is to take a concept that describes processes of collective transformation and struggle and to reterritorialize them on a different register where they lose their importance in contributing to the collective creativity of resistance.

This is the very aspect of the concept that Joseph Heath and Andrew Potter miss in such a vulgar way in their recent book *The Rebel Sell* (2005). Why they do some very good and important work at emphasizing the ways in which countercultural politics have operated in sometimes silly, ineffective, and absurd ways, their position of critique is rather disingenuous. While the book is written as if it's coming from a sympathetic position, critiquing the excesses of counterculture in order to build up a more coherent leftist politics (for instance they seem quite shocked to find out that consumerist individualism is a motor of economic exchange, or must be given the number of time such is repeated as if it's a revelation from god), when it comes down to spelling out their own politics to the end, the mask comes off. First there are appearances of notions like the usefulness of carbon trading schemes and so forth, until eventually it comes clear that the problem they have with most currents of radical counterculture is its opposition to capitalism and the state, which they would both rather keep, in a nice, tidy, more liberal version. This explains why Heath and Potter reject the notion of cooption (not seeing any difference between cooption and recuperation), arguing that acts of counterculture rebellion from the beginning *are already capitalism*, and therefore the idea that they become coopted by such makes no sense. The problem is that if you start from the assumption that all there is or could be is capitalism, then it's hardly very surprising when all you find is more and more capitalism. What else could there possibly be? It would be easier for Spinoza to find a miracle. But enough of these fools.

One of the better more recent attempts exploring dynamics of recuperation is found in the work of Boltanski and Chiapello (2005), even thought they do not use the word itself. Their massive tome sets out in great detail what has long been apparent, that the energies of social resistance and movements provide new fodder and energy for the continued renewal and development of capitalism. As Boltanski and Chiapello show in great detail, this is especially the case for strands of thought emerging out of what might roughly be described as '68 thought. And this is not just the case is more obvious ways (the emphasis on the 'humanization of the workplace,' team working, flexibility, and creativity that started to really emerge as a component of management thought starting in the 1970s), but also in terms of broader political drifts. For instance, one could understand that in part of the Reagan-Thatcher neoliberal turn of the early '80s was at least part in based on rendering the individualistically oriented libertarian streams of post-68 politics in a rightward direction. What Boltanski and Chiapello tend to miss (or at least not emphasize very much) in their work is the way that these recuperative dynamics are not exceptional or that surprising, but rather are embedded deeply within the heart of capitalist dynamics. However, they do point out quite perceptively that the new spirits of capitalism developed both legitimate and constrain the process of accumulation. The book seems written as if the authors had not realized before that such a process was possible, and unfortunately is often used in discussion as a sort of cudgel against anyone who seems to genuinely believe in the possibility of a radical politics that can affect anything. While their overall scope and politics may not add particularly much that is new in some aspects, they do come up with some highly interesting and relevant points about processes of decomposition and recuperation.

Perhaps their most useful observation, which unfortunately does not occur until some 400 pages into the book, is on the difference between collective and individual liberation in processes of recuperation. Boltanski and Chiapello define collective liberation as the liberation of a people (or other form of collective subject) and their deliverance from oppression, as opposed to forms of liberation based around the individual. While it is unfortunate that this is tied in to some degree with their distinction between artistic and social critique (which doesn't hold up very well and seems more a hindrance to understanding than a help), it does add an important nuance to understanding recuperation. Boltanski and Chiapello argue that both forms of liberation are not as available or possible in equal measure at given moments. That, however, is not to say that there always exists tensions between individuals and collectives, although one could make that case. Rather, it is the uneven geography of liberation and its territorializations of individual and collective liberation that acts as a strategic focus for capital, which has a "a tendency to take back on one level what it offers on another" (2005: 435). This process operates through an individuation of collective energies, for turning energies of collective liberation into those of individual liberation, thus rendering them more manageable within a capitalist framework (think for instance of programs based around striving for self-fulfillment and what not). This is very much the process that underlies the transformation previously mentioned of left libertarian sentiments to individualistic impulses by neoliberal ideology. It is interesting to observe how the Free Association attempt to implement this process the other way, asking what sort of collective energies must have been individuated so that they now underlie the various self-help industries (2006).

The SI worked within a heavily Hegelian-Lukacsian subgenre of Marxist thought that still relied heavily on a base-superstructure framework. For them, culture was essentially a reflection of the base, an epiphenomenon. The spectacle, perhaps the concept they are most closely associated with, which is developed mainly within the writing and theorization of Guy Debord, is not then a qualitatively new condition in any sort of epoch making way. Rather, it is a condition where the conditions of capital accumulation as such have reached such intensity that they have become image. The spectacle thus is not a thing, an image, or something that can be reduced to things or images, but rather how capital as a social relation becomes increasingly mediated by images, images that have been produced by the becoming-image of capital as social relationship. How could one possibly fight a class battle on superstructural terms? It seems like a silly idea, and thinking of it within the terms the SI set out, it is one. When one introduces notions of cultural and immaterial labor this would vastly change the terms of engagement. The problem for thinking about arts and culture in the conceptual framework that the SI sets out for basing its radicalism is it creates no space for the very kind of radical politics that the SI practiced. There is no reason to think that the sort of agency that the SI wants to make reference to and work with, this radical subjectivity that it speaks of, according to the analysis it develops, can even exist. It makes no sense. The spectacle flattens out the labor of self-organization and composition.

This explains that animosity that the SI develops to forms of interventions that can be thought of as a strictly cultural politics, or existing as art. For the SI phenomena falling into this realm are attempts to change the structural social base by superstructural means, which are useless at best, and more than likely just another rejuvenation of the symbolic world of the bourgeois as it reincorporates new ideas, tastes, and cultural interactions into its own workings. This also explains the break and split within the SI during the early 1960s, as the faction that wants to be more explicitly political and reject all forms of art and cultural activism as such on these grounds expels the section that still finds (or admits to publicly) some use in cultural activism. It is here that one sees the emergence of what Stewart Home describes as the 'spectro-situationist' international (the section rejected forms of cultural and artistic organizing as distraction, thus opting for a position based upon the analysis of the formation of spectacular society, most closely associated with Debord). Cultural activism reintroduces into the sphere of political action the very form of separation that the

SI is attempting to reject. Specialists in cultural production, the SI argue, most easily resign themselves to their position of separation and the deficiency that accompanies it (1960); as such it is not possible to build a radical politics because it would continually reintroduce a lack which can only be remedied by exterior intervention, or the form of vanguardism the SI continually tries to rid itself of, although never quite succeeding.

The SI sees the introduction of specified roles, or the existence of something separate called the cultural sphere, to be just one more introduction of a Leninist scheme based on the lack of the proletarian revolutionary subject adequate the demands of the situation at hand. For the SI, it is this reality of separation, of the workers from the means of their own social reproduction, which is the greatest problem precisely because this separation is continued by the forced internalization that social existence is not possible without a reliance on capital. It is a separation premised upon reinforcing the idea that there is a lack in the collective subjective capacities of the working class as subject which can only be remedied by a continued reliance as capitalist social relations as making up for this lack, or for the intermediary role of the vanguard party (which the SI sees as nothing more than a mediating mechanism for a new renewal of accumulation under a different guise).

The SI's approach to such questions might indeed have been quite different if they had not conceived of culture and arts within a base / superstructure model. For once you start considering forms of artistic and cultural production as labor, as taking part in what in the base / superstructural model would have to be classed as industrialized cultural production, this throws off the scheme that locks the SI into a certain consideration of arts and culture and the capacities for revolt found within these spheres. Similarly, the moment one introduces the notion that there is a constant reciprocal pattern of interaction between superstructure and base (rather than a mere reflection of one which creates the other), this reopens the very questions the SI has thought it has closed with its totalizing, final and complete critique. While there is no need, purpose, or much gained, for castigating the SI for buying into a relatively staid model of economics and culture, there is still much to be gained from learning from their insights while critiquing parts of their analysis, particularly those which limited the scope available for political intervention and action and tended to paint them into a corner from which no escape seemed possible. Indeed this is perhaps the most important point of such an analysis, because to the degree that large sections of radical movements have worked with ideas coming from the SI (and this is quite the case; the

SI's influence is felt all through contemporary radical politics and the arts, even if paradoxically it finds much less credence given to it within the world of political theory proper), they have also inherited these limitations.

Take for instance the recent attempts of the Retort Collective to work from a politics of spectacle in their analysis of the current age. Their analysis of the relation between different modes of the spectacle, regimes of accumulation, and violence is quite useful. In their wording, when a particular mode of the spectacle enters crisis, the violence of capitalist valorization comes into view, the violence usually hidden by the spectacle: "when a spectacle agonizes, the guns appear at every edge of the image array" (2005: 131). Based on this they attempt to elaborate a notion of the spectacle that is not determined, which is kind of absurd because the spectacle as concept is a determinate formation of capital at a certain stage of accumulative intensity, regardless of whether it has different modes or regimes. To render it otherwise simply turns it into another concept, which might be useful, but wouldn't be the same thing. This the main fault of the SI's analysis, even though it is allegedly founded on a notion of the working class revolutionary subject that lacks nothing, the only actor within its analysis is capital, which is always self-valorizing, which leads to the formation of this thing called the spectacle. The SI falls victim to its own analysis. Futhermore, as Christopher Grey emphasizes in his discussion of the SI (1996), the exclusive focus on developing a complete and total intellectual critique (as if the development of the correct critique would automatically lead on to correct revolutionary action), a magic formula almost, led to their ignoring the emotions and the body.

Raoul Vaneigem makes that intriguing argument that "terrorism is the recuperation of sabotage, its ideology and its separated image" (n.d.: 70). While this at face value may seem to be quite an odd statement, it makes a great deal more sense in the context of the 1970s when forms of social insurgency and movements that had been brewing and simmering from below found themselves confronted by new forms of state power, repression, and controls unleashed to combat groups such as the Red Brigades and Beider-Meinhof, as well as the Weather Underground, the Black Liberation Army, and related factions. While more often than not such factions emerged from the growing frustration with the apparent ineffectiveness and lack of progress of the public and visible movements, and thus argued for an expansion and increase of force coupled with an increasing turn to clandestinity, this also served to separate such factions from the large movements from which they emerged, and usually maintained some sort of connection and alliance with, even if it was usually marked by an ambivalence going in several directions at once. The emergence of terrorism in such a fashion, despite some admitted successes it may have achieved at first (and the support received from various movements, a fact which it is generally forgotten), was all the more problematic not just in the ethical, tactical, and strategic questions around it, but also in the way it reintroduces a logic of passivity and separation back into the structure of organizing: there are those who act towards revolution and those who can at best provide support and infrastructure for them, or at worst act as spectators and bystanders. The point Vaneigem makes here is that recuperation is not only something that occurs as an external structure of power integrates radical politics into itself, but also the ways in which political organizing can introduce elements of separation and alienation into the process of its own self-constitution.

There is a line to be drawn, albeit one that is always thin and in constant motion, between knowing a particular tactic, strategy or campaign has exhausted its effectiveness and potentiality, and lapsing into defeatism and despair. As Sadie Plant wisely emphasizes, making an argument that much can be learned from: "anything which is totally invulnerable to recuperation cannot be used in contestation either" (1992: 180). The subversive potentiality of any particular social field or area is only based on the reality that there is something contained within it that is worth fighting for. It is important to emphasize that recuperation is not a process that occurs because of the malevolent designs and conspiracies of malignant aliens and shrouded cabals who lack ideas of their own. Rather, counterrevolutions take up, absorb, and integrate the concerns of revolutionary movements precisely because, to borrow the argument of Jean Barrot, "revolutionary ideas deal with *real* problems with which the counterrevolution is confronted" (1996: 47). There is a degree of absurdity in criticizing counterrevolutionary currents for addressing the very concerns raised by revolutionary ferment precisely because these concerns could only become part of an emerging revolutionary composition precisely because of the contested space they occupy in the social field.

In other words, and to put it quite bluntly, there's no use fighting over a question or arrangements that is of no great importance to anyone; reactionary forces find themselves bound to address such concerns for the very same reason they acted as point of contestation in the first place, namely that they were of concern to people's livelihoods, existence, being, etc... To make this argument does not mean that there is no room for struggling over the particularities of engagement, particularly as this is the very space where there is continued possibility of political recomposition. Rather, the point is that there is no reason to be surprised that the very issues that form the substance of revolutionary struggle are of the same flesh that composes the body of reactionary thought. It would be more mysterious, and perhaps even miraculous, if this was not the case. As Barrot notes, today all concepts are perverted (or perhaps they always have been); "the subversive moment will only reappropriate them by its own practical and theoretical development" (1996: 47).

This is the peculiar position that focusing on recuperation leaves one in. On one hand if all efforts of social resistance that are completely and totally revolutionary (whatever that may mean) are fated to dig their own graves, to be turned against themselves, and this moment of revolt must be both global and complete, it seems rather absurd, almost impossible that such could even happen. The slide from the political analysis created from a perspective of recuperation into a position of defeatist cynicism is not so far at all. Perhaps the surprising thing isn't Baudrillard's shift into a clever defeatism, but that there weren't more who went with that very direction (although there indeed were many who did). But let us take a second to consider that while it is easy (and sometimes enjoyable) to theoretically beat up on Baudrillard, it is more useful to consider him as a limit case, as the void to stare into which one always risks falling. After all, Baudrillard does not come to such a position from the right, but rather starts from quite a similar position to the Situationists, coming out of an ultra-left tradition with connections to various avant-garde arts groups. His early books, in particular *The System of Objects*, is actually quite close to the analysis put forward by Debord, Vaneigem, the rest of the SI, as well as their commonly ambivalent intellectual progenitor, Henri Lefebvre. The question is how does get there (clever defeatism) from here?

One could perhaps say, to put it crudely, that he's simply missed the joke, or missed the difference between rhetoric and analysis. In other words, gone from the argument that everything is being colonized by the workings of the spectacle, all forms of resistance recuperated and turned against themselves with no hope, *as a means of fomenting a rebellion against this*, versus seeing this as an analysis, as accomplished. But the way that he gets here is quite intriguing. Baudrillard argues that a strategy of intelligent subversion would not be to confront power directly but rather to "force it into occupying this obscene position of absolute obviousness" where "it no longer exists except to violate its own secret" (1990: 79). And this seems fairly sensible, and could be described as being quite close to the spirit that has informed direct action based radical politics for at least the past forty years. It is this idea which Baudrillard says informed the revolts of May '68, but is also paradoxically where for him things end for the possibility of radical politics. Baudrillard argues that by forcing a system of power into generating the image of a greater power to contain the revolt than it actually possessed (by "by obliging power to add repression to the obscenity of repression" (1990: 80) is the phrase he uses to describe such), this puts into motion a new apparatus of power that is founded precisely on simulation. And for Baudrillard once this is started there is no way of stopping it. Strangely, the idea that simulation has a moment of origin quickly disappears from his later work, but he does once identify it. And it is this moment of identification, and more importantly as its erasure, where a theoretical slip occurs, a movement from seeing the determining potentiality as being located in forces of social resistance which lack nothing in their ability to valorize themselves, to a scheme based solely on the power of capital to self-valorize through the power of image and simulation. Once that move is made not even Neo can save him from that condition.

A recent interesting reworking and expansion of the concept of recuperation can be found in the writing of Andrew Robinson (2007), who defines a recuperated project as one that has lost its transformative intentionality. This does not mean that it is easy to differentiate clearly between a recuperated project and one that is not precisely because that would require marking the difference between the stated purpose of the project, campaign, or organization (which is generally fairly obvious), and the "unconscious conversion of means into ends and tools into goals," which needs to be apprehended indirectly. He suggests that such unconscious intentionalities can be deduced from the social relations individuals establish in relation to the project in question. And from this deduction it becomes possible to more make nuanced diagnoses about recuperation. For instance, in cases where an activity is valued in and of itself, Robinson argues that this is most likely an activity which has been recuperated in his sense of the term, a situation more than likely leading to a tendency to convert horizontal relations into vertical ones and to maintain control over the project regardless of its political usefulness or effects. In other words at the moment of institutionalization as recuperation, the orderliness, integrity, and continuity of the organization in question is given a value over the impulses and politics that led to its formation in the first place. This is a dynamic which is not the sole province of recognized forms of institutionalization (i.e., those complete with marquees, corporate slogans, letterhead recognized charters and bylaws, etc) but can also occur through the formalization of relations within radical milieus, even those constituted through the format of allegedly fluid networks and connections. Yes, the much ballyhooed network, despite the often creative and adaptive flexibility it does often possess, is also capable of a social form of ossifying institutionalization perhaps all the more damaging for how easy it is not recognized because of its networked form.

I am not certain that I am totally willing to totally buy into this analysis. For instance, how is one to know that one has correctly ascertained the kinds of relations held to a project? If not, this would not solve the problem of being able to discern a project's recuperation as much as to restate the question on a different register. But despite possible difficulties, Robinson's approach and restatement of the concept reopens it in quite a productive fashion. From it he explores the ways in which the Zapatistas manage to avoid dynamics of recuperation by maintaining a degree of exteriority even when entering a process of dialogue with civil society; by coming from the outside, a sense of otherness that does not prevent dialogue but rather is the precondition for it. Similarly he fruitfully explores tactics for resisting and avoiding dynamics of recuperation, making the case that the point is to stay focused not confusing the means of political organizing with the ends of organizing. This is especially the case where there is a stress on pre-figurative politics, which is not to say there isn't something quite valuable on such tact, but a lot of democratic process is still a means to radical politics, not the politics itself. Thus keeping one's focus on both the conscious and unconscious drives functioning in a project, or its manifest and latent functions, Robinson argues "one can minimize the dangers posed by recuperation and gain the strategic space for effective emancipatory practice." That might not be the end all and be all of thinking through the question, but it's certainly a good position to build from. New imaginal machines do not fall from the sky like pennies from heaven but more often than not are built from reconfiguring the compositions of existing collective imaginaries that have become ossified, or finding ways to reclaim the subversive traces still embedded within the energies of imaginaries that have been turned to other uses. It is where, as Guattari might say (1995), the molecular revolution, composing forms of autonomy and self-organization in everyday life, begins...

Autonomy is not closure but, rather, opening: ontologoical opening, the possibility of going beyond the informational, cognitive, and organizational closure characteristic of self-constituting, but *heteronomous* beings. It is ontological opening, since to go beyond this closure signifies altering the already existing cognitive and organizational 'system,' *therefore* constituting one's world and one's self according to *other* laws, *there-fore* creating a new ontological *eidos*, another self in another world. – Cornelius Castoriadis (1997a: 310)

Notes

1. It would be interesting to think through the relation between recuperation and cultural appropriation, which often basically means the theft and exploitation of ethnic culture, however, this is outside the current context. In particular this would be interesting to explore as often times cultural appropriation gets used in a way that seems to leave little room for conceptualizing cultural exchange and osmosis that does not have some sort of ominous connotations associated with it.
2. For a fuller exploration of the relation between frustrated revolutionary movement and theoretical creativity see the introduction to *Constituent Imagination: Militant Investigations // Collective Theorization* (Shukaitis and Graeber 2007). Also, the recent issue of the *Journal of Aesthetics & Protest* on the theme of failure is quite useful in this regard (Antebi, Dickey, and Herbst: 2007).
3. See Situationist International (1962) "The Fifth SI Conference in Göteborg," note #2. Trans. Ken Knabb. Available at www.bopsecrets.org/SI/7.conf5.htm

:: ∞ Collapsing New Imaginaries ::

All that is visible must grow beyond itself, and extend into the realm of the invisible. – Dumont, *Tron* (1982)

The rhythm of in/visibility is cut time: phantasmic interruptions and fascinations. Stories are propelled by this formation of inhabitable temporal breaks; they are driven by the time they inhabit, violently reproducing, iconizing, improvisizing themselves. – Fred Moten (2003: 71)

One might then say, with good reason, that imaginal machines have life spans, or maybe 'use by' dates. It would be silly to think that an idea that is subversive within a particular social and cultural context will remain so inherently outside of that context, that it could be subversive forever. It very well have subversive potentiality within other times and places, but that is a question of its relations to the particularities of these other contexts rather than something magically inherent to the idea or practice. And this is important to emphasize when thinking about developing collective social architectures against recuperation, in that sometimes the best response to that might not be to try and create permanent structures of configurations, but rather a constantly shifting constellation of relations and affections continually collapsing and rebuilding itself: a machine that works by constantly breaking down and reforming itself, a collapsing new imaginary that is not one of defeat of but continual transformation and constituent power.

The question of finding ways to avoid recuperation is not a new one. Indeed, as already mentioned it is perhaps the question that most haunts this book, pervading all through out. That means that this is not the moment where the question is opened, for it has been coming constantly thus far, even if not taken on fully in and of itself. The question of recuperation might be the one that I've inherited, been blessed with, by particular historical circumstances and conjunctions. Namely arriving in the New York City area, and thus becoming more directly involved in political organizing, at a point where the vitality and energy of the anti-globalization movement was beginning to flag, to lose its creativity. This was easy to ignore, or to fail to be aware of at the time, mainly because it was easier (and made a good deal of sense) to attribute the difficulties faced by the movement to the drastically changed political environment that emerged in the fall of 2001. That is to say, to attribute the majority of difficulties faced by political organizers to the rightward turn of the country in general. While there is some degree of truth in this argument, it also made it possible to obscure and look over the reality that for the most part the innovations of summit protests and the other tactical mobilizations developed had become relatively predictable. Very likely, even without the changes of the political spectrum taking place there would have been somewhat of a flagging of energies as part of the movement's own internal arc, and it is important not to ascribe all such difficulties to external factors and conditions.

Having said that, that does not mean that now is the time, the juncture in the text, where the question of recuperation is finally addressed. It would be silly to say that "now" is that time because it is a question that is already open and has been through out the text. Perhaps it is even the central question that has animated the entire exposition, perhaps much in the way that Guattari argues for a permanent reformism of revolutionary organization on the grounds that it is "better to have ten consecutive failures or insignificant results than a besotted passivity before the mechanisms of retrieval" (1977: 85). To stop now and say, "now is the time for strategizing against recuperation" would be yet another instance of strategic thought as self-pacification rather than a tool for expanding capacities. It would be to cede the question of recomposing radical politics through and against recuperation as something that must occur on the terrain of politics in a separated and reified sphere, rather than as continually process and practice. So, what then are the ways that this question has already been addressed?

The first, and perhaps the most important, is to recognize recuperation as a secondary and reactive dynamic. That is both in the temporal sense (recuperation as a response to the creative power of social insurgency and occurs) and in a more fundamental sense. In other words, to affirm, as Deleuze and Foucault do (in agreement with Tronti) that resistance is the primary, which is to say determining dynamic, to which processes of recuperation are subordinate. It is the reversal of perspective, the key move of autonomist thought, which enables an entirely different reading and understanding of the history of capitalist development, as well as another relation and understanding of capitalism in terms of plotting its demise. This does mean that the idea is to find within every dynamic an exaltation of how it inherently reveals the power of forms of social resistance, and to continually proclaim them even if such is not the case, until the point of absurdity. Rather, it is to concur with the argument of Massimo De Angelis (2006), who observes that the restructuring and renewal of capitalism during the 1980s, does not mean that the claims of autonomist thought were falsified, rather they were temporally bounded. A cycle of composition, a wave of struggles, had been met by a longer period of de-composition. But that does not disprove the potentiality of waves of composition. The problematic then becomes not to find forms of labor, organization, and processes that can fulfill a messianistic role in magically 'solving' these dynamics (a role often attributed to the magical healing wonders of immaterial labor and all its glory), but rather to search for the non-messianistic presence of the multitude, which existed before the advent of capitalism, through it, and within the present. That is, to not wait for a moment of externality which will bring a radical politics into the present (one that could not have been found in the present already), but to work from and through the compositions existing. It could be asked, and somewhat reasonably, isn't this assumption of a working class subjectivity existing before and through capitalism, a subjectivity that maintains a high degree of autonomy, somewhat suspect? One might even suggest that is something of a mythology. And that might not be so far off. Rather it is, much in the same way that Jeffrey Goldfarb describes (2001) the conditions leading to the events of 1989 in eastern Europe, an assumption that one is already free (and a willingness to act on this assumption) that creates the pre-conditions for the realization of that freedom.

From there we encountered various examples and instances that each, in their own way, responded to the problematic of recuperation, from processes of minor recomposition created through clever dé-tournement to other ends, to the development of new symbols and representations of precarious positions and labor through the reappropriation of religious imagery. Pop culture, after all, as Luther Blissett once quipped, is indeed a pre-condition for communism. We explored forms organizing focusing on relationality and social relations themselves (as opposed to reified notions of organizing), and their importance, particularly for the constant renewal of the radical imagination. We also encountered various dead ends that are created within political organizing through various kinds of ossifying separation: whether of the separation of aesthetic from political content within the avant-garde, the separation of class movement from its own potential through a restricted notion of what constitutes value producing labor, or the difficulties faced by the assumption that an organizational form (such as self-management) guarantees in itself that one has gotten past the dynamic of recuperation. At times it might even seem that such dynamics and problems have no way out of them, but this is not the case. Thus, rather than now being the moment where it is time to think strategically about and through recuperation, it is rather another moment of recomposition. That is, to start from the processes and materials that have already been elaborated, and to simultaneously disarticulate the formation they have appeared in, and through that to tease out some other possibilities for articulation.

One way to approach this would be to return to the notion of infrapolitics developed by James Scott (1990) and Robin D.G. Kelley (2002). That is to say the politics of the elaboration of the hidden transcript of power, of the partially hidden public sphere, or some other formulation indicating a space that is somewhat encoded or otherwise made less comprehensible and legible to the view of those in power. But to return to this style of formulating a political space is not to repeat it, if this were even possible. Typically the reason leading to the formation of a hidden transcript or sphere is not really one that is chosen by those existing within it, within the undercommons. It is a form of politics (often times not even recognized as politics) by those in positions who need to communicate in such ways because it would be dangerous to do otherwise: slaves, peasants, the criminalized underclass, and so forth. It is a politics of necessity founded upon finding a way to have a voice under conditions of domination, but not necessarily a voice that makes itself known in the terms and conditions of polite company and rational public debate. But if these are not the conditions that are being addressed, why return to this form of politics? While there is surely some imaginative capacity to be gleamed from these politics of fugitivity, flight, and cloaking, the conditions being addressed here depart from them in significant ways. In other words, many people involved in various social movements may fancy themselves to be pirates, smugglers, and maroons, but for most part this more an imaginative identification than anything else.

Despite this, there is no reason to assume that because the conditions that typically lead to the formation of such infraspace (and infraorganization), that the lessons and principles are only applicable there. To assume this is to risk falling, yet again, into state thought: to assume that visible forms of politics are the only form of politics. It is to risk falling into the assumption because at a given moment there is little going on visibly in terms of radical politics and organizing that means that there is nothing going, that people are caught in the throes of false consciousness, or some other such position. Or, on the flipside, there is the danger of a kneejerk cultural politics of resistance approach, assuming the existence of all sorts of radical acts and forms of resistance like subversively watching a Madonna video and having disdain for it. This still leaves the problem of how a multitude of forms of minor refusals and revolts congeal into anything that goes beyond themselves and their moments (and if possible how such could happen without necessarily being organized by a master narrative or transcendent reference point legitimating such resistance). But the reason to return here is to see what such might offer in terms of thinking through, around, and despite recuperation.

What we can learn from returning to an infrapolitics in relation to questions of recuperation is that positions of visibility and invisibility are not ones that are eternal or universal by any means. It is rather a question of how and by whom one wants be understood, who and how to communicate with, and what that process entails. The dynamics of recuperation fit perfectly with Nietzsche's dictum that an artist would rather by misunderstood than totally understood, for being totally understood renders the space of potentiality and openness over. Exhausted. It does not make sense to respond to the dynamics of recuperation by thinking that it can be avoided, by suggesting, as Rolando Perez has, that "the only way to solve this problem is for the an(archist) to immediately destroy his or her own form of expression immediately, so as to make repetition and incorporation impossible." (1989: 57) Nor does it make much sense to strive for some sort of purely rational acts of communication. Rather, the dynamics of recuperation are questions of political recomposition, questions that require assessing the particularities of entanglements, but rather assessing the compositional effects, affects, and capacities of a particular situations. Recuperation and decomposition may close off certain forms of social action while inadvertently opening other ones. To take an example, the way that the introduction of the factory line and mass production reduced the power and scope of action for the professional worker (introducing great degrees of dehumanization at work), while at the same time through the coordination of the labor process opening avenues for other forms of industrial action such as checkerboard strikes. The visibility or invisibility of forms of social action are questions to be considered as part of the process of recomposition rather than an external factor. In other words, sometimes clandestine struggles do not necessarily have to aspire to become something else, but can remain so because it makes sense compositionally for them to do so.

It is interesting that Debord's later work, which more often than not is ignored in critical analysis, moves precisely in this direction. Both in the sense of exploring the ways which political power today is based upon the ability mechanisms of power to render themselves socially invisible, but also of what the changing relation of visibility and power could mean for the recomposition of social movement. His argument, which was rather prescient for its time (written in 1989) is that the diffuse (Western capitalist) and concentrated spectacles (Soviet state capitalism) have effectively merged, coalescing into an integrated spectacle of power flows and dynamics. Thus states are necessarily enmeshed within flows of power that they themselves cannot directly control, and in the sense it is no longer possible to strategically lead or direct individual states in the ways that it was previously. Conversely, now, the "more important something is, the more it is hidden." (n.d.: 4). In many ways this is quite close to the position that is more well known through the work of Hardt and Negri on the formation of Empire as an integrated global system of power operating through smooth space. One could also see it as being closely related to Huey P. Netwon's theorization (2002) of nation-states having dwindled in their importance, now having been replaced by "reactionary intercommunalism," or networks of power founded on the basis of control over various forms of technology and governance (which are not necessarily state forms of governance).

It was for these reasons that Debord argued for a radical politics based on what he called "necessary incomprehensibility," (n.d.: 7) by which he was indicating not a universal incomprehensibility and wanton nihilism (as fun as that might be), but rather considering the dynamics of who one wants to speak with and how. To not give too much away. Alice Becker-Ho's work has explored such dynamics through her research on Romani slang, argot, and the dynamics of communication within the criminalized underclass, although her work has not been given nearly the attention that it deserves (2000). The neglect of her work is quite regrettable in that it has much to offer in addressing these questions. Thankfully though there have been some growing interest in works, such as Roger Farr's recent essay on anarchist theories of communication and concealment, that draws heavily from Becker-Ho (2007).

This is in many ways not all that far from the position taken by the Situationists in the 1960s, at which point they argued it was more difficult than it would be otherwise for their ideas to be recuperated because they were not being transmitted through any particularly large or visible means of transmission, but rather were the ideas that were already in people's heads. By this they meant several things. Firstly, that many of the arguments and aim they were expressing (focus on pleasure, creativity, non-alienated interactions, and so forth) were not all that different from the forms of interactions and desires found amongst the majority of the population, even if they are more commonly expressed in terms of desire for more leisure, or for particular commodities. Secondly, since their ideas were being disseminated not by official institutions (whether unions, schools, major media, and so forth) but a repertoire of aesthetic interventions, productions, and the creation of situations, they were less open to dynamics of recuperation than they would be otherwise. This is perhaps less the case today where the field of communication and recuperation have learned all too well from this, leading to practices of corporate guerilla graffiti, viral marketing, and other ways that subversive communication has ceased to be subversive in itself and can just as easily be used for purposes of capitalist valorization. Regardless, the point remains the same, namely finding ways to construct what Patricia Pisters recently referred to as "machines of the invisible" (2008), or an "imperceptible politics," as Dimitris Papadopoulos, Niamh Stephenson, and Vassilis Tsianos (2008) suggest in their excellent exploration of the politics of escape routes and exodus. Or one might refine that further and say machines of the infravisible, tools of infra-structure.

Again, this is not something that one has to start from zero with, for this has been a dynamic facing movements and people theorizing social change for some time, even if not explicitly so. Working from spaces where, as Paul Virillio has explored, there are multiple forms of invisibility, disappearance, and their mutations that are always occurring within the framework of everyday life (1991), proved one has developed a sense of attention to the infraordinary. In other words, formed based on the realization that for various reasons (overexposure, recuperation, ossification, etc.) existing forms of social and political action already existing were not sufficient, or were lacking in some aspect, or had exhausted their creativity. Perhaps the clearest example of rethinking politics based on the negotiation of visibility is Hakim Bey's notion of immediatism, which tries to find a space for certain forms of collectivity affectively and intensely modulated, but not necessarily in an openly declared way. This is his response, or reconsideration, of what to do next after formulating the idea of temporary autonomous zones around a notion of a will to invisibility or disappearance in a more general sense. Where the TAZ might alternate between public declaration and disappearance and emergence in a subterranean sense, the immediatist project strives to further preserve itself through a more careful mediation of its visible public expression, namely by trying to avoid having one as much as possible. It is, to employ a strange comparison, somewhat like the moment after the media frenzy and spectacle of the Sex Pistols, the moment where John Lydon / Johnny Rotten and company form Public Image Limited (PiL), declaring in their first release single ("Public Image") a stated aim of having control over the forms of mediation and representation they will be enmeshed in. Of course simply declaring that one will have control over the means of one's public mediation does not mean that this will actually, or simply be the case, the intent is similar.

Some avenues for thinking about developing such a style of politics further can be found in places such as Nathan Martin's analysis (2003) of the Carbon Defense League's work as forms of "parasitic media" and "invisible subversion," forms that are more possible within larger and more complex systems where such deviations would be less likely to be detected. To use the resources of a cultural, artistic, or economic system without contributing to its stated purpose. This is, one might say, a cultural-artistic practice version of Godel's theorem; a system can never be total or complete, and therefore the more varied and complex such a system is, the more spaces and areas tend to avoid being totally accounted for. Forms of parasitic media and cultural subversion grow and thrive not by trying to change, at least at first, the overall the nature and purpose of the host, but in the usage of resources building towards a state where such a shift in tactics become sensible; Martin argues for these practices, "invisibility is our savior... The parasite can operate within the host to slowly create a cellular shift in its primary usage" (2003: 121). This requires knowing the margins of error and systems of tracking found within a given context as for use of resources of growth not to reach a level that would become noticeable. Examples of how this sort of practice has operated include employee theft from stores (included and tolerated until reaching a certain level), hobos riding the rails (and the communication forms and networks they develop them), and the culture jammers' reappropriation of advertising and design motifs.

Another conceptual avenue that has strangely been left somewhat unexplored in recent times is Alexander Trocchi's formulation of an "invisible insurrection of a million minds" (2006). Trocchi was part of the Situationist International, a part like many who found himself purged for being thought to be engaged in an overtly culturalist or questionable form of politics. Despite this, this formulation of his seems quite prescient. In essence his argument is that at the current juncture (written in the early 1960s, although the point remains largely accurate) that it will not be possible to directly confront and/or overthrow systems of state and capitalist power, the goal therefore should be one to moving towards outflanking them through continual renewal and mutation of strategies of intervention. This continual process of transformation and reformulation Trocchi refers to as "sigmatic culture," which is not something that can be planned or forseen per se, but emerges out of a sort of spontaneous university of dialogue and intervention. This is quite close to Joseph Beuys' notion of social sculpture, which likewise takes political-aesthetic practice very much in the direction of intervention, dialogue, relationality as form of intervention, and focusing on keeping open a space. For Trocchi this last element is especially important, for he argues that the act of having a set definition of an insurgent practice is very much necessary part of the process of containing it. Therefore, it is important to direct effort to resisting being contained within a set definition.

This is the tension that Roger Farr (2002, 2007) explores with great precision in his work. The problem is that by falling into forms of dissent and social action that are predictable, defined, and perhaps even expected, there is a tendency to end up facilitating in the very process of recuperation by movements themselves. In this sense it is clearly not a conception of recuperation being a dynamic that comes externally to social movements and descends upon some pure resistant subject, rather through predictability forms of insurgency may inadvertently offer up and facilitate the process of their recuperation. This is, effectively, to create another level of mediation in the communication of dissent, through the effective 'unmarking' process of predictability, the very one that the Situationist's idea of creative intervention into the metropolitan space was working against. This is not to elevate the dynamic of recuperation into over-theorized cynicism, but rather to understand the way in which conventions of dissent (for instance marches, sit-ins, sloganeering, civil disobedience, street theater) both make forms of social action more readily recognizable, but also through the easy recognition can make them more easily containable by that very definition. Farr argues:

> we have entered a phase in which dissent, if it is to retain its power, must anticipate its recuperation, and adopt strategies of surprise and shock. In anticipation of the mechanisms that control opposition, dissent might need to become "unreadable" – but only for those who require the maintenance of coherence, stability, and order to maintain their "grip" on public opinion and, by extension, public space. (2002: 2)

Shifting towards thinking about forms of social illegibility thus contains within it two elements: both forms of social action and dissent which go beyond the expected conventions of political dissent (even if only in subtle ways; not everything has to be over the top or garish to be effective), as well as further developing an infrapolitical, infra-organizational space that by its encoding is at least partially removed from the visibility of public legibility, and through this cloaking, allows for a more open and creative space.

On the Coda, Against Capture

History is thus recognized as the chaos of a multitude of desires become coherent, temporarily, in constituent groups, patterns, or a moment in a process of encounters... Revolution is defined by the continuous movement of a constituent power. Whenever a revolutionary process is closed down in a constituted power – a sovereign identity, a state, a nation – the Revolution ceases to exist. – Michael Hardt (1997: 77/78)

Insurrections, desertions, invention of new organisms of democracy: herein lie the Miracles of the Multitude, and these principles do not cease when the sovereign forbids them... the miraculous exception is not an ineffable 'event,' with no roots, and entirely imponderable. Because it is contained within the magnetic field defined by mutually changing interrelations of Action, Work, and Intellect, the Miracle is rather something that is *awaited but unexpected*... it is an exception that is especially surprising to the one who was awaiting it. It is an anomaly so potent that it completely disorients our conceptual compass, which, however, had precisely signaled the place of its insurgence. – Paolo Virno (1996: 209)

As we stumble towards something resembling a conclusion, even if it is intended to be one that merely pauses rather than ends in closure, perhaps it is fitting to turn towards a discussion of John Holloway. Holloway's work (2002, 2003) has been a major influence in the anti-globalization movement despite being ignored by the academy for the most part (Shukaitis and Graeber 2007). His work has been a constant presence in this text, starting from the role of critical thought as the extension, intensification and development of the scream of dislocation and shock, to avoid the closure of radical thought within a striated, state paradigm. Holloway's thinking emerges out of the state derivation debates of the 1970s, which explored why the state was not really useful as a tool for liberatory struggles. But this argument did not lead to a fetishization of withdrawal premised on the notion that one could magically dispel all relations with the state, but rather the framing of politics based on the ways which one is embedded in state relations and power, and working in and against those.

It is this work that provided the background and subtext for his much better known and more recent work on revolution (2002) without the seizure of state power, which fused together this more nuanced understanding of the state and its function with an approach to politics inspired in large part by the Zapatista revolution in Chiapas. In highly lyrical yet densely analytical prose, Holloway explored the ways in which the scream expressed the horrors of the fracturing of the social flow of doing, that which transforms the beauty and wonder of a world that is indeed created through common efforts, into mechanisms of domination and subordination. It is this process that transforms what he calls power-to into power-over, one that excludes us as active subjects in the process of creation, even as we are enmeshed in it. But this does not mean that that a response of trying to reclaim some lost identity fractured through this process would be all that effective, even if it is understandable. Sovereign and fixed identities are just as much a problem for Holloway in their freezing and fixing of a fluid revolutionary process as they are for Michael Hardt, for they are moments of the closure of a revolutionary process rather than their continuation. For Holloway, liberation is not the liberation of an oppressed identity, but rather of an oppressed non-identity, the ordinary, invisible rumblings of social movement (2002: 136). This is based on an understanding of forms of identification that stops and is frozen there, or ones that negate themselves in the process of identification, or in Holloway's terms, it is the difference between conceptualizing identity on the basis of being or on the basis of doing. Or perhaps even on the basis of a productive disidentity, as Stefano Harney and Nceku Nyathi (2007) show in their revisiting of the relationship between the politics of racialization and revolutionary organization.

This has clear and somewhat drastic implications for that apparently still ongoing snipe hunt of radical politics: the search for the revolutionary subject. Based on Holloway's argument, this, much like snipe hunting in general, is absurd: "To take seriously the idea of self-emancipation we have to look not for a pure subject but rather for the opposite: for the confused and contradictory presence of rebellion in everyday life" (2002: 222). In other words, to we search for processes of revolutionary subjectivization and becoming, the construction of imaginal machines, all throughout the fabric of everyday life and social relations. While the scream itself can be recuperated, as well can an uncritical assertion of positivity, is through these processes of becoming that do not stop in identification and it is possible to enact a "recuperation of doing," or turning the processes of recuperation and retrieval against themselves, even if for only a moment (2002: 208).

Julia Kristeva captures this relation between the emergence and development of collective and individual being when she frames it, rather than as in her framing of Camus' statement "I rebel, therefore we are" as "I revolt, therefore we are still to come" (2002: 42). This changes and reframes the relation between a necessary and direct relation between revolt and collective subjectification, one that strangely seems to stipulate a process of closure through identifying it, with a process that is never finished as we are always to come. This for Kristeva, this is the nature of revolt, a "state of permanent questioning, of transformation, of change, an endless probing of appearances" (2002: 120) and is the same process by which constituent power is kept open; open to the continual construction of imaginal machines. Kristeva seems to think that this process of continual probing and questioning has ceased, or that constituent power has tended to become solidified and no longer open to continued revolt in the broader and deeper sense that she wants to return. While this is always a risk, it is not a process as global or encompassing as it might seem, for it is also continually reopened through renewed insurgency drawing from what Alexander Brener and Barbara Schurz beautifully describe as the "rhythms of rebellion's wisdom" (2005: 71).

Affirmative Abolition

The war machine invents the abolitionist dream and reality –
Gilles Deleuze and Félix Guattari (1987: 385)

Let us return to a concept that may have fallen out of fashion somewhat in recent years, but it is still worth its theoretical salt, namely that of working class self-abolition. To invoke working class self-abolition does not necessarily mean having to fall back on a stagist narrative of capitalist development, to or hold on to any notion of a vanguard party as a necessary directing force, or any of the other assorted accoutrements that might often accompany that style of rhetoric. Autonomist politics has by and large tried to free itself from a stagist narrative, although there exists a lingering desire for a hegemonic subject of resistance, even if this it is known to be both impossible and undesirable. Rather, it is simply this: to the degree that value or worth of any idea or practice is not found inherently within itself, or in some transcendent reference point conferring legitimacy, it can only be found within its compositional capacity, which can only be situated within a particular social historical framework and configuration. A compositional project and class politics is thus from the beginning not designed to find ways to achieve its self-preservation and continuity, but rather is intended from the beginning to work towards the conditions of its own self-dissolution. It is in this sense that working class self-abolition is paradoxically both a negation and preservation, even if this preserved form does not readily seem so at the visible level. Class politics are asserted by the struggle against class domination, where negation is the founding moment of positivity. This is all relatively straight forward within most strands of Marxist thought with any sense of nuance, although despite this it is not surprising that there is often a tendency to focus on keeping together a project, a party, or a network, to sustain itself far beyond the point where it is usefully serving its insurgent function. To put it in Marxist terms: to make the error of preserving a formal party form instead of inaugurating the historic party at the right time. And in this way the conceptual function of self-abolition changes: rather than a forward projected self-abolition providing an outside to the present, it becomes a forward projected communism, that outside is continually present within the manifold forms of already existing communist sociality, and within the continual refraction and composition of ongoing constituent preservation through abolition.

This is to see, as Marina Vishmidt has charted out (2006) for us, in the emergent communism of social struggle, the relations between the working class as the agents of self-abolition, in the emergent communism of social struggle and forms of being-in-common without identity, without fixed identity, or closure. The time of self-activity is the temporality of the abolition of set identities, or their dispersion in representation. But this time is bounded not only by the dynamics of recuperation external to it, but also those introduced from within the process of insurgent movement. Through this process of maintaining itself, and through recuperation not maintaining itself as an open space of constituent potentiality, one is capable of building new imaginal machines. As community can also act as a point of identity, of capture, as well of as a being-in-common, moving towards its dissolution at times is conversely more in line within the founding impulse than its preservation.. This is a strange line of inquiry to follow, particularly to end on, but one that is entirely necessary. The temporary autonomous zone in large degree maintains or is capable of finding spaces of autonomy to occupy precisely because of its temporariness, or the way in which a this territory is animated by a discontinuous continuity, a submerged and underground current not visible until closer inspection. It follows a path charted by Marx's old mole, and then worked out further by further developed by what Sergio

Bologna described as the tribe of moles.

It is a territory marked well by the experience of the Provos, a conglomeration of creative interventionists who emerged in mid-1960s Amsterdam, coming together out of a combination of avant-garde arts, happenings, street theater, Situationist ideas, and the a legacy of anarchist politics. As Richard Kempton (2007) shows in his book on them (the only one currently available in English), the Provos, who took their inspiration from the seemingly random bursts of juvenile criminality and mischief that seemed to haunt the Netherlands at the time, acted as a catalyst, bringing together and connecting a variety of social forces and discontents that normally would have never intersected. And did so in a way that was quite productive in terms of the unleashing of collective creativity and myth making, through construction of symbolic and otherwise disruptions in the metropolitan fabric. But even despite the creativity and vitality of the Provos and their clever but radical demands for the reshaping of the city, they too found within several years of their inception a draining and waning of this energy. That is not to say that they were no longer capable of generating social conflict and antagonism, as that was the case, but, as the Provos themselves would say, the magic was gone. Or was quickly fading. Their conflicts did not generate new ideas or imagery, and in their predictability they found themselves trudging on, propelled only by the power of the myths they had created for themselves. But was the answer to this dwindling compositional power of Provo as an imaginal machine? A move toward electoral politics (a move that some made, with their new Kabouter Party, doing perhaps as well as one could possibly expect given its nature), or an alliance with the student movement? All of these were debated as at a Provo Council roughly modeled, albeit mockingly, on Vatican II.

In the end, it was to end it that was chosen (2007: 105-115). Rather than trudging forward and finding themselves caught up in the very cycles of lifeless and predictable politics they were opposed to, the Provos collectively decided on their self-dissolution. They held a public funeral, an almost as a ritualistic declaration of the suicide of Provo as an entity. This is not too dissimilar from the more well known "death of the hippie" funeral held in 1967, although that event does not seem to have effectively removed hippies from the scene. The important thing was not just the dissolution, but the collectively plotted character of it. An end coming not out of exhaustion or things falling apart (although there probably are some elements of such involved), but a planned dissolution. One could say that if constituent assemblies are mystically founded on the underlying social insurgencies underlying them, that provide the anterior social forces that enable the mystical founding of a constitutional convention that has no means of legitimacy other than its own self-institution, this is something quite different. If the problem is that the constituent assembly, the processes of formalization and institutionalization all too often betrays itself, this is the assembly that preserves by engaging in its own self-destruction and dissolution. A constituent disassembly. It is in this sense that affirmative abolition needs to be tagged to a macrohistorical narrative of capitalist development and its abolition. Self-abolition is not something that occurs once, at the end, at the moment of declared victory preceding the move outside of historical time. Rather, forms of self-abolition, of rendering politics incomprehensible, and encoded at times, are forms that aim for the dissolution of the public and visible forms that provide ways for keeping open the continual construction of imaginal machines, which only work through breaking down. And by breaking down they keep working, by dissolving their own operations are carried on.

This is perhaps what Mario Tronti had in mind when he suggested that if rather than adopting capital's perspective one engaged with struggles from an understanding of their determining role, it would be possible to develop new relationships and forms adequate to these struggles. And more importantly, it would be discovered that "organizational miracles" are always happening and have always been happening (1979: 6). But what does Tronti mean by the organizational miracle, seemingly the same theme picked up by Paolo Virno in his description of the "miracles of the multitude," those disorienting events that are awaited but unexpected? The organizational miracle is perhaps not as grand as its moniker might suggest. It is not something outside of all natural order and reality, just outside the nature of capital's nature, in that the phenomenon is non-homologous to it. The organizational miracle is a necessary feature coming out of the dynamic that while the continuity of struggle is a comparatively simple matter, the continuity of organization is quite a difficult question. Any form of organization created is then recuperated by capitalism, and thus tends to become compromised in its effectiveness in anticapitalist struggle. This is why, as Tronti explains, it is not so surprising that radical movements will abandon forms of organization and social spaces they have only just won.

Tronti's answer to this takes several forms. One is the insistence that this condition demands a specific form of self-organization, one that builds upon the multitude of minor refusals and revolts without coalescing into a fixed form: "an organization, in other words, without organization – which meant not subject to bourgeois institutionalization" (1973). Tronti's organizational miracle is what developed in Italy in the 1970s. It is the form of infra-organization that no longer acts as an intermediary or first step towards state formation, but aims towards the emergence of an entirely new form. Tronti tended to see this as a preliminary version of a new party form. This is somewhat strange in that if it was to be followed out, the forming of a party around an organization-less organization would drastically alter the meaning of the party form altogether. This is evidenced by the development of Autonomia and then network-based organizing, although the tendency then became to shift away from party-building as a framework for organization. It is the formless form through which constituent power is not closed, but remains open to the continual construction of imaginal machines. This segues into Tronti's second answer to the dynamic nature of this formless form, namely the necessity of not having a reactive approach to the utilization and recuperation of struggles by capital. For Tronti, ever the perceptive strategist of class struggle, the struggle is lost if it "fails to immediately grasp the meaning of the coming capitalist initiative," and thus:

> It is first of all a matter of foreseeing these moves and in some cases even of suggesting them. But it is always a matter of anticipating them with the forms of one's own organization in order to render it not only unproductive for capitalist goals, but productive for the labor goals... It must be the attempt to always resist the different forms assumed by labor's attack imperceptibly recognized and, therefore, because of its historical nature and political choice, unpredictable from the organizational viewpoint (1972).

In order to persevere, it must maintain an unpredictable organizational form and strategy, anticipate how struggles will shift the grounds of politics and anticipate capital's response.

This process of continual recomposition as means to maintain a form of composition of struggles non-homologous to capitalist development is the same thing that has been picked up by the various tendrils of autonomist politics and radical movements more generally, even if not always when it is not expressed in the same terms. It is through the continual recomposition of self-organization through which a potential form of autonomy is possible, within and despite capitalism. But not surprisingly, this formula does not, magically solve everything it itself. George Caffentzis (2006), in a discussion of this problem mainly as it occurs in Negri's writing (although it can be seen more broadly in autonomist politics generally), notes that there is a tendency to conflate struggle with the existence of autonomy itself. This is perhaps not so surprising, given that the assumption of autonomy, as argued previously, is often one of the prerequisites for its creation. Caffentzis notes that the existence of struggle implies the possibility of autonomy but not necessarily its actual existence. What then is the criteria for telling the difference between a potential form of autonomy and its actual existence? This is a tricky question. The traditional Marxist answer would be the establishment of a workers' state that then will wither away after capitalism has been abolished. This, notably, is a model that has some problems with it. But moving the focus to the continual creation of forms of self-organization, the animation of imaginal machines and composing forms of autonomous existence and sociality does not really get around this problem to some degree. Rather than the question being about the nature of the state, one could ask similar questions about the nature of the autonomy and self-organization that are created, and whether they are really non-homologous to capitalist development, a very pressing question given the seemingly almost infinite recuperative powers of capital.

This is exactly the question that this text has been addressing. For instance, can forms of worker self-management really build anticapitalist relations and proliferate them under capitalism? To what degree are processes of minor composition truly other to capital? How can affective practices carve out spaces for continued social reproduction outside of capital's measure and rule? Perhaps more importantly than just asking whether various practices and ideas are helpful in creating spaces and forms of sociality outside of capital is the question of how they do so, what sort of compositions they animate, the processes of self-institution, and how they transform the spaces in which they exist. In the beginning, this was marked as a truly titanic task, one likely to end in some form of failure, and with all due luck and skill this promise has indeed been carried through.

Paolo Virno (2004) argues that in the conditions of post-Fordist capitalism it is the faculties of language, communication, and symbolic analysis which become the most productive and contested fields of human interaction, melding together the realms of politics, labor, and communication which have been previously distinct. In this formation it is the working of the General Intellect, or the shared forms of knowledge, experience and expertise, that becomes the score upon which Virno argues that the post-Fordist virtuoso, who becomes the archetype of all waged labor, plays. But rather than using the figure of Glenn Gould as virtuoso (the pianist who used an endless array of takes in the studio and splicing the various recordings together into a flawless performance), or even or even Precarias a la Derivas as a more approachable figure of the affective virtuoso (2005), a compositional approach to formulating intensive social movement and politics suggests an altogether different type of figure. One that is predicated not on trying to find the perfect form of organization or articulation of demands, but through developing intensive social relationships by creatively redirecting the social energies existing in everyday life to new ends, in projects that see failures not as negative but as conditions to learn from in constant renewal and creative social movement.

This is the lesson that is eloquently expressed in *Kafka on the Shore*, a novel by Haruki Marukami, in a scene which the characters Kafka and Oshima discuss the performance of a sonata by Schubert. When discussing why he is drawn to the performance of these particular sonata Oshima notes that it is because of the apparent impossibility of playing all four movements perfectly. It is not that those who have tried lack skill, but rather that the sonata itself is imperfect – and it is this imperfection which draws people into the attempt at playing the piece, which is composed like a pastoral antique. But as new elements are added, adjusting the pace and modulation, soon enough the piece is no longer as Schubert had intended but has indeed become something else. For Oshima this is the beauty of the piece itself, for him listening to these imperfect variations one "can feel the limits of what humans are capable of – that certain type of perfection that can only be realized through a limitless accumulation of the imperfect" (2005: 119-120). It is, as Deleuze and Guattari phrase it: *Each failure is a masterpiece, a branch of the rhizome* (1986: 39). Likewise, it is in these accumulation of different modulations and intensifications of the shared imaginary of social resistance, through the continual recomposition of the radical imagination, that one finds the movement to abolish the current state of things, in which other forms of social life emerge.

"History," Stephen said, "is a nightmare from which from I'm tying to awake." To resist, that is to create, is this waking – in the sense of waking from the nightmare of history: of the accumulation of capital, state power, the vast concentration of hierarchies and fields of power embodied through society – extended through colonization… to resist is to become conscious of them, to tear asunder the forms which replicate and sustain the nightmare of history from which I wish to awake – and to constitute new forms of social life.

We perceive our desires painted on the walls, as gestures and idealizations objectified and staring back at us. The gridded spaces shift, divide and reproduce the void between our body and desire: the space in which the lack is known apart from the sire, as a focal point where our disembodied desires are codified and projected back onto us as means of control – as the sire, the sovereign. In spirals of projection and objectivation these disembodiments come to be perceived as natural. The products of our minds and bodies rule over us alien objects, yet they are of us.

Tu deseos son parte de system: your desires are part of the system (as seen written on a storefront window). Our dreams and longings for transcendence are not opposed to the systems of control and powers of domination, they are very much part of them. The body and its desires may break free from the most blatant iron cages, forms of technocratic and bureaucratic control. But these moments of excess can be contained and recapitulated within systems of control. Moments of desire push beyond the limits of reason and modulate the grids of control but the rupture is not permanent – the bursting and rapture paradoxically maintains the very forms of control we aim to shatter. We may strain to escape the handcuffs, but that only makes them tighter.

Where does that leave us, with no outside, no hope of breaking free from these nightmares of history and control that we have inherited? In the reflections of our desires, the processes through which we externalize ourselves, come to learn ourselves through the processes of relating to others – there contains a possibility of freedom through the rhizomatic unfolding of possible selves. Liberation from the nightmares of history consists not breaking beyond the boundaries of control, but withdrawing from the relations of control into an unfolding of new possibilities. In these constantly folding and unfolding acts of self-creation both collective and individual, the refusal of working towards a unified, unchanging self in opposition: the liberation from domination becomes precisely by refusal of the domination of liberation. – Haduhi Szukis, *I Derived I Saw Myself Last Night* (1524: 1314)

Additional Readings

This book was not written in isolation but in dialogue with the ideas and arguments of many other people. Here is a short-ish list of other texts that either were very important for the formation of arguments contained here or would be for expanding and deepening them:

Silvia Federici – *Caliban and the Witch: Women, the Body, and Primitive Accumulation*

Stephen Duncombe – *Dream: Re-Imagining Progressive Politics in an Age of Fantasy*

Cornelius Castoriadis – *The Imaginary Institution of Society*

Dimitris Papadopoulos, Niamh Stephenson, and Vassilis Tsianos – *Escape Routes: Control and Subversion in the 21st Century*

David Graeber – *Toward an Anthropological Theory of Value: The False Coin of Our Own Dreams*

Midnight Notes – *Auroras of the Zapatistas: Local & Global Struggles of the Fourth World War*

Jacques Attali – *Noise: The Political Economy of Music*

Toni Negri and Félix Guattari – *Communists Like Us*

Stefano Harney – *State Work: Public Administration and Mass Intellectuality*

Franco 'Bifo' Berardi – *Precarious Rhapsody: Semiocapitalism and the pathologies of post-alpha generation*

Nick Thoburn – *Deleuze, Marx, and Politics*

Magazines / Journals:

Mute

Journal of Aesthetics & Protest

Fifth Estate

In the Middle of a Whirwind

ephemera: theory & politics in organization

Anarchy: A Journal of Desire Armed

Bibliography

Activist-Trauma Support (2005) "Activist Trauma: Mutual Support in the Face of Repression," *Shut Them Down! The G8, Gleneagles 2005 and the Movement of Movements*. Ed. David Harvie, Keir Milburn, Ben Trott, and David Watts. West Yorkshire and Brooklyn: Dissent! and Autonomedia: 257-261.

Agamben, Giorgio (1993) *The Coming Community*. Trans. Michael Hardt. Minneapolis: University of Minnesota Press.

Agamben, Giorgio (1998) *Homo Sacer: Sovereign Power and Bare Life*. Trans. Daniel Heller-Roazen. Stanford, CA: Stanford University Press

Agamben, Giorgio (2000) *Means Without Ends: Notes on Politics*. Translated Vincenzo Binetti and Cesare Cesarino. Stanford, CA: Stanford University Press

Agent 083TOM33McC5THY (2008) "Letting It Be: A Red Paper on Terrestrial Art," *Martian Encyclopedia of Terrestrial Life, Volume VIII: Art*. London: Martian Museum of Terrestrial Art.

Alinsky, Saul P. (1977) *Rules for Radicals: A Pragmatic Primer.* New York: Random House.

Alquati, Romano (1970) "The Network of Struggles in Italy." Notes from a presentation. Translation available at libcom.org.

Anonymous (2004) "Multiple Names," *Mail-Art Encyclopedia*. Available at www.sztuka-fabryka.be/encyclopaedia.htm.

Anonymous (2005) "Inside and Outside the G8 Protests," *Shut Them Down! The G8, Gleneagles 2005 and the Movement of Movements*. Ed. David Harvie, Keir Milburn, Ben Trott, and David Watts. West Yorkshire and Brooklyn: Dissent! and Autonomedia: 175-183.

Anonymous (2006) "if we did it, this is how it would have happened." Self-published newspaper. New York City.

Antebi, Nicole, Colin Dickey, and Robby Herbst, Eds. (2007) *Failure: Experiments in Aesthetic and Social Practice*. Los Angeles: Journal of Aesthetics & Protest Press.

Antliff, Alan (2001) *Anarchist Modernism: Art, Politics, and the First American Avant-Garde.* Chicago: University of Chicago Press.

Antliff, Alan (2007) *Anarchy and Art: From the Paris Commune to the Fall of the Berlin Wall.* Vancouver: Arsenal Pulp Press.

Argenti, Filippo (2007) *Nights of Rage: On the Recent Revolts in France.* London: Elephant Editions.

Arzensek, Vladmimir (1972) "A Conflict Model and the Structure of Yugoslav Society," *International Journal of Sociology* 2: 364-383.

Aronowitz, Stanley (2007) "The Ignored Philosopher and Social Theorist: On the Work of Henri Lefebvre," *Situations* Volume 2 Number 1:133-155.

Asimakopoulos, John (2006) "Loot the Rich: Economic Civil Disobedience," Infoshop.org. February 27th, 2006. www.infoshop.org.

Attali, Jacques (1985) *Noise: The Political Economy of Music.* Trans. Brian Masssumi. Minneapolis: University of Minnesota Press.

autonome a.f.r.i.k.a. gruppe (2003) "What is a Communication Guerilla?" *An@rchitexts: Voices from the Global Digital Resistance.* Ed. Joanne Richardson. Brooklyn: Autonomedia: 86-91.

Balfour, Campbell. Ed. (1997) *Participation in Industry.* London: Croom Helm.

Ball, Kirstie (2005) "Organization, Surveillance, and the Body: Towards a Politics of Resistance," *Organization* Volume 12 Number 1: 89-108.

Ballard, J.G. (2000) *Super-Cannes.* London: Flamingo.

Balser, Diane (1987) *Sisterhood and Solidarity: Feminism and Labor in Modern Times.* Cambridge, MA: South End Press.

Barbrook, Richard (2007) *Imaginary Futures: From Thinking Machine to Global Village.* London: Pluto Press.

Barricade Collective (2008) *History of Class Struggle in Hungary, 1919-1945.* Budapest: Hungarian Anarchist Federation.

Barrot, Jean (1996 [1979]) "Critique of the Situationist International." *What is Situationism? A Reader.* Ed. Stewart Home. San Francisco: AK Press: 24-62.

Barthes, Roland (1968) *Writing Degree Zero.* Trans. Annette Lavers and Colin Smith. New York: Hill and Wang.

Bass, Bernard and V.J. Shackleton (1979) "Industrial Democracy and Participative Management: A Case for Synthesis," *Academy of Management Review* Volume 4 Number 3: 393-404.

Baudrillard, Jean (1990 [1983]) *Fatal Strategies.* New York: Semiotexte(e).

Beck, Ulrich (1999) "Goodbye to all that wage slavery," *New Statesman.* March 5, 1999. Available at www.newstatesman.com.

Becker-Ho, Alice (2004) *The Princes of Jargon.* Trans. John McHale.

New York: Edwin Mellen.

Bekken, Jon and Fred Thompson, Eds. (2006) *The Industrial Workers of the World: Its First One Hundred Years 1905-2005*. Philadelphia, PA: Industrial Workers of the World.

Bell, Shannon (1995) *Whore Carnival*. Brooklyn: Autonomedia.

Berardi, Franco "Bifo" (2006) "The Precarious-Euro Insurrection," Interactivist Info.Exchange, April 3rd.

Berardi, Franco "Bifo" (2008) *Félix Guattari: Thought, Friendship, and Visionary Cartography*. Trans. Giuseppina Mecchia. New York: Palgrave.

Berardi, Franco (2009) *Precarious Rhapsody: Semiocapitalism and the pathologies of post-alpha generation*. London/New York: Minor Compositions.

Berger, Dan (2006) *Outlaws of America: The Weather Underground and the Politics of Solidarity*. Oakland: AK Press.

Berman, Matthew (1984) *Workers' self-management in the United States*. Ithaca: Cornell University Press.

Beuys, Joseph (2004) *What is Art?* . Ed. Voler Harlan. East Sussex: Clairview Books.

Bey, Hakim (1994) *Immediatism*. San Francisco: AK Press.

Bey, Hakim (1995) "The Utopian Blues," *Sounding Off! Music as Subversion / Resistance / Revolution*. Ed. Ron Sakolsky and Fred Wei-Han Ho. Brooklyn: Autonomedia.

Biagi, Marco. Ed. (2002) *Quality of Work and Employee Involvement in Europe*. The Hague: Kluwer Law.

Bird, Stewart, Dan Georgakas, and Deborah Shaffer (1985) *Solidarity Forever: An Oral History of the IWW*. Chicago: Lake View Press.

Bishop, Claire (2004) "Antagonism and Relational Aesthetics," *October* No. 110: 51-79.

Blanchot, Maurice (1987) "Everyday Speech," *Yale French Studies Number 73*: 12-20.

Blaug, Ricardo (1998) "The Tyranny of the Visible: Problems in the Evaluation of Anti-institutional Radicalism," *Organization* Volume 6 Number 1: 33-56.

Blissett, Luther (2005) *Q*. London: Harvest Books.

Blumberg, Paul (1968) *The Sociology of Participation*. New Haven: Yale University Press.

Böhm, Steffen (2005) *Repositioning Organization Theory: Impossibilities and Strategies*. London: Palgrave.

Bologna, Sergio (1980) "The Tribe of Moles," *Italy: Autonomia. Post-political politics*. Ed. Sylvere Lotringer and Christian Marazzi. New York: Semiotext: 36-61.

Bologna, Sergio (2007) "An Invisible History of Work." Interviewed by Sabine Grimm and Klaus Ronneberger. Available at www.springerin.at.

Boltanski, Luc and Eve Chiapello (2005) *The New Spirit of Capitalism.* Trans. Gregory Elliot. London: Verso.

Bone, Ian (2006) Bash the Rich: *True-Life Confessions of an Anarchist in the UK.* Bath: Tangent Books.

Bonefeld, Werner (2001) "The Permanence of Primitive Accumulation: Commodity Fetishism and Social Constitution," *the commoner* Number 2.

Bourdieu, Pierre (2003) "Job insecurity is everywhere now," *Firing back: against the tyranny of the market 2.* London: Verso: 81-87.

Bourriaud, Nicolas (2002 [1998]) *Relational Aesthetics.* Trans. Simon Pleassance & Fronza Woods. New York: Les presses due reel.

Bousquet, Marc and Tiziana Terranova (2004) "Recomposing the University," *Mute,* Number 28: 72-81.

Boyle, Maree and Ken Parry. Ed. (2007) *Culture and Organization.* Volume 13 Number 3: 185-266.

Bousquet, Marc (2008) *How the University Works: Higher Education and the Low-Wage Nation.* New York: New York University Press.

Bradley, Keith and Alan Gelb (1983) *Cooperation at Work: The Mondragon Experience.* London: Heineman Educational Books Ltd.

Bradley, Keith and Alan Gelb (1983) *Worker Capitalism: The New Industrial Relations.* London: Heineman Educational Books Ltd.

Bratich, Jack Z. (2008) *Conspiracy Panics: Political Rationality and Popular Culture.* Binghamton: SUNY Press.

Bratsis, Peter (2006) *Everyday Life and the State.* Boulder, CO: Paradigm Publishers.

Brener, Alexander and Barbara Schurz (2005) *The Art of Destruction.* Ljubjana: Blossom vs. Fruit Samizdat.

Brenner, Johanna and Barbara Laslett (1991) "Gender, Social Reproduction, and Women's Self-Organization," *Gender & Society* Volume 5 Number 3: 311-333.

Brewer, Norman (2005) "Victorious Students Unleashed Rally – Next Stop: May Day Rally and Contingent," Melbourne Indymedia. May 1, 2005. Available at www.melbourne.indymedia.org.

Brinton, Maurice (2004 [1974]) *For Workers' Power.* Ed. David Goodway. Oakland, CA: AK Press.

Brosnan, John (1978) *Future Tense: The Cinema of Science Fiction.* New York: St. Martin's Press.

Brown, Wendy (1995) *States of Injury.* Princeton: Princeton University Press.

Buchanan, Ian (1997) "Deleuze and Pop Music," *Australian Humanities Review.* Available at www.australianhumanitiesreview.orgl

Buchloh, Benjamin (1984) "From Faktura to Factography," *October* Volume 30: 82-119.

Buchloh, Benjamin (2001) *Neo-avantgarde and Culture Industry: Essays on European and American Art from 1955 to 1975.* Cambridge: MIT Press.

Buhle, Paul (2004) *Wobblies! A Graphic History of the Industrial Workers of the World.* New York: Verso.

Burawoy, Michael (1983) "Between the Labor Process and the State: The Changing Face of Factory Regimes Under Advanced Capitalism," *American Sociological Review* Volume 48 Number 5: 587-605.

Burger, Peter (1984) *Theory of the Avant-Garde.* Trans. Michael Shaw. Minneapolis: University of Minnesota Press.

Caffentizis, George (1999) "On the Notion of a Crisis of Social Reproduction: A Theoretical Review," *Women, Development and Labor of Reproduction.* Ed. Mariarosa Dalla Costa and Giovanna Dalla Costa. Trenton, NJ: Africa World Press: 153-187.

Caffentzis, George (2005) "Dr. Sachs, Live8, and Neoliberalism's 'Plan B,'" *Shut Them Down! The G8, Gleneagles 2005 and the Movement of Movements.* Ed. David Harvie, Keir Milburn, Ben Trott, and David Watts. West Yorkshire and Brooklyn: Dissent! and Autonomedia: 51-60.

Caffentzis, George (2006) "Acts of God and Enclosures in New Orleans," *Mute.* May 24, 2006. Available at www.metamute.org.

Caffentzis, George (2006a) "Notes for a talk on Autonomism Beyond Borders." Left Forum, March 12th, 2006.

Caffentzis, George (2006b) "The "Si Se Puede" Insurrection: A Class Analysis," *Mute.* June 23rd, 2006. Available at www.metamute.org.

Camatte, Jacques (1995) *The World We Must Leave and Other Essays.* Brooklyn: Autonomedia.

Camus, Albert (1983) *The Myth of Sisyphus and Other Essays.* New York: Vintage Books.

Carlsson, Chris (2006) "May Day 2006," *The Nowtopian.* Available at lipmagazine.org.

Carr, James (2002) Bad: *The Autobiography of James Carr.* Oakland: AK Press.

Castoriadis, Cornelius (1975) *The Imaginary Institution of Society.* London: Polity Press.

Castoriadis, Cornelius (1997) *World in Fragments: Writings on Politics,* Society, Psychoanalysis, and the Imagination. Ed./Trans. David Ames Curtis. Stanford, CA: Stanford University Press.

Castoriadis, Cornelius (1997a) *The Castoriadis Reader.* Ed. David Ames Curtis. Oxford: Blackwell Publishers.

Cesaire, Suzanne (1996) "A Civilization's Discontent," *Refusal of the*

Shadow: Surrealism and the Caribbean. Ed. Michael Richardson. Trans. Michael Richardson and Krzysztof Fijalkowski. New York: Verso.

Chaplin, Brian and John Coyne (1977) *Can Workers Manage?* Sussex: Institute of Economic Affairs.

Ciaperoni, Anna (1991 [1982]) "What If there Were Only Thorns?" *Italian Feminist Thought: A Reader.* Ed. Paola Bono and Sandra Kemp. Oxford: Blackwell

Churchill, Ward (1998) *Pacifism as Pathology: Reflections on the Role of Armed Struggle in North America.* Winnipeg: Arbeiter Ring.

Clark, Gordon (1984) "A Theory of Local Autonomy," *Annals of the Association of American Geographers* Volume 74 Number 2: 195-208.

Clarke, Simon (1992) "The Global Accumulation of Capital and the Periodisation of the Capitalist State Form," *Open Marxism Volume 1: Dialectics and History.* Ed. Werner Bonefeld, Richard Gunn, and Kosmas Psychopedis. London: Pluto Books: 133-150.

Clastres, Pierre (1977) *Society Against the State: The Leader as Servant and the Human Uses of Power Among Indians of the Americas.* Trans. Robert Hurley and Abe Stein. New York: Urizen Books.

Cleaver, Harry (1979) *Reading Capital Politically.* Austin, TX: University of Texas Press.

Cleaver, Harry (19988) "The Uses of an Eathquake," *Midnight Notes* Number 9: 10-14.

Cleaver, Harry (1998) "The Zapatistas and the Electronic Factory of Struggle," *Zapatista! Reinventing Revolution in Mexico.* Ed. John Holloway and Eloina Peláez. London: Pluto Press: 81-103

Cleveland, William (2008) *Art and Upheaval.* Oakland: New Village Press.

Clough, Patricia Ticineto (1992) *The Ends of Ethnography: From Realism to Social Criticism.* London: Sage Publications.

Clough, Patricia Ticineto (2001) *Autoaffection: Unconscious Thought in the Age of Teletechnology.* Minneapolis, MI: University of Minnesota Press.

Clough, Patricia Ticineto with Jean Halley, Eds. (2007) *The Affective Turn: Theorizing the Social.* Durham, NC: Duke University Press.

Cohn, Norman (1993) *The Pursuit of the Millenium: Revolutionary Millenarians and Mystical Anarchists of the Middle Ages.* London: Pimlico.

Cole, G.D.H. (1972 [1917]) *Self-Government in Industry.* London: Hutchinson Educational Ltd.

Colectivo Situaciones (2005) "Something More on Research Militancy: Footnotes on Procedures and (In)Decisions," *ephemera.* Trans. Nate Holdren and Sebastian Touza. Volume 5 Number 4. Fall 2005: 602-614.

Colectivo Situaciones (forthcoming) *19 & 20: Notes on a New Social*

Protagonism. Brooklyn: Autonomedia.

Comrades of Kronstadt Editions (1990) *Worker's Autonomy.* London: Elephant Editions.

Consemi, Carla (1991 [1982]) "Without Polemics: Reasons for a Debate," (1991) *Italian Feminist Thought: A Reader.* Ed. Paola Bono and Sandra Kemp. Oxford: Blackwell.

Corbin, Henry (1969) *Creative Imagination in the Sufism of Ibn Arabi.* Trans. Ralph Manheim. Princeton: Princeton University Press.

Corsani, Antonella (2007) "Beyond the Myth of Woman: The Becoming-Transfeminist of (Post-)Marxism. *SubStance* Volume 36 Number 1: 107-138.

Curious George Brigade (2002) "The End of Arrogance: Decentralization and Anarchist Organizing," *After The Fall* August 2002.

Curious George Brigade (2003) "Beyond Duty and Joy," *Anarchy in the Age of Dinosaurs.* New York: CrimethInc Ex-Workers Collective: 33-40.

Cutler, Chris (1992) *File Under Popular: Theoretical and Critical Writing on Music.* Brooklyn: Autonomedia.

Dalla Costa, Mariarosa and Giovanna Dalla Costa, Eds. (1995) *Paying the Price: Women and the Politics of International Economic Development.* London: Zed Books.

Dalla Costa, Mariarosa and Selma James (1972) *The Power of Women and the Subversion of Community.* Bristol: Falling Wall Press.

Dauvé, Gilles (n.d.) *When Insurrections Die.* Austin: Institute for Experimental Freedom. Also available at www.geocities.com/Capitol-Hill/Lobby/3909/whenidie.

Davis, Angela (1981) *Women, Race, and Class.* New York: Vintage.

Day, Dorothy (2006 [1952]) "Poverty and Precarity," *Great Catholic Writings: Thought, Literature, Spirituality, Social Action* Ed. J.D. Childs and Robert Feduccia. Winona, MN: Saint Mary's Press: 234-238.

Day, Richard (2005) *Gramsci is Dead: Anarchist Currents in the Newest Social Movements.* London: Pluto Books.

De Angelis, Massimo (2000) *Keynesianism, Social Conflict, and Political Economy.* Basingstoke: Macmillan.

De Angelis, Massimo (2001) "Marx and Primitive Accumulation: The Continuous Character of Capital's 'Enclosures'," *the commoner* Number 2.

De Angelis, Massimo (2006) "Reflections on Tronti," Info.Interactivist. December 14th, 2006. Available at info.interactivist.net.

De Certeau, Michel (1984) *The Practice of Everyday Day Life.* Trans. Steven Rendall. Berkeley: University of California Press.

Dean, Kenneth and Brian Massumi (1992) *First & Last Emperors: The Absolute State and the Body of the Despot.* Brooklyn: Autonomedia.

Debord, Guy (1958) "Theory of the Dérive." Available at www.bopsecrets.org/SI/2.derive.htm.

Debord, Guy (1983) *Society of the Spectacle.* Detroit, MI: Red & Black.

Debord, Guy (n.d.) *Comments on the Society of the Spectacle.* Sheffield: Pirate Press.

Del Re, Alisa (1996) "Women and Welfare: Where is Jocasta?" *Radical Thought in Italy: A Potential Politics.* Ed. Michael Hardt and Paolo Virno. Trans. Ed Emery. Minneapolis, MN: University of Minnesota Press: 99-113.

Deleuze, Gilles and Félix Guattari (1977) "Balance Sheet-Program for Desiring-Machines," *Anti-Oedipus: From Psychoanalysis to Schizoanalysis, Semiotext(e)* Volume 2 Number 3: 117-129.

Deleuze, Gilles and Félix Guattari (1994) *What is Philosophy?* Trans. Graham Burchell and Hugh Tomlinson.

Deleuze, Gilles and Félix Guattari (1986) *Kafka: Towards a Minor Literature.* Trans. Dana Polen. Minneapolis: University of Minnesota Press.

Deleuze, Gilles (2004) "Nomadic Thought," *Desert Islands and Other Texts.* Ed. David Lapoujade. Trans. Michael Taormina. New York: Semiotext(e): 252-261.

Denz, Diva (2005) "Billionaires Rush to the Aid of Starbucks," NYC Indymedia, August 10, 2005. Available at nyc.indymedia.org.

Derrida, Jacques (1992) "Force of Law: The 'Mystical Foundation of Authority'," *Deconstruction and the Possibility of Justice.* Ed. Drucilla Cornell, Michel Rosenfeld, David Gray Carlson. New York: Routledge.

Dery, Mark (1993) *Culture Jamming: Hacking, Slashing, and Sniping in the Empire of Signs.* Open Magazine Pamphlet Series.

Dery, Mark (1995) "Black to the Future: Afro-Futurism 1.0." Available at www.levity.com/markdery/black.html.

Desroche, Henri (1979) *The Sociology of Hope.* Trans. Carol Martin-Sperry. London: Routledge.

Disconaut, Neil (2000) "Mission accomplished but the beat goes on: the Fantastic Voyage of the Association of Autonomous Astronauts," *See you in Space: the Fifth Annual Report of the Association of Autonomous Astronaut.* London: Association of Autonomous Astronauts.

Dixon, Frederick Markatos (2001) "Here is Folk Science!" *Days of War, Nights of Love: A Beginner's Guide to Crimethink.* Atlanta, GA: CrimehInc. Free Press: 230-233.

Dolgoff, Sam (1974) *The Anarchist Collectives: Workers' Self-Management in the Spanish Revolution 1936-1939.* Montreal: Black Rose Books.

Dominijanni, Ida (2006) "Heiresses at Twilight. The End of Politics and the Politics of Difference," *the commoner* Number 11: 89-109.

Dorfman, Ariel and Arman Mattelart (2003 [1971]) *How to Read Donald Duck: Imperialist Ideology in the Disney Comic.* Somewhere: Kinko's Bootlegging Facility.

Drew, Jesse (2004) "Technopranks. Carving Out a Message in Electronic Space," *Processed World 2005:* 39-43

Duncombe, Stephen (2007) *Dream: Re-Imagining Progressive Politics in an Age of Fantasy.* New York: New Press.

Durkheim, Emile (1984) *The Division of Labor in Society.* Trans. WD Halls. New York: Free Press.

Eden, Dave (2005) "Treasonous Minds: Capital & Universities, the Ideology of the Intellectual and the Desire for Mutiny," *ephemera* Volume 5 Number 4: 580-594.

Ehrenreich, Barbara and Arlie Roschild, Eds. (2002) *Global Women: Nannies, Maids, and Sex Workers in the Global Economy.* London: Granta Books.

Eisenstadt, Shmuel (1966) *Modernization: Protest and Change.* Englewood-Cliffs, NJ: Prentice-Hall.

Elliot, Charlene (2001) "Consuming Caffeine: The Discourse of Starbucks and Coffee," *Consumption, Markets, and Culture.* Volume 4 Number 4: 369-382.

Elms, Anthony, John Corbett, and Terri Kapalsis, Eds. (2007) *Pathways to Unknown Worlds: Sun Ra, El Saturn and Chicago's Afro-Futurist Underground, 1954-68.* Chicago: WhiteWalls.

Engels, Frederick (1968) *The Role of Force in History: A Study of Bismarck's Policy of Blood and Iron.* London: Lawrence & Wishart.

Erickson, Rebecca J. and Christian Ritter (2001) "Emotional Labor, Burnout, and Inauthenticity: Does Gender Matter?" *Social Psychology Quarterly* Volume 64 Number 2: 146-163.

Eshun, Kodwo (2003) "Further Considerations on Afrofuturism," *CR: The New Centennial Review* Volume 3, Number 2: 287-302.

Fantone, Laura (2007) "Precarious Changes: gender and generational politics in contemporary Italy," *Feminist Review* 87: 5–20.

Farr, Roger (2002) "Protest Genres and the Pragmatics of Dissent," presentation for the "Studies in Practical Negation" series at the Kootenay School of Writing, May 2002. Notes, personal communication August 2007.

Farr, Roger (2007) "Strategy of Concealment," *Fifth Estate* Number 375.

Federici, Silvia (1980) "Wages Against Housework," *The Politics of Housework.* Ed. Ellen Malos. London: Allison & Busby: 253-261.

Federici, Silvia (2004) *Caliban and the Witch: Women, the Body, and Primitive Accumulation.* Brooklyn: Autonomedia.

Federici, Silvia (2008) "Precarious Labor: A Feminist Viewpoint," *In The Middle of a Whirlwind: 2008 Convention Protests, Movement, and Movement.* Los Angeles: Journal of Aesthetics & Protest Press. Available at www.inthemiddleofawhirlwind.info.

Federici, Silvia and Nicol Cox (1975) *Counter-planning from the Kitchen.* Bristol: Falling Wall Press.

Federici, Silvia and George Caffentzis (1982) "Mormons in Space," *Midnight Notes*: 3-12.

Federici, Silvia and Leopoldina Fortunati (1981) "High Tide: Women in Motion." From the Red Notes Archives. London.

Federici, Silvia and George Caffentzis (2001) "A Brief History of Resistance to Structural Adjustment," *Democratizing the Global Economy.* Ed. Kevin Danaher. New York: Common Courage Press.

Fenwick, and Jon Olson (1986) "Support for Worker Participation: Attitudes Among Union and Non-union Workers," *American Sociological Review* Volume 51 Number 4: 505-522.

Ferguson, Ann Arnett (1991) "Managing Without Managers: Crisis and Resolution in a Collective Bakery," *Ethnography Unbound: Power and Resistance in the Modern Metropolis.* Ed. Michael Burawoy et al. Berkeley, CA: University of California Press.

Fine, Michelle (1994) "Working the hyphens: Reinventing self and other in qualitative research," N. K. Denzin & Y. S. Lincoln (Eds.), *Handbook of qualitative research.* Thousand Oaks, CA: Sage: 70-82.

Fisher, Virginia and Nicholas Tabor (2006) "Wobbly Union Gets Support," *Harvard Crimson.* October 17, 2006. Available at www.thecrimson.com/article.aspx?ref=514996.

Fleming, Peter and André Spicer (2007) *Contesting the Corporation: Struggle, Power and Resistance in Organizations.* Cambridge: Cambridge University Press.

Florida, Richard (2002) *The Rise of the Creative Class. And How It's Transforming Work, Leisure and Everyday Life.* New York: Basic Books.

Flynn, Elizabeth Gurley, Walker C. Smith, William E. Trautman (1997) *Direct Action & Sabotage: Three Classic IWW Pamphlets From The 1910s.* Chicago: Charles H. Kerr.

Fortunati, Leopoldina (1995 [1981]). *The Arcane of Reproduction: House, Prostitution, Labor and Capital.* Brooklyn: Autonomedia.

Fortunati, Leopoldina (2007) "Immaterial Labor and its Machinization," *ephemera* Volume 7 Number 1: 139-157.

Fortunati, Leopoldina, James Katz, and Raiminda Riccini, Eds. (2003) *Mediating the Human Body: Technology, Communication, and Fashion.* Mahwah, NJ: Lawrence Erlbaum Associates.

Foucault, Michel (1984) *The Care of the Self. The History of Sexuality: Volume 3.* Trans. Robert Hurley. London: Penguin Press.

Foucault, Michel (1991) *Remarks on Marx*. Trans R. James Goldstein. New York: Semiotext(e).

Foti, Alex (2004) "Precarity and n/european Identity," *Mute*. Available at www.metamute.org.

Frake, Charles O. (1968) "The Ethnographic Study of Cognitive Systems," *Cognitive Anthropology*. Ed. Stephen Tyler. New York: Holt, Rinehart and Winston, Inc: 28-41.

Free Association (2006) *What is a Life?* Leeds: self-published. Available at www.nadir.org.uk.`

Frere Dupont (2007) "Forty, or, The Most Average Length Suicide Note in History," pressessence. July 27th, 2007. Available at pressessence.livejournal.com.

Ginsborg, Paul (2003) *A History of Contemporary Italy: Society and Politics 1943-1988*. New York: Palgrave.

Godbout, Jacques with Allain Caille (1998) *The World of the Gift*. Trans. Donald Winkler. Montreal: McGill-Queen University Press.

Godfrey, Richard, Gavin Jack, and Campbell Jones (2004) "Sucking, Bleeding, Breaking: On the Dialectics of Vampirism, Capital, and Time," *Culture and Organization*. Volume 10 Number 1: 25-36.

Goldfarb, Jeffrey (2001) "1989 and the Creativity of the Political," *Social Research* Winter 2001.

Goldman, Emma (1998) "The Tragedy of Women's Emancipation," *Red Emma Speaks: An Emma Goldman Reader, 3rd Edition*. Ed. Alice Kats Shulman. Amherst, MA: Humanity Books.

Goldner, Loren (2006) "Marx and Makhno Meet McDonald's," Mute. January 9th, 2006. Available at www.metamute.org.

Grady, Robert C. (1990) "Workplace Democracy and Possessive Individualism," *Journal of Politics* Volume 52 Number 1: 146-166.

Graeber, David (2001) *Toward an Anthropological Theory of Value: The False Coin of Our Own Dreams*. New York: Palgrave.

Graeber, David (2002) "The New Anarchists," *New Left Review* 13. Available at www.newleftreview.org/A2368

Graeber, David (2002a) "Direct Democracy and the Global Justice Movement," DualPower.net. New York: DualPower.net Worker's Collective. Available at sandiego.indymedia.org.

Graeber, David (2004) *Fragments of an Anarchist Anthropology*. Chicago: Prickly Paradigm Press.

Graeber, David (2007) *Possibilities: Essays on Hierarchy, Rebellion, and Desire*. San Francisco: AK Press.

Greenberg, Edward (1986) *Workplace Democracy: The Political Effects of Workplace Participation*. Ithaca: Cornell University Press.

Greenberg, Edward, Leon Grunberg, and Kelley Daniel (1966) "Industrial Work and Political Participation: Beyond Simple

Spillover," *Political Research Quarterly* Volume 49 Number 2: 305-330.

Gregoire, Roger and Fredy Perlman (1969) *Worker-Student Action Committees France May '68.* Detroit: Black & Red.

Grey, Christopher (1996) "Essays from Leaving the 20th Century," *What is Situationism? A Reader.* San Francisco: AK Press: 3-23.

Grindon, Gavin (2007) "The Breath of the Possible," *Constituent Imagination: Militant Investigations // Collective Theorization.* Ed. Stevphen Shukaitis and David Graeber with Erika Biddle. Oakland, CA: AK Press: 94-107.

Gross, Daniel and Joe Tessone (2006) "How to Make Work Safe with Direct Action," Znet. September 8, 2006. Available at www.zmag.org.

Grossberg, Lawrence (1992) *We Gotta Get Out of This Place: Popular Conservatism and Postmodern Culture.* London: Routledge.

Guattari, Félix (1977) "Psychoanalysis and Schizoanalysis," *Anti-Oedipus: From Psychoanalysis to Schizopolitics. Semiotext(e)* Volume 2 Number 3: 77-85.

Guattari, Félix (1995) *Chaosophy.* Ed. Sylvere Lotringer. New York: Semiotext(e).

Gunn, Christopher (1986) *Workers' Self-Management in the United States.* Albany: State University of New York Press.

Habermas, Jurgen (1989) "The New Obscurity: The Crisis of the Welfare State and the Exhaustion of Utopian Energies," *The New Conservatism: Cultural Criticism and the Historians' Debate* Ed. and Trans. Shierry Weber Nicholsen. Cambridge: MIT Press: 48-70.

Haeffler, Ross (2006) *Straight Edge: Hardcore Punk, Clean-Living Youth, and Social Change.* New Brunswick, NJ: Rutgers University Press.

Hardt, Michael (1997) "Prison Time," *Yale French Studies* Number 91: 64-79.

Hardt, Michael (1999) "Affective Labor," *boundary 2* 26:2: 89-100.

Hardt, Michael (2002) "Sovereignty," *Theory & Event.* Volume 4 Number.

Harney, Stefano (2002) *State Work: Public Administration and Mass Intellectuality.* Durham: Duke University Press.

Harney, Stefano (2005) "Why is Management a Cliché?" *Critical Perspectives on Accounting* Volume 16 Number 5: 579-591.

Harney, Stefano (2006) "Programming Immaterial Labor," *Social Semiotics* Volume 16 Number 1: 75-87.

Harney, Stefano (2008) "Governance and the Undercommons." Available at info.interactivist.net.

Harney, Stefano and Nceku Q. Nyathi (2007) "Disidentity," *Exploring Identity: Concepts and Methods.* Ed. Alison Pullen, Nic Beach, and

David Sims. London: Palgrave: 185-197.

Hart, Richard (1985) *Slaves Who Abolished Slavery: Blacks in Rebellion.* Barbados: University of the West Indies Press.

Harvie, David (2006) "Value-production and struggle in the classroom," *Capital and Class* 88: 1-32

Harvie, David, Keir Milburn, Ben Trott, and David Watts, Eds. (2005) *Shut Them Down! The G8, Gleaneagles 2005 and the Movement of Movements.* West Yorkshire and New York: Dissent! And Autonomedia.

Heath, Joseph and Andrew Potter (2005) *The Rebel Sell: How the Counterculture Became Consumer Culture.* London: Capstone.

Helliwell, Paul (2007) "Zombie Nation," *Mute* Volume 2 #5: 74-84. Available at www.metamute.org.

Herd, Pamela and Madonna Harrington Meyer (2002) "Care Work: Invisible Civic Engagement," *Gender & Society.* Volume 16 Number 5: 665-688.

Herold, Conrad (2002) "On Financial Crisis as a Disciplinary Device of Empire: Emergence and the Crisis of the Crisis," *the commoner* Number 5: 1-16.

Highleyman, Liz (2007) "A John of All Trades," available at anarchistnews.org.

Hill, Christopher (1972) *The World Upside Down: Radical Ideas During the English Civil War.* London: Penguin.

Hirsch, Joachim (1991) "From the Fordist to the Post-Fordist State," *The Politics of Flexibility: Restructuring State and Industry in Britain, Germany, and Scandinavia.* Ed. Bob Jessop et al. Hants: Edward Elgar: 67-81.

Holdren, Nate (2007) "Why is there no precarity discourse in the US?" *Understanding Precarity.* Available at precariousunderstanding.blogsome.com.

Holloway, John (2002) *Change the World Without Taking Power: The Meaning of Revolution Today.* London: Pluto Press.

Holloway, John (2003) "In the Beginning Was the Scream," *Revolutionary Writing: Common Sense Essays in Post-Political Politics.* Ed. Werner Bonefeld. Brooklyn: Autonomedia.

Holloway, John and Marina Sitrin (2004) "Walking We Ask Questions: An Interview with John Holloway," *Perspectives on Anarchist Theory* Fall 2004. Interactivist Info.Exchange, March 2, 2005. Available at info.interactivist.net.

Holloway, John (2006) "Gleneagles: Breaking Time," *Shut Them Down! The G8, Gleneagles 2005 and the Movement of Movements.* Ed. David Harvie, Keir Milburn, Ben Trott, and David Watts. West Yorkshire and Brooklyn: Dissent! and Autonomedia.

Holmes, Brian (2004) "Artistic Autonomy and Communication Society," *Third Text* Volume 18 Issue 6.

Holmes, Brian (2006) "Images of Fire," Nettime. March 29th, 2006.

Holmes, Brian (2007) "Excerpts from Free Cooperation and After," *The Art of Free Cooperation*. Ed. Ggert Lovink and Trebor Scholz: 27-28.

Holmes, Brian (2007) *Unleashing the Collective Phantoms: Essays in Reverse Imagineering*. Brooklyn: Autonomedia.

Holtzman, Ben, Craig Hughes, and Kevin Van Meter (2004) "Do It Yourself...and the movement beyond capitalism," *Radical Society* Volume 31 Number 1: 7-20.

Home, Stewart (1991) *The Assault on Culture: Utopian Currents from Lettrisme to Class War.* Edinburgh: AK Press.

Home, Stewart (1995) *Neoism, Plagarism, & Praxis*. San Francisco: AK Press.

Home, Stewart (1997) *Mind Invaders: A Reader in Psychic Warfare, Cultural Sabotage and Semiotic Terrorism*. London: Serpent's Tail.

Hunter-Hendersen, Roberta (1973) "A Sense of Liberation," Papers from the Women's Liberation and Socialism Conference 22/23. September 1973. London: 41-45.

Hurchalla, George (2005) *Going Underground: American Punk 1979-1992*. Stuart, FL: Zuo Press.

Huws, Ursula (2003) *The Making of a Cyberteriat: Virtual Work in a Real World*. New York: Monthly Review Press.

Hydrarchist (2005) "Disobbedienti, Ciao," *Mute* Issue 29: 36-38.

Jansson, Sune and Ann-Britt Hellmark, Eds. (1986) *Labor-Owned Firms and Workers' Cooperatives*. Hants: Gower Publishing.

Jenkins, Mark and Mark Andersen (2000) *The Dance of Days: Two Decades of Punk in the Nation's Capital*. New York City: Akashic Books.

Jones, Andrew W. (2001) "Caring Labor and Class Consciousness: Dynamics of Gendered Work," *Sociological Forum* Volume 16 Number 2: 281-299.

Jones, Campbell (2002) "Foucault's inheritance/Inheriting Foucault," *Culture & Organization*, 8(3): 225-238.

Jones, Campbell (2005) "Practical Deconstructivist Feminst Marxist Organization Theory: Gayatri Chakravorty Spivak," *Contemporary Organization Theory*. Ed. Jones, Campbell and Roland Munro. Oxford: Blackwell: 228-244.

Jones, Campbell and Roland Munro, Eds. (2005) *Contemporary Organization Theory*. Oxford: Blackwell: 228-244.

Jonynas, Antanas (2002) *Inclusions in Time*. Ed. Jonas Zdanys. Trans. Jonas Zdanys, Antanas Danielius, and Craig Czury. Vilnius:

Lithuanian Writer's Union Publishers.

Katsiaficas, George (1987) *The Imagination of the New Left: A Global Analysis of 1968*. Boston: South End Press.

Katsiaficas, George (2001) *The Subversion of Politics: European Autonomous Movements and the Decolonization of Everyday Life*. New Jersey: Humanities Press.

Kelley, Robin D.G. (2002) *Freedom Dreams: The Black Radical Imagination*. Boston: Beacon Press.

Kempton, Richard (2007) *Provo: Amsterdam's Anarchist Revolt*. Brooklyn: Autonomedia.

Kendra and Lauren (2003) *Beyond Gallery Walls and Dead White Men*. New York: self-published.

Kerouac, Jack (1958) *The Dharma Bums*. London: Pan Books.

Kiaer, Christina (2005) *Imagine No Possessions: The Socialist Objects of Russian Constructivism*. Cambridge: MIT University Press.

King Mob Echo (2000) *English Section of the Situationist International*. Edinburgh: Dark Star.

Klein, Naomi (2007) *The Shock Doctrine: The Rise of Disaster Capitalism*. London: Penguin Books.

Klein, Naomi and Avi Lewis (2004) *The Take*. Toronto: First Run Films.

Knights, David and Hugh Willmott (2002) "Autonomy and utopia or dystopia," *Utopia and Organization*. Ed. Martin Parker. Oxford: Blackwell: 59-81.

Koehline, James and Ron Sakolsky, Eds. (1994) *Gone to Croatan: The Origins of North American Dropout Culture*. Brooklyn: Autonomedia

Kohl, Paul (1993) "Looking Through a Glass Onion: Rock and Roll as Modern Manifestation of Carnival," *Journal of Popular Culture*, 27(1).

Kousha, M. (1994) "African American Private Households and 'Control' of the Labor Process in Domestic Service," *Sociological Focus* Volume 27 Number 3: 211-226.

Kramer, Darren (2002) "The Working Class and the Democratic Economy." Available at process.grenpeppermagazine.org

Krauthamer, Diane (2007) "The People Business Serving Coffee?" *Bread and Roses* Volume 2 Issue 7: 3.

Kristeva, Julia (1984) *Revolution in Poetic Language*. Trans. Margaret Waller. New York: Columbia University Press.

Kristeva, Julia (2000) *The Sense and Non-Sense of Revolt: The Powers and Limits of Psychoanalysis*. Trans. Jeanine Herman. New York: Columbia University Press.

Kristeva, Julia (2002) *Revolt, She Said*. New York: Semiotext(e).

Kubler, George (1962) *The Shape of Time: Remarks on the History of*

Things. New Haven, CT: Yale University Press.

Kuspit, Donald (1993) *The Cult of the Avant-Garde Artist.* Cambridge: Cambridge University Press.

Lafargue, Paul (1989 [1883]]) *The Right to Be Lazy.* Chicago: Charles H. Kerr Publishing Company.

Lalich, Janja (2004) *Bounded Choice: True Believers and Charismatic Cults.* Berkeley: University of California Press.

Landeur, Gustav (1973) *Prophet of Community: The Romantic Socialism of Gustav Landeur.* Berkeley: University of California Press.

Landstreicher, Wolfi (n.d.) *Autonomous Self-Organization and Anarchist Intervention.* Somewhereville: Institute for Experimental Freedom.

Lasn, Kalle (2000) *Culture Jam: How to Reverse America's Suicidal Consumer Binge.* New York City: Harpers.

Lazzarato, Maurizio (1996) "Immaterial Labor," *Radical Thought in Italy.* Ed. Paolo Virno & Michael Hardt. Trans. Paul Colilli & Ed Emory. Minneapolis: University of Minnesota Press: 132-146.

Leason, Jean (2007) "Music on the March: How Protest Learned to Dance," *Fifth Estate* 374: 21-24.

Leblanc, Lauraine (1999) *Pretty in Punk: Girl's Gender Resistance in a Boy's Subculture.* New Brunswick, NJ: Rutgers University Press.

Leeds May Day Group (2004) "Moments of Excess." Available at www.nadir.org.uk/excess.html

Lefebvre, Henri (2002/2006) *Critique of Everyday Life. Volumes 1-3.* New York: Verso.

Lewis, Helena (1990) *Dada Turns Red: Politics of Surrealism.* Edinburgh: Edinburgh University Press.

Linebaugh, Peter (1992) *The London Hanged: Crime & Civil Society in the Eighteenth Century.* Cambridge: Cambridge University Press.

Linebaugh, Peter (2008) *The Magna Carta Manifesto: Liberties and Commons for All.* London: Verso.

Linstead, Stephen and Heather Hopfl (2004) *The Aesthetics of Organization.* London: Sage.

Maher, Kris (2006) "IWW Branches Out in Bid to Recruit Starbucks Baristas," *Wall Street Journal.* May 17, 2006. Available at www.starbucksunion.org.

Malos, Ellen. Ed. (1980) "Introduction," *The Politics of Housework.* Ed. Ellen Malos. London: Allison & Busby: 7-43.

Mandarini, Matteo (2006) "Marx and Deleuze: Money, Time, and Crisis," *Polygraph* 18: 73-97.

Mandarini, Matteo (2008) "Not Fear but Hope in the Apocalypse," *ephemera: theory & politics in organization* Volume 8 Number 2.

Mannheim, Karl (1936) *Ideology and Utopia: An Introduction to the Sociology of Knowledge.* Trans. Louis Wirth and Edward Shils. New York:

Harcourt, Brace & World.

Marazzi, Christian and Sylvère Lotringer, Eds. (1980) *Italy: Autonomia. Post-political politics*. New York: Semiotext(e): 28-35.

Marchand, Roland (1998) *Creating the Corporate Soul: The Rise of Public Relations and Corporate Imagery in American Big Business*. Berkeley, CA: University of California Press.

Martin, Nathan (2003) "Parasites and Other Forms of Tactical Augmentation," *An@rchitexts: Voices from the Global Digital Resistance*. Ed. Joanne Richardson. Brooklyn: Autonomedia: 115-122.

Martin, Randy (1994) *Socialist Ensembles: Theater and State in Nicaragua and Cuba*. Minneapolis: University of Minnesota Press.

Martin, Randy (2002) *On Your Marx: Rethinking Socialism and the Left*. Minneapolis: University of Minnesota Press.

Marcus, Greil (1989) *Lipstick Traces: A Secret History of the Twentieth Century*. Cambridge: Harvard University Press.

Marx, Karl (1973) *Capital Volume 1: A Critique of Political Economy*. Trans. Ben Fowkes. New York: Penguin.

Mason, Ronald (1982) *Participatory and Workplace Democracy*. Carbdondale: Southern Illinois University Press.

McCarthy, Kevin and Ed Gorman (1999) *"They're Here..." Invasion of the Body Snatchers: A Tribute*. Berkeley: Berkeley Boulevard Books.

McKay, George (1998) *DIY Culture: Party & Protest in Nineties Britain*. New York: Verso.

McKay, John Henry (1999 [1891]) *The Anarchists*. Trans. George Schumm. Brooklyn: Autonomedia.

McNally, David (1993) *Against the Market: Political Economy, Market Socialism, and the Marxist Critique*. London: Verso.

Michels, Robert (2001) *Political Parties: A Sociological Study of the Oligarchical Tendencies of Modern Democracy*. Kitchener, Ontario: Batoche Books.

Middleton, John and David Tait, Eds. (1970) *Tribes Without Rulers: Studies in African Segmentary Societies*. New York: Humanities Press.

Midnight Notes (1990) "Introduction to the New Enclosures," *The New Enclosures. Midnight Notes* Number 10: 1-9.

Miéville, China (2007) "The Struggle for Intergalactic Socialism," *Socialist Review*. January 2007. Available at www.socialistreview.org.uk.

Miles, Maria (1999) *Patriarchy and Accumulation on a World Scale: Women in the International Division of Labor*. London: Zed Books.

Miller, Paul (1999) "Afro-Futurism: A Statement of Intentions – Outside In, Inside Out." Available at www.afrofuturism.net

Mitropolous, Angela (2005) "Precari-us?" *Mute* Issue 29: 88-92.

Mitropolous, Angela (2006) "The Demography of Time and the

Times," *ephemera* Volume 6 Number 1.

Mitropolous, Angela (2007) "Autonomy, Recognition, Movement," *Constituent Imagination: Militant Investigations // Collective Theorization.* Ed. Stevphen Shukaitis and David Graeber with Erika Biddle. Oakland, CA: AK Press: 127-136.

Miyazaki, Hajime (1984) "On Success and Dissolution of the Labor-managed Firm in the Capitalist Economy," *Journal of Political Economy* Volume 92 Number 5: 909-931.

Monroe, Alexei (2005) *Interrogation Machine: Laibach and the NSK.* Cambridge, MA: MIT Press.

Moore, Barrington (1977) *Social Origins of Dictatorship and Democracy: Lord and Peasant in the Making of the Modern World.* New York: Penguin Books.

Morris, William (1993) *Art and Society: Lectures and Essays by William Morris.* Ed. Gary Zabel. Boston: George's Hill.

Moten, Fred (2003) *In The Break: The Aesthetics of the Black Radical Tradition.* Minneapolis: University of Minnesota Press.

Moynihan, Daniel Patrick (1973) *The Politics of a Guaranteed Income.* New York: Random House.

Murakami, Haruki (2003 [1987]) *Norweigan Wood.* Trans. Jay Rubin. London: Vintage.

Murakami, Haruki (2005) *Kafka on the Shore.* London: Vintage.

Muraro, Luisa (1991 [1985]) "Bonding and Freedom" *Italian Feminist Thought: A Reader.* Ed. Paola Bono and Sandra Kemp. Oxford: Blackwell: 123-129.

Nancy, Jean-Luc (1991) *The Inoperative Community.* Minneapolis: University of Minnesota Press.

Negation (1975 [1973]) *Lip and the Self-Managed Counter-Revolution.* Trans. Peter Rachleff and Alan Walllach. Detroit: Black & Red.

Negri, Antonio (1988) "Keynes and the Capitalist Theory of the State Post-1929," *Revolution Retrieved: Selected Writings on Marx, Keynes, Capitalist Crisis and New Social Subjects 1967-1983.* Trans. Ed Emery and John Merrington, Red Notes, London: 9-42.

Negri, Antonio (1991) *Marx Beyond Marx: Lessons on the Grundrisse.* Ed. Jim Fleming. Trans. Harry Cleaver, Michael Ryan, Maurizio Viano. Brooklyn: Autonomedia

Negri, Antonio (1999) *Insurgencies: Constituent Power and the Modern State.* Trans. Maurizio Boscagli. Minneapolis, MN: University of Minnesota Press.

Negri, Antonio (1999) "Value and Affect," *boundary 2* Volume 26 Number 2: 77-88.

Negri, Antonio (2002) "Letter to Nanni, On Construction," *Arte y multitudo. Ocho cartas.* Ed. Raul Sanchez. Trans. Nate Holdren. Private communication October 1st, 2004.

Negri, Antonio (2003)"The Ripe Fruit of Redemption," Generation On-Line. Available at www.generation-online.org

Negri, Antonio (2003) *Time for Revolution.* Trans. Matteo Mandarini. London: Continuum.

Negri, Antonio (2004) "Back to the Future," MakeWorlds. Available at www.makeworlds.org/node/140

Negri, Antonio (2007) *Political Descartes: Reason, Ideology, and the Bourgeois Project.* Trans. Matteo Mandarini and Alberto Toscano. New York: Verso.

Negri, Toni and Félix Guattari (1990) *Communists Like Us.* Trans. Michael Ryan. New York: Semiotext(e).

Negt, Oskar and Alexander Kluge (1993) *Public Sphere and Experience: Toward an Analysis of the Bourgeois and Proletarian Public Sphere.* Minneapolis: University of Minnesota Press.

Neill, Monty (2001) "Rethinking Class Composition in Light of the Zapatistas," *Auroras of the Zapatistas: Local & Global Struggles of the Fourth World War.* Brooklyn: Autonomedia: 119 – 143.

Neilson, Brett and Ned Rossitter (2005) "From Precarity to Precariousness and Back Again: Labor, Life and Unstable Networks," *fibreculture* Issue 5. Available at journal.fibreculture.org.

Nelson, Alondra (2000) "Afrofuturism: Past Future Visions," *Colorlines.* Available at www.arc.org.

Nelson, Alondra (2001) *Afrofuturism: A Special Issue of Social Text.*

Neundlinger, Klaus (2004) "Fuzzy Production Logics. Experience and Reflection in the Laboratory of Insecurity," republicart. Net.

Newton, Huey P. (2002) *The Huey P. Newton Reader.* Ed. David Hilliard and Donald Weise. New York: Seven Stories Press.

Niedzviecki, Hal (2006) *Hello, I'm Special: How Individuality Became the New Conformity.* San Francisco: City Light Books.

Nietzsche, Friedrich (1990) *Beyond Good and Evil.* Trans. R.J. Hollingdale. New York: Penguin Books.

Nunes, Rodrigo (2005) "Nothing is What Democracy Looks Like," *Shut Them Down! The G8, Gleneagles 2005, and the Movement of Movements.* Brooklyn: Autonomedia.

O'Connor, Flannery (1956) *Everything That Rises Must Converge.* New York: Noonday Press.

O'Connor, Lynn, Wallace Russell, Pat Mialoca (1978) *The Office Workers' Manifesto.* New York: Freeway Press.

O'Hara, Craig (1999) *The Philosophy of Punk: More Than Noise.* San Francisco: AK Press.

Olmedo, Clara and Martin J. Murray (2002) "The Formalization of Informal/Precarious Labor in Contemporary Argentina," *Interna-*

tional Sociology. Vol. 17(3): 421–443.

Ong, Aiwa (1987) *Spirits of Resistance and Capitalist Discipline: Factory Women in Malaysia.* Albany, NY: SUNY Press.

Ong, Aiwa (1991) "The gender and labor politics of postmodernity," *Annual Review of Anthropology* 20:279-309

Osterweil, Michal (2007) "'Becoming Woman?' In theory or practice?" *Turbulence: Ideas for Movement* Issue 1. Available at www.turbulence.org.uk.

Palmer, Phyllis (1984) "Housework and Domestic Labor: Racial and Technological Change," *My Troubles Are Going to Have Trouble With Me: Everyday Trials and Triumphs of Women Workers.* Ed. K.B. Sacks and D. Remy. New Brunswick, NJ: Rutgers University Press: 80-91.

Pannekoek, Anton (2005) *Workers' Councils.* Oakland: AK Press.

Papadopoulos, Dimitris, Niamh Stephenson, and Vassilis Tsianos (2008) *Escape Routes: Control and Subversion in the 21st Century.* London: Pluto Press.

Paoli, Guillaume (2004) "Demotivational Training. Anecdote on the drop in economic optimism," republicart.net.

Parker, Martin, Warren Smith, Matthew Higgins, and Geoff Lightfoot, Eds. (2001) *Science Fiction and Organization.* London: Routledge.

Parker, Martin. Ed. (2002) *Utopia and Organization.* Oxford: Blackwell.

Parker et al, Eds. (2007) *The Dictionary of Alternatives: Utopianism and Organization.* London: Zed Books.

Parker, Martin (2005) "Organizational Gothic," *Culture and Organization.* Volume 11 Number 3: 153-156.

Panzieri, Raniero (1976) "Surplus Value and Planning: Notes on a Reading of Capital," *The Labor Process & Class Strategies.* Trans. Julian Bees. London: Stage 1: 4-25.

Pasquinelli, Matteo (2007) "ICW – Immaterial Civil War: Prototypes of Conflict within Cognitive Capitalism," *MyCreativity Reader: A Critique of Creative Industries.* Ed. Geert Lovink and Ned Rossiter. Amsterdam: Institute of Network Cultures: 69-79.

Patton, Paul (2000) *Deleuze & the Political.* New York: Routledge.

Perez, Rolando (1990) *On An (archy) and Schizoanalysis.* Brooklyn: Autonomedia.

Pisters, Patricia (2008) "Machines of the Invisible: Manifesto for a Schizo-analysis of Media Culture." May 25, 2008. Available at mastersofmedia.hum.uva.nl.

Plant, Sadie (1992) *The Most Radical Gesture: The Situationist International in a Postmodern Age.* London: Routledge.

p.m. (1995) *bolo'bolo.* New York: Semiotext(e).

Poggioli, Renato (1965) *The Theory of the Avant-Garde*. Cambridge: Harvard University Press.

Precarias a la Deriva (2003) "Close encounters in the second phase: The communication continuum: care-sex-attention." Available at www.sindominio.net/karakola/antigua_casa/precarias.htm

Precarias a la Deriva (2003) "First Stutterings of Precarias a la Deriva." Available at www.sindominio.net/karakola/antigua_casa/precarias.htm

Precarias a la Deriva (2005) "Precarious Lexicon." Available at www.sindominio.net/karakola/antigua_casa/precarias.htm

Precarias a la Deriva (2005) "Bodies, Lies, and Videotape: Between the Logic of Security and the Logic of Care." Available at www.sindominio.net/karakola/antigua_casa/precarias.htm

Precarias a la Deriva (2006) "A Very Careful Strike – Four Hypotheses," *the commoner* Number 11: 33-45.

Quadrelli, Emillio (2007) "Grassroots Political Militant: Banlieusards and Politics," *Nights of Rage*. London: Mute Magazine: 7-60. Also available at www.metamute.org.

Ra, Sun (1968) *Outer Spaceways Incorporated*. El Saturn Records.

Ra, Sun (1974) *Space is the Place*. Directed John Coney. El Saturn Records.

Rachleff, Peter (1996) "The Independent Union of All Workers: Community-Based Unionism," *"We are all leaders": the alternative unionism of the early 1930s*. Ed. Staughton Lynd. Urbana: University of Illinois Press.

Rachleff, Peter (2008 [1993]) *Organizing Wall to Wall*. Chicago: Chicago IWW.

Ranciere, Jacques (1989) *The Nights of Labor: The Workers' Dream in Nineteenth Century France*. Philadelphia: Temple University Press.

Rasy, Elisabetta (1991 [1978]) "An Interpretation: Marching in the Night." *Italian Feminist Thought: A Reader*. Ed. Paola Bono and Sandra Kemp. Oxford: Blackwell.

Raunig, Gerald (2007) *Art and Revolution: Transversal Activism in the Long Twentieth Century*. Trans. Aileen Derieg. New York: Semiotext(e).

Raventós, Daniel (2007) *Basic Income: The Material Conditions of Freedom*. London: Pluto Books.

Readings, Bill (1997) *The University in Ruins*. Cambridge: Harvard University Press.

Redding, Paul (1999) *The Logic of Affect*. Melbourne: Melbourne University Press.

Reeves, Martha and Mark Bego (1994) *Dancing in the Street: Confessions of a Motown Diva*. New York: Hyperion Books.

Reinsborough, Patrick (2003) "De-colonizing the Revolutionary

Imagination," *Journal of Aesthetics & Protest* Volume 1 Number 3: 37-41.

Renshaw, Patrick (1999) *The Wobblies: The Story of the IWW and Syndicalism in the United States.* Chicago: Ivan R. Dee, Publisher.

Retort (2005) *Afflicted Powers: Capital and Spectacle in a New Age of War.* London: Verso.

Reverend Billy (2003) *What Should I Do if Reverend Billy is in My Store?* New York: New Press.

Rhodes, Carl (2007) "Outside the Gates of Eden: Utopia and Work in Rock Music," *Group and Organization Management* Volume 32 Number 1: 22-49.

Rio, Cecilia (2005) "'On the Move': African American Women's Paid Domestic Labor and the Class Transition to Independent Commodity Production," *Rethinking Marxism.* Volume 17 Number 4. October 2005: 489-510.

Robinson, Andrew (2007) "Thinking from the Outside: Avoiding Recuperation," *Anarchy: A Journal of Desire Armed.* Number 64.

Rock Bloc Collective (n.d.) *Stick It To The Manarchy.* A-Infos News Service March 16, 2001. Available at www.ainfos.ca.

Rosemont, Franklin (2002) *Joe Hill: The IWW & the Making of a Revolutionary Working Class Counterculture.* Chicago: Charles H. Kerr Publishing.

Rosemont, Franklin and Charles Radcliffe, Eds. (2005) *Dancin' in the Streets: Anarchists, IWWs, Surrealists, Situationists & Provos in the 1960s.* Chicago: Charles H. Kerr Publishing Company.

Ross, Andrew (2003) *No Collar: The Human Workplace and Its Hidden Costs.* New York: Basic Books.

Rothe, Eduardo (1969) "The Conquest of Space in Time and Power," *Internationale Situationniste* No. 12. Trans. Ken Knabb. Available at www.bopsecrets.org/SI/12.space.htm.

Rubenstein, Richard (1970) *Rebels in Eden: Mass Political Violence in the United States.* Boston: Little, Brown & Company.

Rucker, Rudy, Robert Anton Wilson, Peter Lamborn Wilson, and Bart Plantenga (1991) *Semiotext(e) SF.* New York: Semiotext(e).

Ryle, Gilbert (2000 [1949]) *The Concept of Mind.* Chicago: University of Chicago Press.

Sacks, Shelley (2007) "Seeing the Phenomenon and Imaginal Thought," *Imagination Inspiration Intuition: Joseph Beuys & Rudolph Steiner.* Victoria: Victoria National Gallery: 37-47.

Salusbury, Matt (2003) "Posadism for Beginners," Fortean Times. Available at www.forteantimes.com.

Scott, James C. (1979) "Revolution in the Revolution: Peasants and Commisars," *Theory and Society* Volume 7 Number 1 & 2: 97-134.

Scott, James C. (1990) *Domination and the Arts of Resistance: Hidden Transcripts*. New Haven, CT: Yale University Press.

Scott-Heron, Gil (1971) "Whitey on the Moon," Pieces of a Man. New York: Flying Dutchman Records.

Sewell, Graham and Barry Wilkinson (1992) "Someone to Watch Over Me: Surveillance, Discipline and the Just-in-Time Labor Process," *Sociology* Volume 26 Number 2: 271-289.

Sharp, Hasana (2005) "Why Spinoza Today? Or, 'A Strategy of Anti-Fear'," *Rethinking Marxism*. Volume 17 Number 4. October 2005: 591-608.

Shepard, Ben (2007) "Towards a Ludic Counterpublic: Play, Creativity, and the New Street Activism," *Drain*. Available at www.drain-mag.com.

Shukaitis, Stevphen (2003) "Contesto, creazione, comunità" (Context, creation, community), *DeriveApprodi* Volume 13 Number 3: 59-63.

Shukaitis, Stevphen (2004) "An Ethnography of Nowhere: Notes Towards a Re-envisioning of Utopian Thinking," *Social Anarchism* Number 35. January 2004: 5-13

Shukaitis, Stevphen (2005) "Space. Imagination // Rupture: The Cognitive Architecture of Utopian Political Thought in the Global Justice Movement," *Sussex Journal of Contemporary History* 8: 1-14.

Shukaitis, Stevphen and David Graeber (2007) "Introduction," *Constituent Imagination: Militant Investigations // Collective Theorization*. Ed. Stevphen Shukaitis and David Graeber with Erika Biddle: 11-34.

Shukaitis, Stevphen (2009) "Infrapolitics and the Nomadic Educational Machine," *Contemporary Anarchist Studies: An Introduction to Anarchy in the Academy*. Ed. Randall Amster et al. New York: Routledge.

Shukaitis, Stevphen (2009a) "Workers' Inquiry, Militant Research, and the Business School" *Fifth Estate* Volume 44 Number 1.

Sitirin, Marina. Ed. (2006) *Horizontalism: Voices of Popular Power in Argentina*. Oakland / Edinburgh: AK Press.

Situationist International (1960) "The Situationist Frontier," *Internationale Situationniste* #5. Trans. Paul Hammond (December 1960). www.cddc.vt.edu/sionline/si/frontier.html.

Situationist International (1962) "The Fifth SI Conference in Göteborg," note #2. Trans. Ken Knabb. Available at www.bopsecrets.org/SI/7.conf5.htm.

Situationist International (1966) "Decomposition and Recuperation," *Internationale Situationniste* #10. Trans. Reuben Keehan. Available at www.cddc.vt.edu/sionline

Situationist International (1969) "Faces of Recuperation," *Situationist*

International #1. Available at www.cddc.vt.edu/sionline.

Smith, Gibbs M. (1984) *Joe Hill.* New York: Gibbs Smith.

Smith, Suzanne (2001) *Dancing in the Street: Motown and the Cultural Politics of Detroit.* Harvard University Press.

Sorokin, Pitirim (1950) *Leaves from a Russian Diary.* Boston: Beacon Press.

Spencer, Wayne (2007) "Gasping from Out the Shadows: Reflections of Revolutions in the Early 21st Century." Available at libcom.org.

Spinoza, Baruch (1949) *Ethics.* New York: Hafner Publishing.

Spinoza, Baruch (2004) *A Theological-Political Treatise.* Trans. R.H.M. Elwes. Mineola, NY: Dover Publications.

Spivak, Gayatri Chakravorty (1985) "Scattered Speculations on the Question of Value," *Diacritics* Volume 15 Number 4: 73-93.

Spivak, Gayatri (1996) *The Spivak Reader.* London: Routledge.

Stallybrass, Peter and Allon White (1986) *The Politics of Poetics of Transgression.* Ithaca: Cornell University Press.

Stansill, Peter and David Zane, Eds. (1999) *BAMN (By Any Means Necessary): Outlaw Manifestos & Ephemera, 1965-1970.* Brooklyn: Autonomedia.

Starman, Neil (2005) "Nostalgia for the Future: The Darker the Night, the Brighter the Stars." Talk given at the "Art is not Terrorism" event on April 23rd, 2005, Paris. Available at www.geocities.com/redgiantsite/paris.html.

Stimson, Blake and Greg Sholette, Eds. (2007) *Collectivism After Modernism: The Art of Social Imagination After 1945.* Minneapolis: University of Minnesota Press.

Stone, C.J. (1996) *Fierce Dancing: Adventures in the Underground.* London: Faber and Faber.

Strange, Gerard and Jim Shorthouse (2004) "The New Cultural Economy, the Artist and the Social Configuration of Autonomy," *Capital & Class* Issue 84.

Strauss, David Levi (1999) *Between Dog & Wolf: Essays on Art and Politics.* Brooklyn: Autonomedia.

Sullivan, Laura (2005) "Wages for Anyone is Bad Business," *Mute* Issue 29. Available at www.metamute.org.

Szwed, John (1998) *Space Is the Place: The Lives and Times of Sun Ra.* Cambridge: De Capo Press.

Szukis, Haduhi (1524) *The Lithuanian Book of the Undead.* Trans. Roberto Bui. Vilnius: Insurgent Peasant Publishing.

Tarì, Marcello and Ilaria Vanni (2005) "On the Life and Deeds of San Precario, Patron Saint of Precarious Workers and Lives," *fibreculture* Issue 5. Available at journal.fibreculture.org.

Tarrow, Sidney (1994) *Power in Movement: Collective Action, Social*

Movements and Politics. Cambridge: Cambridge University Press.

Taylor, Charles (2004) *Modern Social Imaginaries*. Durham: Duke University Press.

Terranova, Tiziana (2004) *Network Culture: Politics for the Information Age*. London: Pluto Press.

Theroux, Louis (2005) *The Call of the Weird*. New York: Pan Macmillan.

Thoburn, Nick (2003) *Deleuze, Marx, and Politics*. London: Routledge.

Thoburn, Nick (2003a) "The Hobo Anomalous: Class, Minorities and Political Invention in the Industrial Workers of the World," *Social Movement Studies*, 2(1): 61–84.

Thoburn, Nick (2006) "Vacuoles of Non-communication: Minor Politics, Communist Style and the Multitude," *Deleuze and the Contemporary World*. Ed. Ian Buchanan and Adrian Parr. Edinburgh: Edinburgh University Press: 42-56.

Thompson, E.P. (1966) *The Making of the English Working Class*. London: Vintage.

Thornley, Jenny (1981) *Workers' Cooperatives*. London: Heineman Educational Books Ltd.

Tilly, Charles (2004) *Social Movements, 1768-2004*. London: Paradigm Publishers.

Titchener, E.B. (1895) "Affective Memory," *Philosophical Review*. Volume 4 Number 1: 65-76.

Trocchi, Alexander (2006) *A Life in Pieces: Reflections on Alexander Trocchi*. Ed. Allen Campbell and Tim Niell. Edinburgh: Rebel Inc.: 164-176.

Tronti, Mario (1972) "Workers and Capital," *Telos:* 68-83.

Tronti, Mario (1973) "Social Capital," *Telos* 17: 98-121.

Tronti, Mario (1979) "Lenin in England," *Working Class Autonomy and the Crisis: Italian Marxist Texts of the Theory and Practice of a Class Movement: 1964-79*. London: Red Notes: 1-6.

Tronti, Mario (1980) "The Strategy of Refusal," *Italy: Autonomia. Post-Political Politics*. Ed. Sylvere Lotringer and Christian Marazzi. New York: Semiotext(e): 28-35. Also available at libcom.org.

Trott, Ben (2005) "Gleneagles, Activism, and Ordinary Rebelliousnes," *Shut Them Down! The G8, Gleneagles 2005 and the Movement of Movements*. Ed. David Harvie, Keir Milburn, Ben Trott, and David Watts. West Yorkshire and Brooklyn: Dissent! and Autonomedia: 213-233.

Turner, Mary, Ed. (1995) *From Chattel Slaves to Wage Slaves: The Dynamics of Labor Bargaining in the Americas*. London: Indiana University Press.

Vague, Tom (2005) *The Red Army Faction Story 1963-1993*. Oakland:

AK Press.

Vallas, Steven P. (2003) "Why Teamwork Fails: Obstacles to Workplace Change in Four Manufacturing Plants," *American Sociological Review* Volume 68: 223-250.

Van Meter, Kevin (2006) "Of Floods and Flows in New Orleans: Self-Activity, Struggle and 'the Commons' After the Storm." Available at www.warmachines.info.

Van Raaphorst, D.L. (1988) *Union Maids Not Wanted: Organizing Domestic Workers 1870-1940*. New York: Praeger Publishers.

Vandenbroeck, Andre (1990) *Al-Kemi: A Memoir: Hermetic, Occult, Political, and Private Aspects of R.A. Schwaller de Lubicz*. Herndon: Lindisfarne Books.

Vaneigem, Raoul (n.d.) *Collection of Desires*. Richmond, VA: Paper Street.

Vaneigem, Raoul (1994) *The Movement of the Free Spirit*. Trans. Randall Cherry and Ian Patterson. New York: Zone Books.

Vaneigem, Raoul (1994 [1967]) *Revolution of Everyday Life*. Trans. Donald Nicholson-Smith. London: Rebel Press.

Vanek, Jaroslav (1970) *The general theory of labor-managed market economies*. Ithaca, NY: Cornell University Press.

Vanek, Jaroslav (1975) *Self-Management Economics: Economic Liberation of Man*. Hammondsworth: Penguin.

Vanek, Jaroslav (1977) *The Labor-Managed Economy*. Ithaca, NY: Cornell University Press.

Vaughan, Genevieve (2002) *For-Giving: A Feminist Criticism of Exchange*. Austin, TX. Plain View Press.

Verba, Sidney and Goldie Shabad (1978) "Workers' Councils the Political Stratification," *American Political Science Review* Volume 72 Number 1.

Vercellone, Carlo (2008) "The New Articulation of Wages, Rent, and Profit in Cognitive Capitalism." Available at www.generation-online.org/c/fc_rent2.htm.

Vienet, Rene (1992 [1968]) *Enrages and Situationists in the Occupation Movement*. France, May '68. New York and London: Autonomedia / Rebel Press.

Virillio, Paul (1991) *The Aesthetics of Disappearance*. Trans. Phillip Beitchman. New York: Semiotext(e).

Virno, Paolo (1996) "Virtuosity and Revolution: A Political Theory of Exodus," *Radical Thought in Italy: A Potential Politics*. Ed. Michael Hardt and Paolo Virno. Minneapolis, MN: University of Minnesota Press.

Virno, Paolo (2004) *A Grammar of the Multitude: For an Analysis of Contemporary Forms of Life*. Trans. Isabella Bertoletti, James Cascaito, and Andrea Casson. New York: Semiotext(e).

Virno, Paolo and Michael, Eds. (1996) *Radical Thought in Italy*. Minnesota: University of Minnesota Press.

Vishmidt, Marina (2004) "de-, dis-, ex- on Immaterial Labor," Republicart.net.

Vishmidt, Marina (2006) "The Auto-Destructive Community: The Torsion of the Common in Local Sites of Antagonism," *ephemera* Volume 6 Number 4: 454-465.

Von Gunden, Kenneth and Stuart H. Stock (1982) *Twenty All-Time Great Science Fiction Films*. Arlington: Arlington House.

Waits, Tom (2005) *Innocent When You Dream: The Tom Waits Reader*. Ed. Mac Montandon. New York: Thunder's Mouth Press.

Watson, David (1996) *Beyond Bookchin*. Brooklyn: Autonomedia.

Weiner, Jonah (2008) "Lil Wayne and the Afronaut Invasion," *Slate* June 2008. Available at www.slate.com.

Weir, David (1997) *Anarchy & Culture: The Aesthetic Politics of Modernism*. Amherst, MA: University of Massachusetts Press.

Weiss, Jeffrey (1994) *The Popular Culture of Modern Art: Picasso, Duchamp, and Avant-Gardism*. New Haven: Yale University Press.

Wharton, Amy (1999) "The Psychosocial Consequences of Emotional Labor," *Annals* 561: 158-176.

Whitney, Jennifer (2003) "Infernal Noise: The Soundtrack to Insurrection," *We Are Everywhere: The Irresistible Rise of Global Anticapitalism*. Ed. Notes from Nowhere. London: Verso.

Wiener, Hans with Robert Oakeshott (1987) *Worker-Owners. Mondragon Revisited*. London: George Over Ltd.

Wildcat Dodge Truck Strike 1974 (1996) Detroit, MI: Red & Black.

Williams, Ben (2001) "Black Secret Technology: Detroit Techno and the Information Age," *Technicolor: Race, Technology, and Everyday Life*. Eds. Alondra Nelson and Thuy Linh Tu. New York: New York University Press: 154-176.

Wilson, Peter Lamborn (1988) *Scandal: Essays on the Margins on Islam*. Brooklyn: Autonomedia.

Wilson, Peter Lamborn (1996) *Shower of Stars: The Initiatic Dream in Sufism and Taoism*. Brooklyn: Autonomedia.

Wilson, Peter Lamborn (1996a) "Cybernetics & Entheogenics: From Cyberspaace to Neurospace." Presentation at the Next Five Minutes conference, Amsterdam. Available at www.t0.or.at.

Wilson, Peter Lamborn (1998) "The Sacred and the Profane History of Money," *Whole Earth Spring* 1998.

Wilson, Peter Lamborn (2003) Pirate Utopias: Moorish Corsairs & European Renegades. Brookyln: Autonomedia.

Witz, Anne, Chris Warhurst, and Dennis Nickson (2003) "The Labor of Aesthetics of Organization," *Organization* Volume 18 Number 1: 33-54.

Wolf, James and Helmet Geerken (2006) *Sun Ra: The Immeasurable Equation: The Collected Poetry and Prose.* Herrsching: Waitawhile.

Wonder, Stevie (1976) "Saturn," *Songs in the Key of Life.* Detroit: Motown Records.

Wright, David (1979) *Cooperatives & Community: The Theory and Practice of Producers Cooperatives.* London: Bedford Square Press.

Wright, Steve (2003) *Storming Heaven: Class Composition and Struggle in Italian Autonomist Marxism.* London: Pluto Press.

Yaszek, Lisa (2005) "Afrofuturism: Science Fiction and the History of the Future," *Socialism and Democracy* Volume 2 Number 3.

Zerowork Collective (1992 [1975]) "Introduction to Zerowork I," *Midnight Oil: Work, Energy, War, 1973 – 1992.* Brooklyn: Autonomedia: 109 – 114.

Zerubavel, Eviatar (1991) *The Fine Line: Making Distinctions in Everyday Life.* Chicago: University of Chicago Press.

Zerzan, John (1999) "Organized Labor Versus 'The Revolt Against Work,'" *Elements of Refusal.* Columbia, MI: CAL Press.

Forthcoming Titles

Precarias a la Deriva
Aeffective Revolts
Intimate Bureaucracies
Beneath the Commons

you can find them at yr local undercommons...

...or better yet,

create your own....

www.minorcompositions.info

Lightning Source UK Ltd.
Milton Keynes UK
24 September 2009

144133UK00002B/2/P